RUDY WIEBE

# of this earth

~

A MENNONITE BOYHOOD
IN THE BOREAL FOREST

*Vintage Canada*

VINTAGE CANADA EDITION, 2007

Copyright © 2006 Jackpine House Ltd.

Published in Canada by Vintage Canada, a division of Random House of Canada Limited, Toronto, in 2007. Originally published in hardcover in Canada by Alfred A. Knopf Canada, a division of Random House of Canada Limited, Toronto, in 2006. Distributed by Random House of Canada Limited, Toronto.

www.randomhouse.ca

Grateful acknowledgment is made to the University of Alberta Press to reprint from "Conversation #2" from *The Snowbird Poems* by Robert Kroetsch, University of Alberta Press, Edmonton, 2004.

LIBRARY AND ARCHIVES CANADA CATALOGUING IN PUBLICATION

Wiebe, Rudy, 1934–
Of this earth : a Mennonite boyhood in the boreal forest / Rudy Wiebe.

ISBN 978-0-676-97753-0

1. Wiebe, Rudy, 1934– —Childhood and youth. 2. Mennonites—Saskatchewan—Speedwell—Biography. 3. Farm life—Saskatchewan—Speedwell. 4. Speedwell (Sask.)—Biography. 5. Authors, Canadian (English)—20th century—Biography. I. Title.

PS8545.I38Z47 2007          971.24'2          C2006-904700-6

Text design: CS Richardson

Printed and bound in the United States of America

2 4 6 8 9 7 5 3 1

THIS BOOK IS FOR

Rocio Michaela
Camilo Aaron
Anna Helen

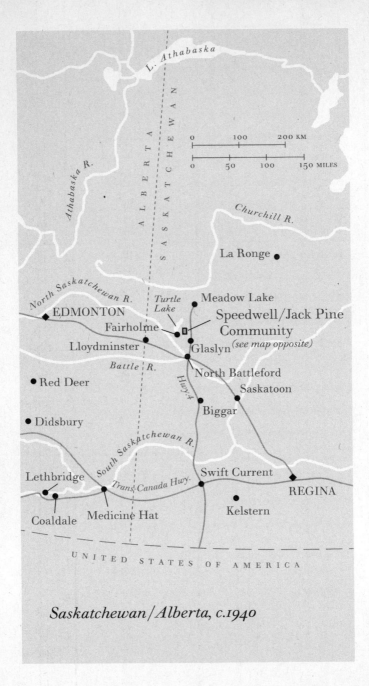

*Saskatchewan/Alberta, c.1940*

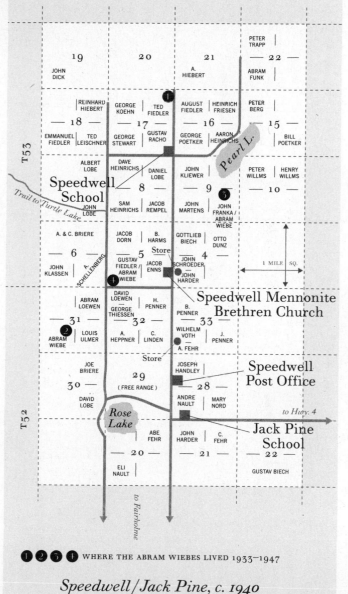

Speedwell/Jack Pine, c. 1940

BASED ON THE ORIGINAL AARON HEINRICHS MAP, 1930

What do you do for a living? I asked.
I remember, she replied.

—ROBERT KROETSCH,
*The Snowbird Poems*, "Conversation #2"

~

Daut wia soo lang tridj, daut es meist nijch meea soo.
That was so long ago, it is almost no longer so.

—Russian Mennonite proverb

# CONTENTS

OF THIS EARTH

# NOW

~

"Nu es et Tiet," my mother would say in the Russian Mennonite Low German our family always spoke together. Now it is time. And my father would get up to wrap his bare feet in foot-cloths and pull on his felt boots with rubbers over them, hook his heavy mackinaw and fur cap off the pegs by the door and go outside with the neighbour we were visiting. They would lead Prince and Jerry out of the barn and hitch them to our bobsled and we would drive home to a rhythm of harness bells, always, as I remember it, in blue darkness and covered by blankets and stiff cowhide in the sledbox.

We are travelling between winter poplars, momentarily open fields, along massive black walls of spruce; the horses feeling in the snow the trail of their own hoofprints home like the narrow path of sky above us, bright heaven sprinkled with light but sometimes, abruptly, flaming out like an exploded sun, a shower of fire and frightening until it swims away into waves fading out in rainbows: there, God lives in such light eternally and so far away I may never get there beyond the stars. Though my mother certainly will, and also, perhaps, my father.

They are singing. My father's favourite hymn, which they have carried with them from their Mennonite villages on the steppes of Ukraine and Russia to sing in Saskatchewan's boreal forest:

Hier auf Erden bin ich ein Pilger,
Und mein Pilgern, und mein Pilgern währt
nicht lang. . . .

Here on earth I am a pilgrim
And my pilgrimage will not be very long. . . .

In the crystalline cold my mother's soprano weaves the high notes on "Pi-il-ger" back and forth into my father's tenor like wind breathing through the leaves of summer aspen. My oldest sister, Tina, is married and my oldest brother, Abe, in Bible school, they are not there, and Dan is standing at the open back of the sledbox, tall and silent; but we four younger siblings are humming inside our layered clothes under the covers, Mary especially because she can already thread alto between Mam and Pah's voices, make three-part harmony, and if only Dan would open his mouth, as Mary tells him often enough, we could have a family quartet even if Helen and Liz and I are too little for anything yet except melody.

We are driving home in the boreal forest that wraps itself like an immense muffler around the shoulders of North America; the isolated spot where once my particular life appeared. A physical place in western Canada not difficult to find: north of North Battleford halfway to Meadow Lake, west off Highway 4 where the Saskatchewan Official Highway Map is blank except for tiny blue streams beginning and running in every direction; not a settlement name north of Glaslyn, for ninety kilometres; in the space cornered by Turtle and Stony and Midnight lakes. The ground of whatever I was or would be, root and spirit.

There, before I could speak any language, I heard Psalm 90, a Prayer of Moses, read aloud, and recited at home and in church:

Herr, Gott, du bist unsere Zuflucht für und
für. . . .

Lord, God, you have been our refuge in all
generations.
Before the mountains were brought forth,
or ever you had formed the earth,
from everlasting to everlasting you are God.
All our days pass away under the shadow of your
wrath,
our years come to an end like a sigh.
The years of our life are threescore and ten,
or perhaps by reason of strength fourscore,
yet their span is but toil and trouble,
they are soon cut off, and we fly away.

Threescore and ten years ago my life began on
the stony, glacier-haunted earth of western Canada.
Seventy years of refuge, under the shadow of wrath.
As my mother said, "Now it is time."

—On board MS *Dnieper Princess,*
the Black Sea, October 4, 2004

# HOMESTEAD

~

An arc of water spouts from a steel kettle. It steams against the darkness under the roof rafters like a curve of light. And a scream. My sister Liz—she is five years old, or six—has stepped into the family washtub too quickly, at the instant Helen, certainly nine, began to pour boiling water into the tepid, slightly scummy bathwater I have just scrambled out of. The boiling water slaps down Liz's leg, that's her scream, and with a cry Helen drops the steel kettle to the floor, the water splashes out with the crash, pours over the bumpy boards as the kettle lid rings away and I am screaming too.

Our mother would have been there in a second. Kettles with long spouts are a dangerous story in our family; even as a baby I knew how in Russia my oldest brother, Abe, at six, ran in from play outside and inexplicably tipped the spout of the kettle boiling on the stove into his mouth for a drink and scalded his tongue and throat almost to the point of death. Steel kettles squatted on every kitchen stove, Russia or Canada, often steaming and dangerous, but they were as necessary as continuous fire in the grate.

This must have happened on our CPR homestead before I turned three, certainly in summer when we had washtub baths on Saturday evening, though we washed our feet, dirty from running barefoot all day, every night before bed. First I hunkered down in the tin tub used for washing clothes, then my three sisters bathed in the order of their ages, just adding more hot water each time to what had already grown cold around the person washing before. Until Mary, thirteen with curly blond hair, who would sometimes seize the tub by its handle, drag it to the kitchen doorstep and dump it out, she'd rather wash herself *in a cup* than sit down in everyone else's Schwienarie, piggish filth!

My first memory: water arcing and the length of Liz's small leg scalded; which is not as dreadful as

Abe's throat, but why are the rafters there? Why would we bathe upstairs in the sleeping loft? Where is Mary? The extremely hot, very heavy kettle would have had to be hoisted up the ladder stairs you needed two hands to clutch and climb—hoisted somehow by Helen who was always sickly, never strong? This should have happened in our lean-to kitchen, as usual, beside the woodstove where Mary would simply swing the kettle around by its handle, off the firebox and tilt it over the washtub.

But in this, the first undeniable memory of my life, nothing is more fixed than that low, open jaw of roof rafters and three of us screaming. Childhood can only remain what you have not forgotten.

~

The pole rafters were in the log house our family built on our original Saskatchewan homestead. It stood on a quarter section of land my father acquired in 1934 from the Canadian Pacific Railway—the CPR owned every odd-numbered section in the area— by making a down payment of "Tien dohla fe daut wille Bosch," he told me: ten dollars for that wild bush.

According to Gust Fiedler, my sister Tina's husband for over sixty years, the first people to clear land for farming in the northernmost area of what would become the Speedwell school district were his cousins the John Lobes. The Lobe–Fiedler–Dunz clan were not Mennonites but ethnic Germans originally from Bessarabia (now in Moldova) who had emigrated to Harvey, North Dakota, before World War I. However, they were extremely poor there and wanted better land, closer together for their extended families, so several clan sons, including Gust, moved again, north into Canada to look for the "free" homesteads Saskatchewan was advertising. By 1925 they found what they wanted north of Glaslyn on the highway to Meadow Lake, west and north on the Jack Pine School Road: a whole township of land available for homestead settlement. Within the next five years they filed on some twelve to fifteen quarters north of Jack Pine School. As Gust said, "We were close together and the land really cost nothing, just work."

"But solid bush wilderness?"

"We weren't scared of work, clearing land! There was some good bottom land and hay sloughs and lots of big spruce and pine, so we Fiedlers set up a sawmill, John Lobe brought in a steamer and breaking plow to bust sod and Otto Dunz a good threshing machine. And in '26 and '27 lots of Mennonites were coming too, immigrants, everybody wanted land. Poplars can be chopped down and rooted out."

Jack Pine School had been organized in 1920 by the Joe Handley (English) and Elie Nault (Metis) families for the few homesteaders who already lived in Township 52, northeast of shallow Stony Lake, but north beyond them, in Township 53, the Lobe–Fiedler–Dunz clan began settlement and Russian Mennonite immigrants from the Soviet Union followed them. Area population grew fast during the Depression because immigrants prefer to settle land in language and racial groups—a practice Canada has always encouraged for stability and development—and also because the Saskatchewan government wanted farmers in its aspen parkland north, away from the dried-out prairie south. As *Maclean's Magazine* reported on April 1, 1932, in an article called "The Trek to Meadow Lake":

> Starting gradually in spring, the Northward flow of farmers increased as the failure of the 1931 [prairie area] crop became certain, until the movement became the greatest internal migration Canada has seen. . . . Before winter set in some 10,000 persons had moved from the prairies to find new homes in the Northern bush. . . . It was to a greater extent a pilgrimage of the middle-aged, beaten once but trying again. Number Four Highway of Saskatchewan was the main channel of the northward stream.

So Township 53, where the Speedwell School had been organized in 1930, grew quickly into a cul-de-sac community of log and mud-plastered houses, of sod-roofed barns and tiny fields surrounded by boreal forest west and north and east. A single trail led in, cleared more or less along the road allowance survey line over the esker hills and around the swamps north from the Jack Pine School corner. When my family arrived from the dusted-out Saskatchewan prairie in May 1933, every quarter-section homestead along the only road between Jack Pine and Speedwell schools (see map, p. vii) was, except for Joe Handley, settled by the Lobe–Fiedlers or Mennonites. Dad found our "CPR quarter," as we called our 160 acres, at the end of a bush track a mile and a half west of the main road.

Boreal forest continued endlessly west of us, but walk on "our" land in any direction and aspen, black poplar, birch, clumps of spruce towered over you, here and there a ragged jack pine or a tiny hay slough rimmed by willows with spring water for singing frogs and mosquitoes. A quarter square mile of basically flat land—good to clear for fields—except for a long esker knoll that ran across our neighbour Louis Ulmer's west field and over our eastern boundary to end in a shallow slough. A well beside a slough was always good for watering cattle:

my father and brothers cleared that knoll of aspen to make our farmyard.

~

As the people of the Thunderchild Cree or Saulteaux Indian reserves might have told us, whose ancestors had hunted animals and gathered berries and roots and collected poplar sap on that land for hundreds of generations, we Russian Mennonite Wiebes were the first people since creation to build a house of wood on that place; to try and live there by farming. But the Cree and Saulteaux people were isolated by Treaty Six, restricted to live on their reserves twenty miles apart, in bush beyond Turtle Lake to the west and Midnight Lake to the east. I don't know if anyone in my family ever met them, or even exchanged a word with one of them when they drove by on the road allowances in summer, their wagons filled with children. I know I never did. And though I waved, only the man driving waved back.

We lived on the edge of white settlement with only endless "empty" bush, as it seemed to us, west of our CPR land, but we never trapped wild animals or hunted them for food. My parents would not have a rifle in their house, not so much as a .22 for rabbits or the partridges that burrowed into the grain stooks when the snow caught us in fall before Otto Dunz's threshing machine reached our place, and we had to haul the oats through the snow for cowfeed and wait with threshing what was left of the barley till winter was over. One spring we heard that Alex Sahar, a Russian homesteader beyond the Aaron Heinrichses near Highway 4, had shot four thousand rabbits that winter, sold the pelts for eight to ten cents each and fed the carcasses to his pigs, but no, our Pah said, we're Mennonite farmers, we raise our food, we grow gardens, grain, raise chickens for eggs and meat, pigs for meat and cows for milk and cream. Daut Wille enne Wildnis es nijch fe uns, animals in the wild aren't for us.

Nevertheless, like the Cree and Saulteaux, we did eat jackfish caught in Turtle Lake when we went there for summer picnics with the Fiedlers; we traded eggs and chickens for frozen fish when occasional pedlars came around in winter. And we certainly picked wild berries, especially blueberries and saskatoons, ate them with cream or baked them into Plautz, open-faced fruit pastry, or canned them for winter—though we did not know how to dry them and pound them into dried meat to make pemmican the way the Cree had once preserved their food. And, like them, we also dug seneca roots.

We knew nothing about making medicines from them, but Voth's or Schroeder's store paid thirty cents a pound for dried seneca roots which, they said, a company bought from them to make into cough remedies. Robin Hood flour cost two dollars for a one-hundred-pound bag: if we found enough good seneca patches in early summer, Mam, Mary and Helen could maybe dig and sun-dry eight pounds in three days, or four. That was a burlap sack full of tiny sun-wrinkled roots, and Liz and I were too little to dig but I could find the plants as easily as anyone; their flowers were instantly recognizable, a ring of tiny white spears among all the green, like two hands cupped upwards together with flowers on every fingertip. And at their centre the unseen root: the thicker the flowers, the bigger the root.

Seneca plants grow best at the moist edges of aspen groves, and by the time I was big enough to dig them out, my brother Dan had made us diggers from the cut, sharpened leaf of a car spring bolted to the broken spoke of a wagon wheel. I have one still, though I have never found a seneca plant in the aspen forests I wander west of Edmonton. I know I would instantly recognize that ring of flowers, delicate white and low against the earth; it is an image painted on my memory like the face of my mother bent down, smiling, her broad fingers sifting the earth for every gram of root that will buy her one more handful of flour to feed her family.

~

Our CPR house was built of peeled spruce plastered with mud. The only complete photo of it is a distant side view from the south: a bare yard with the bush a ragged wall peering over its vertical slab roof. A man with his hands behind his back and wearing a hat stands against the left window; on the right five children and a woman wearing an apron are lined in a row up to the lean-to door; between them, stretched out on bare ground, two men lie on their elbows in the Russian Mennonite style of taking group pictures, a white-and-black dog at their feet. A two-horse cutter stands beside the willow fence in the right foreground, something we certainly used in winter, but I have no winter memory of that yard; everything is green summer.

The man with his hands behind his back is my father. The spot of white shirt farthest from him in front of the screen door is me, with my mother and her Sunday white apron beside me. Liz is almost invisible, her dress so dark against the butt-ends of the house logs. The taller girl in white beside her is Helen, who died too young. Her hands are folded up together at her lips as if in prayer.

~

The earth along that house is packed grey and bare, especially around the screen door of the kitchen lean-to. And I know Onkel Fout, Mr. Wilhelm Voth, the storekeeper, is very close to me. There are neighbours standing on the yard grass that slopes down towards the barn and the hay corral, the scraggly jack pine beyond the pasture fence; they are laughing, telling stories, but Onkel Fout is crouched down low, staring at me. Slowly he pushes his right hand into his mouth.

So many people of all ages seem to be there, it must be Sunday afternoon, time for spezeare gohne, going visiting. Mennonites in Russia lived side by side in farm villages, but in Canada the Dominion Land Act requires homesteaders to live in a house built on the land they settle and so to us Speedwellers, isolated behind bush, visiting is as important as going to church on Sunday morning. I may still be wearing my Sunday white shirt and short black pants and Onkel Fout is the centre of attention. He owns a store filled with anything you could want to buy and also the only truck in the Speedwell–Jack Pine area; everyone has been listening to him talk about a place called Coaldale. Later I will understand that Coaldale is a town four hundred miles away in southern Alberta where many Mennonites live, where there is always good summer work which any-one can do for steady cash pay in sugar beet fields that stretch to the horizon, that Onkel Fout has taken a load of our young people, including my brother Dan, away to work there for the summer and has just come back, but now I understand nothing except "Coaldale," a word I will never be able to forget.

It is a place where apparently no one has to raka, slave himself to death, clearing trees to finally create one small field, stump by rooted stump dragged out by a team of horses throwing its full strength against a

chain wrapped high around the stump while someone chops furiously at the cracking, anchoring roots,
Coaldale where there are no trees at all, nor so much
as a rock or slough whose moss can swallow you slow
as torture in its brown stinking water. People just
grow sugar beets on a steppe like in Russia—but without the terrible Communists—with water running
between rows of plants whenever you want to open
your ditch, everyone has the right to an irrigation ditch
full of mountain water all summer long and a huge
cash crop every year, sugar, sugar, not like our endless
poplars, nobody will ever sprinkle spruce sawdust on
their porridge for breakfast! But in Coaldale, land of
sugar, far away, the world is completely sweet.

Onkel Fout is shorter than my Pah, who is not as
tall as my oldest brother, Abe, though broader, and
I know my brother Dan is even taller: if Onkel Fout
got into Dan's clothes, more than half of Dan would
be left over for sure. I know he has taken Dan away;
Mam says Dan will be gone all summer. I watch
Onkel Fout drink water out of our dipper from the
pail standing ready for visitors on our best chair in
the shade of the lean-to. Above the dipper rim his
eyes shift, look through me, away south across our
small stumpy clearing of potential grain field and
the stones picked and already piled along its edges
like walls. I say in Low German:

"Will Dan be different?"

"Na?" With a flip he throws the water beside me, so close I feel spray, and hooks the dipper back on the edge of the pail. Suddenly he looks down at me as if I were von jistre, born yesterday.

"Different," I say, "when he comes home . . . you don't look different."

"Du tjliena Tjnirps," he tells me: you little twerp. And he folds down onto his heels so close to me I see the grey sheen of his shaven whiskers. "Can you do this?"

One after the other he pushes his hands, all his fingers, into his gaping mouth. Then slowly he pulls out the inside of his face. Teeth and pink flesh, first the top, then the bottom. His wide fingers hold all that under my nose.

He says, "Can you do it?"

His face is caved in, his words hiss. Appalled, I can only scream. My mother comes quickly, the people all over the yard are staring at me and I burrow my face against her thigh. She shakes me, her big hands grip my head and shoulder shaking me.

"Be still, still! What's the matter with you?"

She has to push me away, pull both my hands out of my mouth before my howling stops and she can understand me.

"Why can't I do that! What's wrong with my mouth!"

Behind me Onkel Fout is laughing. Mam looks up at him, all around us our neighbours are laughing and gradually she smiles just a little.

I ask, "Why can't I take my mouth out?"

When she smiles my mother's teeth do not shine white like the perfect curves in Onkel Fout's hand. They are mostly brownish stumps, almost grey, with gaps; she cuts her meat very small and when she chews I have seen that she holds the food mostly at the front of her mouth, when it shifts back she grimaces. My stern and loving Mam always so afraid of sin for her children, arms warm and tight around me, is in dreadful pain when she eats, though she says nothing. Sometimes she says, "Nu mot etj wada beize," now I have to again—but I don't know exactly what *beize* means, she has never done it to me and I watch her place a lump of salt carefully in a particular spot inside her mouth and I do not know she is pressing it against an eroded stump to try and destroy its relentless pain, I only see pain move in waves between her hands as she clutches her head. Sometimes she even uses a cloth soaked in kerosene. This is poison, she tells me, never you do this! but she holds it inside her mouth with her finger until tears run down her cheeks and after that she spits it out, washes her mouth with water from our pail and spits: *beize* is something too horrible to ask about, or to explain. It means something like killing.

I tell her, reasonably enough, "I want them too. Coaldale teeth."

Behind me Onkel Fout says quietly, "No no, you have all the luck. Born in Canada, the youngest, you'll never need them."

~

Before they leave for their own evening chores, our Sunday afternoon visitors will eat Vaspa with us—the Mennonite custom of "late afternoon tea," which, Onkel Fout has told us, the fancy Englische do too only with a different name—taking turns crowded around the kitchen table where the screen door offers some protection from summer mosquitoes. Tweeback, doubled buns, to eat and Pripps, roasted barley brewed like coffee, to drink, probably with rhubarb stems cooked to a dessert puree, the first edible spring plant to sting your winter-blah mouth, but add a heaping spoon of sugar to your bowl, or even two—"Benjeltje! Dauts jenuag!" You little imp, that's enough! and a slap hovering above my hard head—with a thick swash of whipped cream and you could never gulp enough.

Eaten with Vaspa Tweeback, those inexpressible buns baked of butter and flour, two cups of one to ten cups of the other and mixed between Mam's powerful hands in milk and boiled-potato water, a food carried over four centuries from the Netherlands to Poland/Prussia to Russia/Ukraine, often roasted to preserve them for long journeys over land or sea, gnawed dry or dipped in Pripps or tea or coffee if there ever was any money to buy them. And now when neighbours visited here in bush Canada, Tweeback could be opened, parted completely, and both parts skimmed over with wild cranberry or pincherry jelly, blueberry jam. My first solid food: roasted Tweeback crushed to crumbs and mixed with warm milk: Tjreemel senn uck Broot, crumbs are also bread, and the enduring proverb of the poor: Broot schleit den Hunga doot: bread strikes all hunger dead.

~

Our house in the clearing on the CPR knoll was built of white spruce my father and brothers cut on our 160 acres of bush. They selected the trees tall and straight from various spruce stands scattered among the dense poplars, cut them down with a two-man crosscut saw and dragged them through bush to the knoll with our team of horses; nothing to pay but sweat. Peeling was easy: the trees were so strong with sap that a strip cut loose at one end could often be tugged off the complete length of log, round golden wood drying in the sun. It seems I was born while they were notching and stacking the cured logs up into walls, round by round, until they reached eight feet and could lay the ceiling beams across the width of them.

In a family photo taken several years later, the log ends of those ceiling beams protrude from the house wall, and clearly the roof rafters above these beams are thin peeled poles as well, probably black spruce or lodgepole pine. From the width of the two windows you can estimate the house was either twenty-two or twenty-four feet long, with an eight-foot lean-to kitchen added on the eastern gable end. No picture shows the width of the gable. The house is eleven logs high to the ceiling beams, and either two or three logs above that to the pole rafters and the roof of tarpaper and rough-cut slabs, so my bath memory could be right: there was plenty of space for sleeping under the roof, and with six children at home (Tina married Gust Fiedler and they moved onto his homestead the winter before our house was built) the two oldest boys at least would have wanted to.

My mother told me she bore me in a log hut, a temporary, first-summer shack with earth for a floor they built on the site before starting the house, so they could move onto the homestead in 1934 as fast as possible. The hut stood in the hollow west of the knoll and later, she said, was used as our chicken barn. My birth certificate states I was born at the Canadian geographical co-ordinates of "S. W. 31–52–17 West 3rd" on Thursday, October 4, 1934, and they must have been building the house very fast so late in the season, perhaps they just barely got the roof slabbed horizontally over the pole rafters, tarpapered and slabbed again vertically and the walls chinked with plaster in time to move in before winter hit. If they were very lucky the frost and snow came really late that fall, and my three sisters, aged ten, seven and three, would have helped make the mud plaster in the way my father had learned on the Russian steppes, how to mix water and clay with straw and cow manure and grass by tramping it out in a mud pit with their little bare feet, bare legs shivering under their skirts lifted in the autumn air of wet mud and coming cold. There is unbelievably much labour to building a house by hand in Saskatchewan bush, so you can live safely through the long northern darkness of winter with a daughter who is often ill and a final, squalling, son.

But no matter how hard or long the work, you needed to buy almost nothing. You could even work at the Fiedlers' sawmill to earn the floorboards and roof slabs, so only the windows, the tarpaper and nails and stovepipes actually cost money. And, Gott sei Dank, thanks be to God, there was also no need to build house walls from Pautzen, clay bricks, as my father did in 1917 after the Russian war offensive collapsed into disaster and he rode freight trains back to the treeless steppe of Romanovka village, and built, at the landless-worker end of the settlement, an entire house of sun-dried clay bricks for himself, Mam and their two infants. Though Canadian bush was hard labour to clear for grain fields, it did provide superb wood for farm buildings, endless fuel to keep you warm in winter and dense shelter from the wind and driving, white-out blizzards of the open steppe.

And here and there on our quarter square mile of mostly tall trembling aspen lay small water sloughs hidden by willows that nubbled into silver pussy willows in spring long before leaves appeared; and also clumps of paper birch. Birch, Pah said, like the great forests where he had served for three years as a Mennonite conscientious objector during the Great War on the Kiva River near Zurskoi Lienichstvo in central Siberia; cluster birch I would see all my Canadian life spraying up from the blue silence of snow, suddenly there, like hoarfrost spirits among the winter aspen.

~

The south wall of that CPR house on the knoll was the background for the first photograph of our entire family.

Angled against the logs so as to face into the light, Mam and Pah sit on high-backed chairs whose carved rungs are visible between their legs. We seven children circle around and between them under the overhang of the pole-and-slab roof. The slab door of the kitchen stands open behind my sister Helen's left shoulder, beyond her face squinting into the evening sun. The heavy shadow of the photographer—someone who seems wrapped in a heavy cloak—is thicker than any of us; the shadow reaches across the bare foreground and up the right side of the picture, it cuts a black angle through Helen's legs just above her ankles and the shapeless bump of its head blots the corner of her skirt. Helen will be the first of us to die, in late March when World War II in Europe is at last coming to an end, and thirty years before our father seated beside her, who will be next. The shoulder bulge of the long shadow barely misses Pah's left foot so close to Helen's right, but his large worker hands lying on his knees are already balled into fists, and ready.

The click of a box camera exposed my slightly unfocused family in a place and position no memory could retain so absolutely. An image to fit in your palm, several aged cracks across its surface. All proper in our Speedwell Mennonite Brethren Church best, Pah and Abe and Dan in suits and ties, Tina, Mary, Helen and Liz in dresses and stockings, Mam in a flowered dress with triangular dark collar and a black cloche hat whose buttons shine above her forehead lifted high into the sun. No one faces the low light as openly as she.

I stand at her knee. Or it may be I am being held tight against her knee, because my mother's right leg is angled against my chest, her right arm tight around my back, her right hand grips my right elbow and her left hand holds my right hand down on her thigh as if, were she to relax for an instant, I would vanish. Aus du tjleen weascht, she often told me, when you were small you never crawled; you walked, you ran before eight months.

Tjleene Tjinja klunje o'pe Schoot,
Groote Tjinja klunje op'em Hoat.

Little children trample your lap,
Grown children trample your heart.

In our meagre photo collection from various times on two continents, this is the first in which I appear. It must have been an important event—someone's first box camera?—because we have four photos taken on the same spot on the same day.

In the other three photos, all without the shadow, I have been released, small me, to stand on one of the ornate chairs. Once I am flanked by Abe and Dan, who are so tall that my head barely reaches the crooks of their elbows; then again I am surrounded by six girls, three of whom are my youngest sisters but the other three I do not recognize. All the girls look into the camera, except Helen, who is exactly my height on the chair and looking at me, her mouth open. Perhaps she is already telling me a story.

In the fourth photo taken that day, I stand alone on the chair. My mouth is opening, my right arm rising as if I am about to orate. Compared to the standard height of a chair, I could be seventy-five centimetres—thirty inches—tall. How old is that?

I contemplate the four photos; gradually I am drawn to my oldest sister, who appears only once, in the picture with the shadow. Tina stands at the back, so slender between Abe and Dan, her face tilted down and it seems her eyes are closed. Or it is possible, to judge from the angle of her head, that she is looking down over Mam's shoulder at me, and it comes to me that memory in these images is like the ineffability of the love she and I gave each other, oldest and youngest, always separated except for a few days, or a few hours, of visit year after year; a love we felt that needed no comment or overt demonstration.

There were either twenty or nineteen years between us: twenty if you accept the "1914" written on Mam's February 1930 German refugee camp identity papers, nineteen if you accept Tina's personal word. "Anyways," she shrugged, "what does it matter, a year so far back?" She was simply Katerina and Abram Wiebe's first child, born in Village Number Eight, Romanovka, Orenburg Mennonite Colony, near the Ural Mountains in eastern European Russia, and I, their last child, was born in a place that was nameless but profusely numbered, the southwest quarter of Section 31, Township 52, Range 17, west of the 3rd meridian in Saskatchewan, Canada. Born on the same latitude, 53.5 degrees north, but on opposite bends of the globe, she October 25, 1914, and I October 4, 1934.

And there is, as well, a photograph of infant Tina standing on a chair. But taken in a studio, in Russia. She balances herself, not as I do against the chair back, but by hooking her right hand into the cummerbund of a woman who stands beside her in a floor-length dress trimmed with white lace, her hair and eyes black, her face calmly beautiful, someone I would never recognize as my careworn mother. But when I receive this picture in 1997 from the aged daughter of Mam's half-sister, who has lived out her Soviet exile life in "stony Tajikistan," as she calls it, she declares that this sweet, elegant woman truly is my mother at twenty, and the tiny girl on the chair my oldest sister.

Tina herself was staggered by the photo. She saw it for the first time in her memory the year before she died at the age of eighty-four. When we together pondered where our mother might have gone to get such a studio portrait—it must have been in the city of Orenburg over a hundred kilometres away, a journey possible only by horse and wagon—Tina thought it likely was taken to send to Pah, who served out the First World War in the Forstei, the Czar's forestry service, and who had never yet seen his first child.

The young, handsome woman and man in these photographs were my parents, married in Romanovka on January 19, 1914; Tina was born there in October 1914, and she married Gustav Fiedler on January 15, 1934, in stony bush Canada. I was born the following October, so my mother must have conceived me about the time of Tina's wedding. Seven children in twenty years, all evenly spaced with never a miscarriage or infant death: how did my mother, working ceaselessly and often ill with stomach, leg and teeth ailments, manage that? Most of her contemporaries who survived middle age gave birth fifteen times in twenty years with barely half their babies living past infancy. Mam was not one to talk about such things as birth control: the birth of children was not "controlled," they were "a gift from God," and after I became a parent myself and jokingly told her I thought that nevertheless she had had quite a bit to do with it, to say nothing of Pah, she turned to the potatoes frying on her stove with a curt, "Jung, sie doch jescheit." Boy, do be decent.

Even Tina had no explanation when we talked about our varying ages years after our mother's death. She did not remember Mam nursing any baby very long in Russia—there was never enough good food, and she knew she held the bottle for baby Abe when she was three, she thought, or at most four— but she did have one particular memory about me, from before I was born. The summer our mother was pregnant with me, Mam was ashamed.

"What?"

"Ashamed to go to church, to be seen. Here I was, her daughter, young and married seven, eight months and still thin as a stick, nothing, and here she was, an old woman and sticking out"—Tina's hands shape an impossible mound over her lap—"you were big!"

"Old? She just turned thirty-nine."

"It's true." Tina laughs high and quick. "So we had to get going."

Gust snorts happily. "And we caught up, seven kids too!"

Tina's smile fades a little. After a moment she says, "That wasn't so easy. Five children under fifteen and then all of a sudden two more in a year and a half, when I'm close to forty."

Gust's elbows are propped on the table, his head in his hands. "Always good kids though," he says quietly, "all seven."

Tony was the first, born in late August 1935, nearly eleven months after me. But he is not in the family picture, nor is his father; only slender Tina standing between our broad brothers, her hair pulled severely back, her body angled away from the shadow reaching across the ground.

Judging by my size and the height of the ornate chair, I believe those first family pictures were taken in the spring or early summer of 1936, when I was one and a half years old. Gust clicked the camera—he would have bought it—in the low evening light and baby Tony, perhaps nine months old, was somewhere behind the window curtains thankfully already asleep.

## 2.

# MOTHER TONGUES

~

Saskatchewan tried, wherever possible, to ensure that all its children between the ages of seven and fifteen had access to a public school within three miles of their home, and so our cul-de-sac community off Highway 4, still being chopped as farmsteads and fields out of the forest, was divided into two school districts. The boundary between them was the east–west township road allowance: everyone living south in Township 52 attended Jack Pine School, while those who lived in Township 53 went to Speedwell School four miles north (see map, p. vii). Each school was a one-room building for grades one to eight, together with space for a playground, a horse barn for students driving or riding to school and a small teacherage where the teacher could live if she or he chose not to board with a local family.

The road connecting the two schools was the busiest in the community, not only because there were settlers on every quarter section but also because the Speedwell Mennonite Brethren Church, the Speedwell post office—which served both school districts—run by the postmistress, Lucille (Mrs. Joe) Handley, and also Schroeder's (later Harder's) and Voth's general stores were on that road. At the Jack Pine corner the road turned either east to the highway or continued south through the Clarkville School District, past homesteads and the Evangelical Mennonite Brethren Church, which we sometimes attended for harvest and mission services, to the hamlet of Fairholme on the Canadian National Railroad with almost a hundred people, two elevators and a tiny red passenger station, nine miles of twisting road allowance from Jack Pine School, thirteen from Speedwell.

Our CPR homestead was half a mile south of the school district boundaries and so, beginning in spring 1934, Helen, Mary and Dan attended Jack Pine. By the time I grew to consciousness Liz would soon be going too, but Dan was no longer at school: he was nine when they arrived in Canada and when he turned fifteen on January 26, 1935, he was a six-foot bony boy, struggling and uncomfortable in grade five. And Pah said now the Canada school law was passed, he could leave and go work. And he did: John Lobe had a government contract for cutting railroad ties and he received a relief grant of $15 a month for every man he hired: $7.50 was to pay the wages for the worker and $7.50 his keep. So Dan joined Lobe's crew; they chopped down spruce in the snow, sawed them into eight-foot tie lengths and then flattened them on two sides with a flat-face broadaxe: nine-inch face for a grade 1 tie, seven-inch face for a grade 3. Exhausting, heavy labour for a fifteen-year-old, but John Lobe was a good man: he paid Dan the whole grant and fed and boarded him besides, so Dan had the whole fifteen dollars to bring home to our family.

Dan never attended school again. "But I wrecked my back lifting logs, always the heavy end," he tells me, retired from a lifetime of ranching in northern Alberta. "I had a lot of trouble. I went to chiropractors till I was about seventy-five years old, then my back must have fused, now I have no back problems, praise the Lord."

The language in both schools was of course English, but no one spoke it at home except Joe

Handley's family and perhaps the Metis Brieres and Naults—and Old Man Stewart who lived alone in his cluttered shack and, it was said, talked very fancy English to his dog and had been seen walking back and forth preaching something incomprehensible to the trees. The Fiedler–Lobe–Dunz clan from Bessarabia spoke mostly High German—or sometimes Swaebisch between the elders—but everyone else in a community of about three hundred people was Mennonite, 1920s immigrants or refugees from the Soviet Union and their day-to-day language was the one we Wiebe children spoke to our parents all their lives: Russian Mennonite Low German.

A comic, self-deprecating poem brought from Russia was sometimes recited in our homes when neighbours visited each other on long winter evenings, heard always with laughter and more laughing stories. I remember one verse:

MIENE MUTTASPROAK

Daut disse Sproak dee baste es,
Wea haft duat wohl besträde?
Sest haud dee Mutta gaunz jewess
See mie nie leahd too räde.


MY MOTHER TONGUE

This language is the very best,

Who ever could dispute it?
Or else my mother certainly
Would never have taught me to speak it.

The Mennonite variation of European Low Country German is rooted in Old Saxon and was carried by our ancestors from Friesland, Holland, where the Mennonites originated during the religious disputes, wars and martyrdoms of the early sixteenth century. Die Wereloose Christenen, the "Defenseless Christians," as they called themselves for their committed discipleship to the teachings of Jesus and their pacifism, carried their language with them on their journeys—which were often flights from persecution simply to stay alive—along the European Lowlands of the North Sea, always borrowing more vocabulary and practices from surrounding languages over four centuries, from the Netherlands to Poland/Prussia to Ukraine and Russia, and eventually to North and South America. It grew into a distinct language as closely related to English as it is to modern Dutch and German.

In the spring of 1938, when I was three, our family had been in Canada for eight years, but my parents had learned only a few words of English. Like many other Canadian immigrants, they had always lived in communities of their own people: several months with relatives in Didsbury, Alberta, when they arrived in 1930, three years working on the dryland farm of my mother's uncle Henry Knelsen in the Kelstern dust bowl of southern Saskatchewan, and now five years in Speedwell. In all the strangeness of Canada and "de Englische," the English, which to them meant anyone who did not speak Low German, they found groups of Mennonite people they could live and work with and, even more important, a church where they could worship. This was the most powerful way in which they came to feel at home in Canada.

~

But school in western Canada is only English, and when Helen and Mary got home late in the afternoon from their three-mile trudge back from Jack Pine School along road allowance and cow trails and said something English to me, I knew it as easily as anything my mother spoke all day. Because different languages meant nothing to me, words were sounds made with your mouth that meant whatever anyone said they did, and I swallowed them whole without thinking. To a child of three or four, words are a continuing revelation of arbitrary mysteries that everyone older agrees about, and I learned to make the right sounds so that everyone understood me and no one would laugh: my parents simply made certain sounds, my siblings at times others.

And even better, my sisters could show me what their words looked like in the school readers they were sometimes allowed to bring home for one evening—they could not leave the reader at home for me to look at all day, never, school rules! I can still feel the ribbed, heavy blue covers of *Highroads to Reading*, Book Two under my fingertips, see the smooth, beautifully tinted pictures inside, and the exact shape of English words:

If the moon came from heaven,
Talking all the way,
What could she have to tell us,
And what could she say?

"That's *moon*," ten-year-old Helen points up with the same finger that has led her voice and my eyes across the page, speaking out loud the tiny black tracks on the perfect white paper. In the long northern evening light she is multiplying meaning from sound to sight and back again. "It's almost like *Mohn*, just a little different."

And of course I believe her instantly; I will understand these shifty differences for the rest of my life. For Helen and me anything can have as many names as it wants: that giant ball of light rising out of the black aspen across the field on Louis Ulmer's homestead can change its sound from Mam's Low German *de Mohn* to the church preacher's High German *der Mond* to school English "the moon" as easily as it will, I already know, change its shape night after night sailing across the sky. There are marks on its orange face now, they could be eyes—or scars, maybe from torture like they do in Russia, maybe the moon has a Russian name too, Pah could name it in Russian if he wanted to, and Mam as well, but they never do, never, not another word in that Communist Stalin language now be still about it.

Perhaps, if Mam dared to ask it in Russian, the moon would say something nice about her youngest brother Heinrich Knelsen, the terrible Communist, but so sad-eyed, who sent her his picture from Russia wearing that Red Army uniform, a huge red star on his pointed military cap. Or tell us something, anything, about her older brother Johann, whom Stalin's police have disappeared. If only she dared ask—would God answer her about her brothers and horrible Stalin if she prayed in Russian? She never does, nor in Low German; my mother prays only in High German, and weeping.

~

The poplar leaves shiver like fear in the night wind, their branches groan above us in the moonlight. And it comes to me now that Helen and I, and Liz as well, yes, we are in a tent under the trees in the hollow behind our log house. In the dark where any sound could suddenly shift into a different, dangerous story. But there are three of us and we are safe together on our CPR homestead, warm, we have our barn lantern burning under the sloped canvas, a tiny flame enclosed by glass among our good sheets and quilts and pillows piled high around us safe as our bed. Safe from everything. Today we helped carry all the family bedding out of the house into the yard as we do every year, we stripped our fingers tight down every quilt and pillow seam, we opened all the mattresses and shook out their oat straw—crushed fine by a winter of sleep—into a heap and watched as the quick bonfire flamed it into light, air and ashes. Work all day and now the story can start, a story just a little bit scary but not too much, okay now, start:

It is time. Mother Duck has to go out of the house for food. She warns her six ducklings once more about the red fox: they must stay inside, they must lock the door behind her and not open it, no, never, only when she returns and they hear her voice call, only her voice. Then she goes out and instantly the six ducklings slam the house door shut behind her. And they lock it!

Our house has no lock, only a latch, but we are not inside. In the long summer twilight we youngest, Helen and Liz and I, crowd together around the globe of light, so safe and cozy under all our bedding in a tent set up near our root cellar and the various well holes now filled back in again because my brothers could not find water in them, and actually we're under the tall poplars close to the Betjhüs, the toilet; it won't be far to go in the dark if one of us has to. Our log house is sealed as tightly as possible, every crack closed with mud or rags, and there will soon be nothing alive inside, not even the mice who will have all scurried out by now, Helen says, because the horrible stink of formaldehyde is burning slowly in pails, it must burn for at least three days to kill all the Waunztje, the lice, bedbugs, that hide in every mud-plaster crack, the log joints and splits where they wait to come out at night to bite us, suck blood from the folds of our necks, from behind our ears and around our eyes when we're asleep against the straw mattress and the deep pillows made of feathers plucked from our chickens.

My straw and feather bed is soft and very warm, but the lice and wood fleas are worse than mosquitoes because they creep in, Mam says, unstoppably day and night from the endless bush all around us. The lice like the warm seams of our bedding too and they hide in every fold, waiting there for our warm blood; sometimes I wake up at night crying in pain. But no fox can sneak out of the bush to get into a house where the door is wedged shut, and the ducklings won't open when a fox knocks, most certainly not when they hear his voice. Never.

"Go away!" they all shout. "Our mother has a sweet voice but your voice is rough! You are the red fox, go away!"

And Red Fox will go away—to the grocery store. He says to the grocer, "Give me a big piece of chalk, I want to eat it!" The grocer is worried; he thinks this fox wants to trick someone again, but he is also very afraid and so he gives him what he wants. That's the way it is with people who are afraid.

Red Fox chews the chalk and goes back to the ducklings again. "Open the door, my darlings," his voice now so soft and sweet, "I have a present for each of you!"

And of course the ducklings know such a sweet voice can only be their mother, they unlock and open the door—but there are the horrible teeth of Red Fox! They scatter in every direction, hide among the firewood, inside the stove, even behind the chamber pot under the bed but Red Fox finds them, wherever they are, and gobbles them up, gulp!

Yes, every one—well, no, only five, because the littlest duckling is so smart it jumps up on the window sill and hides behind the curtain. Red Fox's stomach is stuffed with five fat ducklings but he wants the sixth too, foxes never leave a scrap or feather, and he looks and looks, but the littlest duckling stays so perfectly still, barely breathing, that finally Red Fox thinks, why bother, such a little Tjnirps, I'm sure he doesn't even taste good!

And he wobbles out of the house, he's so-o-o full, lies down on the grass beside the river, it's such hard work catching lunch, he stretches out and falls asleep in the warm sunshine.

I'm the littlest in our family so I'm often called du Tjnirps, you little twerp! and I know for sure I'd be the smart duckling and I'd save everyone, no fox would ever find me behind the window curtains. Though I have never seen a river. Sometimes in spring, when the snow melts, water runs past for several days like a creek through this hollow below our locked house with formaldehyde smoking through it. The ugly scrabbling Waunztje will be falling inside, out of the cracks and mud plaster between the logs like snow, my mother and sisters will sweep them into black drifts and shovel them out when we open the doors and windows wide, let the wind whistle through and blow out the stink.

I hear this story inside our summer Waunztje tent behind the CPR house on the knoll. We lived there only four years; we had not yet cleared thirty acres of cropland—all the men had to work for pay whenever they could to support the family, and there was no time to clear bush; perhaps we had not even paid the CPR any more than the down payment— and though it seems our mother did not want to leave, in 1938 Pah insisted we move. John Franka had proved up on a quarter near Speedwell School, but he was moving away: that was better, more cleared land, and we should go there.

This happened before I turned four, and I remember nothing about chickens roosting and laying eggs in the log shack in which the local midwife Mary (Mrs. Gottlieb) Biech once assisted my mother to give birth to me. I do not retain the faintest image of a room inside that good CPR house, not a curtain or a windowsill, nor can I recall whether the interior walls were nailed over diagonally with slim willows and smeared smooth with plaster for whitewash. Nevertheless, this detailed story is as sharp a memory as I have of our first homestead: ducklings, a fox, the tent in the hollow under poplars, our house sealed thick with poison gas, the bush vermin my mother detested: Waunztje.

~

The story is like a folktale Mam might have known from her High German Mennonite school in Russia, but the only stories she told were either about her life in Russia or from the Bible, and there are no talking ducks in the Bible, leave alone in a Mennonite village. It seems only Helen could have told the duckling story; she must have found it in a Jack Pine School book. Did I know that much English before I was four?

Nonethcless, the story continues:

Mother Duck returns to the horror of her door hanging open, her house empty and furniture thrown around like feathers, oh-oh-oh, she is crying her worst fears for her children, lost forever because of horrible Red Fox—but the sixth duckling bumbles against the curtain, drops to the floor with stubby wings beating, Oh smart little Sixth! He'll tell Mother everything, together they follow the tired tracks to the bank of the river where Red Fox lies snoring. With his belly bulging . . . and they see it ripple, yes, it is stirring a little.

Mother Duck does what a mother has to do: she takes from her apron pocket her scissors, her needle and thread. Swiftly she begins to snip Red Fox's belly open, the first duckling already has its head out and, as she snips more, all five hop out one by one. Then Mother sends them down to the river for stones.

This first story I remember being told is a story completed by stones. My father groaned there were stones like lice on that CPR land, and even as a toddler I knew that when he and my brothers had finally cleared the first ten acres, chopping trees and brush and digging at roots and leaving tall stumps to give leverage for tearing them out with chains and straining horses, even after John Lobe's steam tractor with steam-lug wheels as wide as I was long had blasted itself over the land and its giant breaking-shares had ripped the sod over into stripes glistening with more peeled roots and clay, I knew that when Pah worked the breaking down with our smaller plows and disks, more and more stones would emerge. We heard the crack! of steel on stone all day long.

Thirty acres was too much everlasting labour, how could you ever grow a saleable crop? My sister Mary remembered that land angrily all her life, uggh, good for nothing but mosquitoes and stone soup!

"I think," John Lobe told Pah sadly beside his panting steamer, "you found one of these real good stone quarters, like me. Nine years we've plowed, and every year there's a new crop of stones to pick. They grow even better than the weeds."

Sixty years later I again find the cellar hole of
the house on the knoll. Every farm building long
vanished: the aboriginal bush is grown back as
tangled and tall as aspen will grow. What was once
yard, hay corral, fields, is now so thick with trees
I can sometimes only wedge myself through sideways. My son Chris discovers a crushed, rusted
Stelco waterpail where the willow fence once
marked our quarter boundary, and also the edge of
the field my father and brothers cleared south of
the farmyard: a wide, pyramidal ridge of gathered
stones with poplars sprouting through it, a ridge
winding out of sight into seemingly untouched
boreal forest like the relentless esker of a human
glaciation momentarily passing.

The ducklings, little Sixth too, each bring a stone
as big as they can carry up from the river. They
lay them neatly inside the opened belly and
Mother sews it shut so lightly Red Fox will never
dream he has so much as a scar. And then they're
off, up the hill, inside the house, lock the door
and talk, oh! all at once:

"I got stuck half-way down . . ."

"He's so greedy, he just gulped . . ."

"I was really cozy between . . ."

"The gurgling, ugggh! his stomach . . ."

"I felt sour all over!"

and beside the river Red Fox wakes up. He has a
dreadful thirst and, strangely, his stomach feels
so heavy, so hard. He staggers to the river and
bends down and opens his long mouth to drink;
the heavy stones slide forward, he tips over head-
first, he falls, he drowns.

On our homestead we had many chickens but
never ducks or geese like the Russian villagers
always had, Mam said. Nor were there any foxes in
our area. However, we and all our neighbours scattered throughout the bush had farm dogs: never as
pets in the house, but working dogs who remained
outside or in the barn like every other farm animal.
Sometimes towards evening our black dog Carlo—or

Louis Ulmer's or David Loewen's dogs in their yards far beyond the darkening trees—would answer the howls of the coyotes hunting in the free range west of us, in the tangled deadfall and hills and muskegs that stretched for miles, it was said, until they disappeared into the white sand beaches of enormous Turtle Lake. At four I had not yet seen Turtle Lake often enough to remember it, but I recognized the high laughter of coyotes easily, in the same way that I heard and recognized our several cowbells far away in summer on the free range. I knew what our cowbells meant, and our calves and cows bawling: they were hungry, they were thirsty, they wanted each other. But what did coyotes cry in their strange, yipping language, and what did Carlo answer?

Their wild ululations rise like mist where the last twilight fades against the western clouds; I go into the house and pull the door shut. And perhaps it is because Mary has read aloud from her blue *Highroads to Reading*, Book Four that I lean my ear against the inside of the slab door:

Some one came knocking
At my wee, small door;
Some one came knocking,
I'm sure—sure—sure;

I listened, I opened,
I looked to left and right,
But nought there was a-stirring
In the still dark night. . . .

I do not lift the latch to open the door, nor do I look to left or right. I am listening for a knock: our farmyard is so completely alone at the end of a winding trail that no one ever is just "passing by," no one ever visits us except on Sundays; and I know if I open the door the summer night will not be still. Outside there is breathing high among the aspen leaves; small creatures scurry past your feet; somewhere in the darkness robins scold an owl fiercely and then, before you can sense it coming, the owl has passed with the *swish!* of its feathered body tilting huge and gone between branches. You trust the dark around the house, it always remains in the same place, the same shape, your bare feet feel the hollow path you need to walk along shifting pale or greyer, and certainly ahead is the black Betjhüs, literally "house for bending," with its two high ovals in the seat for big people and a little bench beside it with an opening rounded perfectly for my small buttocks.

Often I don't need to go as far as the toilet, I'm a boy, just around the corner of the house is enough to swing my Stengelji, my Zoagel, my little Schwenjeltje, my little stem . . . tail . . . handle/clapper, Low German has all kinds of sounds for it, every one a giggle when a sibling says it out loud, probably so many because sometimes it changes in your hands, funny how it will feel different though you are always doing one thing, standing there, pushing, letting it pour. You're a boy, when you feel full you don't need to find a bush to crouch behind like your sisters, day or night you just turn your back and point, wave, shoot, spray anywhere among the weeds and low brush and go in to sleep feeling just fine, you've acted as direct and manly as any big brother.

Like Mam says, smiling a little, "Doa räagent daut aus haulf maun-huach." It's raining there half-a-man high.

~

The fox and ducks story comes of course from *Die Märchen der Brüder Grimm—The Grimm Brothers' Folk Tales*. Jacob and Wilhelm Grimm gathered two hundred of them, and published them in 1812. "Diese unschuldige Hausmärchen . . ." these innocent little house stories, through which flows ". . . jene Reinheit um derentwillen uns Kinder so wunderbar and selig erschienen," innocent stories . . . through which flows that purity that makes children appear so marvellous and blessed to us.

I read these editorial comments now in a collection of the tales I bought in 1958 while I was a student at the University of Tübingen, West Germany. And even as my memory insists on three children snug in blankets around a lantern in a tent hidden in the Canadian boreal forest, I try to disassemble what I cannot forget: the Grimms' story number four is "Märchen von einem, der auszog das Fürchten zu lernen," "The Tale of One Who Went Out to Learn How to Be Afraid," and number five is our tent story, but different: "Der Wolf und die sieben jungen Geisslein."

There are neither fox nor ducklings in it, rather a wolf and seven young goats, kids. The wolf gets into the house not only by threatening the grocer for chalk to soften his dreadful voice, but by frightening the village miller into giving him flour to whiten his black paws; the smallest, seventh, kid escapes the wolf by hiding, not behind window curtains, but high in the clock hanging on the wall. When the wolf awakens with his belly sewn shut, he staggers to a well (not a river) to drink, and as he walks the stones inside him clatter together. And then that Bösewicht, that devil of a wolf, bursts inexplicably into song:

> Was rumpelt und pumpelt
> In meinem Bauch herum?

Ich meinte, es wären sechs Geisslein,
So sind's lauter Wackerstein.

What rumbles and pumbles
Around in my gut?
I thought it was six little goats' bones,
But actually it's stony stones.

Amazing. At the moment of his death, the villain is granted an epiphany; before he drowns, the murderous wolf sings a song of profound self-recognition.

I don't think gentle Helen sang the wolf's rumble song. But the mirrored, multiplied differences between my memory and the text echo perfectly our pioneer community of three hundred people isolated by landscape, language, belief and custom. There every child knew by instinct that, whatever had literally happened, the story of that happening, if you wanted to listen, would be told by any mouth into any ear in any of three different languages: an endlessly circulating stew of gossip and humour and "Shush!" and implication and malicious or jealous or hilarious laughter cavorting through an immensity of detail only a literal contortionist could attempt to reorder. Stories were facts for retelling.

~

The light and dark I lived in as a boy were the day and night of the sun; it was changed very little by barn lanterns or the solitary kerosene lamp with its elegant glass chimney on our kitchen table. But wherever I was, I was inside family, and the kitchen, lit or unlit, shifted its shadows however I moved, behind the stove or the wood piled there, in the corners by the curtained cupboards and under the benches and table or beside the waterpail and washstand by the door: the light and the dark of the house, inside or out, held no fear. Not even the startling *crack!* of a wall log splitting as it dried in the winter cold. Wherever I walked or sat, whatever happened I had already seen or heard it before, smelled, or at the very least touched.

But every child, no matter how beloved, discovers some unknown to fear, and the earliest I remember was not the dark, or the wild weather of thunderstorms or blizzards, and certainly not the rustling boreal forest; it was fear of the bull. On a thirties homestead where no electricity or engines existed, the work and food animals can be as much fun and chaseable as a dog or squawky, scolding chickens, as frisky as calves sucking your fingers for milk or a mousing cat curled around your leg, but some farm animals are squat, thick, immovable as pigs, or enormous like cows and horses. One slight movement of their huge legs or heads, to say nothing of their gigantic bodies, can be unexpected and disastrous for a child. The horses I first became aware of were usually harnessed, attached to a wagon or farming machine, always haltered and bridled for control and you learned before you knew it from the very movements of adults, from the way father or brother handled them, your mother and sisters walked wide to climb into the wagon far from the huge heads tossing themselves against flies and mosquitoes and bulldogs (as we called biting horseflies), stomping hooves and the endless slash of tails, you understood these bodies had such immense, startling power that you would never climb through the barbed-wire fence into a pasture where they were grazing loose. Even at three you were not that stupid.

Nevertheless, farm animals were not necessarily easy to control. We lived on the outermost edge of the community and in summer anyone could herd their cattle on the unsettled free range west of us, wherever they found a hay slough or open clearing. Some even let their animals graze unattended for days because there were sloughs for watering everywhere, no large wild animals to fear and no possible thieves. So we're CPR lucky again, Pah said, forever optimistic, a quarter right beside empty land, no need to chase our cattle for miles, all the free range we want right beside us. Nah yoh, well yes, our Mam was inclined by nature and grim experience to anticipate the worst, and so we also have the endless trample of neighbours' cattle across our land to and from the free range. And they were both right.

Individual farm herds were small, at most fifteen animals in the general poverty of the Depression, and each herd was belled for identification. Every morning my mother and sister milked our two or three cows, and then we would open the rails of the corral and our entire little herd would file away to graze for the day. We all knew the distinctive sound of our several bells and throughout the day we listened, tracking the distance they wandered to find grass. At times those sounds would vanish, sometimes when wavering summer heat lay over the wooded hills, when mosquitoes and bulldogs swarmed them, the cattle would lie motionless among thick willows to escape those pests and chew their cud. Then not a sound could be heard, and by early afternoon Mam would pull on her canvas shoes, slit to fit her painful bunions, and walk the cattle trails west with a saskatoon stick, taking Mary or perhaps even Helen along to help her listen to find them. And sometimes, in that wild land, it became a question of who was lost, the cattle or the searchers?

In our family, our mother did what needed to be done, always. For us small children the thought of Mam not knowing what to do on the farm was incredible; that she would not do whatever was necessary we could not imagine. But she had lived the first thirty-five years of her life in a Mennonite row village on the immense steppes sloping up to the wide Romanovka hills; she often could not recognize the features of this Canadian boreal landscape: it was empty in a way, yes, but also wildly endless and crowded, you could see nothing for bush! Walking, listening, straining to see while struggling over deadfall and through muskeg and around water sloughs and up the repeated rolls of hills, she lost any sense of where our house clearing might be. The search for cows became desperate then: they had to be found so they could lead her home. Where her children waited.

But a bull was coming! Mam and Mary and Carlo were searching for cattle again and only we three youngest were in our yard, playing tag and laughing and often standing still, listening for the cowbells we knew were ours, listening them closer, come, come home. And suddenly we heard a bull bellow, and saw it, and we ran into the house terrified.

The bull came across Louis Ulmer's field and through the willow fence beside our house as if it wasn't there, bellowing, his enormous head, his horns curled forward above his wiry, white face, red body solid and thick as a steamer smoking across our yard, snuffling at the barn and manure pile, tossing chunks high with his horns and lifting his head, lips twisting back above his gigantic teeth as he roared the smell into the sky; we could see the steel ring in his nose flip upwards as we peered through the useless glass of windows. If he saw us move he'd charge the house, the kitchen door would crumple with one heave of his head, we'd have to be up the stairs like lightning before—but Mam! Mary!—if they came home with the cows he'd trample and horn them into dust, we were all three crying and trying not to move to attract the bull's attention, but we had to look out to know where he was, to see what that wille Tiea, wild beast was doing—Pah was there!

Walking straight from where our wagon trail bent out of the trees and across the yard to the barn, a long poplar in his hand. The bull turned, stared, hooked up a sod of rage with his left hoof and Pah hit him smash on the ring in his nose so hard we could hear the *thud!* in the house and the bull wheeled and Pah sliced him one across both flanks and the bull galumphed away, kicking up his heels as if he was doing exactly what he wanted but he was running— towards us staring from the window!—past the corner of the kitchen, crashing through the fence back into Louis Ulmer's field again, his tail up and bucking high, the thin green summer shit squirting from his smeared buttocks. We ran out the door, Pah was home and Mam and Mary were coming waving poplar branches to fend off mosquitoes, we could hear the cowbells just beyond the barn and Carlo barking, we were laughing and crying at the same time.

"You don't have to be scared," Pah said. "Just Loewen's scrub Mejchel."

Mejchel, prejchel, loht mie läwe
Dee baste Koo woa etj die gäwe. . . .

Michael, prichael, let me live
The best cow to you I'll give. . . .

That Low German skipping song goes on for as many verses as you can invent, but we were running wildly down the slope of the yard towards the cattle corral, shouting, swinging the empty milk pails over our heads.

~

Our mother sang at her continual and endless work, though never skipping songs about bulls. Her soprano was clear, high as a child's and it roamed through the countless High German hymns she knew, hundreds truly by heart. They were often sad Heimatlieder, home-songs of longing for the heavenly rest all earthbound Christians must desire, as she said, but at times sudden, surprising exclamations of joy would rise from her farm drudgery as well. Like Allelujah! Schöner Morgen, Hallelujah! Lovely morning:

Ach, wie schmeck ich Gottes Güte
Recht als einen Morgentau,
Da mein sehnendes Gemüte
Wandelt auf der Grünen Au;
Da hat wohl die Morgenstund
Edlen Schatz und Gold im Mund.

Ah, today I taste God's goodness
Sweeter than the morning dew,
As my longing spirit wanders
Happily green meadows through;
This sweet morning's gifts unfold
In my mouth like purest gold.

Singing on the flat of our yard near the barn, among the unnameable grasses and weeds growing there and picking tiny yellow-cone flowers of what she called Kamille, camomile, to brew into a tea only she drank, for her stomach she said, which was always part of her various and continual ailments. The golden camomile tufts on their tiny stalks smelled like her mouth, and tasted like it too, their flecks sparkling on your fingers in the sun to the sound of her song and the dreadful bush emptiness, as she said, this Canada where the law said every family had to live on its own land, by itself, and our nearest neighbour was a bachelor, Louis Ulmer, who was a very good person, he let us chop a wagon trail across his land and directly through his yard so we had the shortest distance to the road allowance, but he was no Mennonite, he never darkened our church door, not even for funerals.

Who was he, with a strange name like Louis Ulmer? He never said and if we knew then, no one remembers now. His small cabin built of sawn lumber, not logs, my father said was already there when we bought the quarter west behind him, and we built our house right beside his biggest field that opened east down the knoll, every tree cleared away for a quarter of a mile so we could see the sun rise over his oats, and in fall the northern lights burn above his stooks.

In fact, the photo of our house on the knoll shows that our kitchen lean-to was less than ten feet from Louis Ulmer's grain field. The border between us was a rail fence interwoven with vertical willows where clothes on washday could be draped to dry, and the Süa'romp, sorrel leaves, for soup and the sour-sweet rhubarb stems for Plautz, open-face fruit pastry, both the first green plants that could be eaten in spring, grew along the fence down the slope where the late April sun could best brighten over their unfolding underground shoots.

It seems to me now that Louis Ulmer was a short stocky man who often lent us his machinery when ours broke on our stony land. Because of "Louis" we thought for a time he might be related to the Metis Briere family that lived a mile north of us and stayed in the Speedwell district almost as long as we did, or even the many Naults farther south, but "Ulmer" doesn't fit with Metis names and Louis disappeared before I could remember him personally. Nevertheless, his name remains indelible; when I hear "Louis," "Ulmer" follows like a distant, Low German echo of "Just wait, we're almost home," and between the swinging heads of our horses I see the bright notch in the sky made by the poplars where the road allowance cuts over the esker ridge towards his cabin, and it may be the sky is burning, shifting with northern lights and I know the wagon track that begins there on his yard will end half a mile farther west, deeper in the darkening forest but the sky will still be aflame with light. Tüss: home.

Tüss es Tüss,
Enn hinj'rem Owe
Es tweemol Tüss.

Home is home,
And behind the stove
Is doubly home.

3.

# WRATH

~

It was said a stranger had been seen, walking on the road past the Mennonite Brethren Church. The Watkins or Raleigh medicine pedlars, the stud-horse man leading his giant dapple-grey Percheron stallion, the knife-and-axe-and-scissor sharpener with his many grinding stones, even an occasional pedlar of used but clean clothes would appear in the district at some time every summer, but always with a good trotter pulling a buggy; and travelling evangelists or the Dispensations Bible teachers who drew timelines and beautiful chalk pictures of die Entrückung, the Rapture, on charts usually arrived in someone's Model T or even Model A Ford. From where would a solitary man come to Speedwell on foot? Why?

~

By 1938 our Wiebe family had lived and worked at every available labouring job in Canada during eight years of worldwide Depression. The five children born in Russia were learning to speak English so well that all their lives they spoke it without an accent. And even while trying to homestead on land never cleared before, we managed to feed ourselves for years with barely a bit of government relief; besides Dan's fifteen dollars a month earned cutting railroad ties, we may have received, at most, two or three twenty-five-dollar vouchers to order winter clothes. And once I remember standing in a lineup of farmers with Pah during an early autumn snowfall when he was handed a wooden box of red Nova Scotia apples—the end-label with beautiful, shining apples was right!—out of a boxcar beside the Fairholme Pool elevator.

Our family was fortunate to have two grown sons; they worked at everything from cutting cordwood for groceries to hoeing sugar beets, working on threshing or railroad building crews, to logging and cattle feeding. But clearing the CPR quarter for a crop was too hard, there was other land already cleared available, and in 1938 we moved all our Oam'seelijchtjeiten, our paltry possessions, and few cattle four miles from our CPR homestead north into Township 53, to the John Franka land half a mile east off the road between Speedwell and Jack Pine.

That main road itself could not follow the surveyed road allowance very often because of the rolling terrain: it was mostly wagon ruts worn wide and winding around hay sloughs and along ridges or hills to avoid muskeg, but in short sections it was cut as straight as the surveyors marked it; it was even ditched and graded, especially where it led down to plank culverts crossing two creeks that ran in spring or prolonged summer rain. The road's surface was whatever the land offered: black topsoil, clay, sandy hillsides, swamp, gravel ridges and mudholes. Your horses simply had to be strong enough to haul your wagon through or around these mudholes that widened and deepened with the seasons, especially during spring thaw. In winter tracks could be hard, but breaking through drifts blown by heavy blizzards with a cutter or family caboose or sleigh-rack loaded high with hay was even harder.

My mother remembered the exact day that our family, for the first time, drove north along this road. May 9, 1933, she told me when I was writing Pah's obituary; in a small rented truck. They wanted to be farmers, but after three years in Canada they did not own a single animal, not a cow, not so much as a dog. They were coming from Kelstern in southern Saskatchewan where since May 1930 the family had worked on the large grain farm owned by Mam's uncle Henry Knelsen, who had emigrated to Canada early in the century. Like all of southern Saskatchewan, the Knelsen farm was being buried in the blowing dust of the thirties.

Dan tells me—he was then thirteen—that around Kelstern it was so dry that if anyone dipped a pail of water out of a slough, a hole was left in the slough. "So we left, the whole family with our little stuff hardly filled a ton truck, and we drove down a street and Dad was standing in the back eating a chicken leg and he waved it at people on the sidewalk, 'See!' He was so happy in Canada we still had something to eat." I presume Mam and baby Liz, born at Kelstern, were in the truck cab and did not hear this declaration, the only story that remains of the more than three-hundred-mile travel up the desert length of Depression Saskatchewan, and which ever after was told in our family as a bit of laughter or chagrin. Apparently "See!" was our father's one English word after three years in Canada; very useful, he said.

Pracha'oam, de tjenne nijch e'mol den Hund
von hinj'rem Owe locke.

Beggar-poor, they can't so much as lure a dog
from behind the stove.

Since they moved from Kelstern, now a three-building spot well south of the Trans-Canada Highway, the street with the sidewalk must have been in Swift Current, and Highway 4, which then began at Orkney near the Montana border and was more or less cleared and laid out north to Meadow Lake in what was then called "Good Grade 2 Highway," the road they travelled. On it they would have found a ferry to cross the South Saskatchewan River and at Battleford a steel bridge to drive over the Battle and the North Saskatchewan rivers.

When I ask Dan why, of all possible places, they hauled themselves to stony Speedwell, he replies, "There was really no work in the south, and Mam and Pah wanted their own land to work. Things didn't go so good working for Henry Knelsen anyway, and all that drought and grasshoppers and foreclosures down south. Then Pah heard the government had lots of homestead land up north, even new Mennonite immigrants from Russia were getting land to file on up there. And good rain and snow too, you just had to build a house, clear ten acres a year and break it. He heard through some connection with Fiedlers, they met somewheres."

Dan's eighty-four-year-old memory does not know if Pah somehow met Gust Fiedler, Tina's future husband, or August, the thick and venerable Fiedler patriarch, but in May 1933 their groaning truck trundled off Highway 4 and when it reached Jack Pine School turned north, ground along past the clearing on the Enns hill where the cellar for the future Mennonite Brethren Church was being dug by men with shovels, on past Speedwell School where Annie Born had taught the first forty children in eight grades in the fall of 1931, half a mile farther to the August Fiedler homestead cut into the outermost northern edge of the community. Pauline and August had nine children—the oldest, Gustav, was twenty-six—a few acres of bush farm cleared and a steam sawmill.

"I still have my steam engineer papers," Gust tells me in September 1995. "I ran our mill for twelve years."

"He was an old bachelor then," my sister Tina says slyly. Her face has grown into the folds I remember of our mother. "I worked a bit for the Fiedlers, in the house, but I didn't want anything to do with him!"

We laugh, drinking herbal tea around the table in their Lethbridge, Alberta, condo; by 1995 Tina and Gust have been married for sixty-two years.

"When we got to Speedwell on that miserable truck," Tina says, "they let us live on his brother Ted's homestead, half a mile through the bush from old Fiedlers. Dan, Mary and Helen started school in Speedwell."

"Ted wasn't married yet," Gust says, "but he took over the quarter west of us when the Lemkeys moved away. There was a log cabin with a barn on the side so they saved building one wall."

"Like the old Mennonite house-barn style, in Russia?"

"Sort of. We had no place, and they took us in, for a whole year, till we got the CPR quarter."

"But you didn't really like Gust?"

"Well, men, you know . . ." We all laugh again at her tone, and then she continues seriously, "We were always so poor in Canada, when we'd been a few months at Henry Knelsen's I turned sixteen so Pah and Mam sent me to Manitoba to work for my keep. To Mam's aunt, a Mrs. Siemens, and I was warned to watch myself, there was the old guy and four sons and their youngest daughter Nancy warned me 'You better watch my dad,' and sure enough he came after me, the old goat, but Mrs. Siemens was suspicious of *me*. She opened my letters from the folks and read them when they came to the post office and it got too much, I left. But wherever I worked the men were always grabbing me so I wrote to Mam and I went back to Kelstern.

"But Mam wanted to get away from Kelstern too. They worked there three years and her uncles had been in Canada thirty years and had big farms but the Depression got worse and they said they couldn't help us. Jake Knelsen was a preacher and couldn't help anyway but Henry had this great big farm though he wouldn't sponsor us to come to Canada—it was Mam's aunt in Alberta that did that—there was something not very good there and Mam wanted to get away from them."

Sad family stories that fade but never vanish, hard edges that remain irrefutable as fossils.

But Gust is full of Speedwell and sawmills. "There was lots of good pine and spruce there then," he says. "In winter we had different guys cutting for us, Abe and your Pah too, skidding in the logs, and then we traded the sawed lumber in Fairholme for groceries—two-day trip with horses."

"That's how the Fiedlers paid," Tina says, "with lumber and groceries."

"Then in fall I went harvesting near Mervin," Gust is grinning across the table at Tina, "stooking, field pitcher for the thresher, and you come there to cook for the threshing crew. I came to see you."

"And I slammed the door in your face! I was sleeping in the hayloft on that farm."

Gust bursts out, "And in three months we got married!"

"How did that happen?"

"Oh, it was Mam," Tina says. "She thought Gust was a really good man, she told me she'd pray about it."

We are laughing aloud now. Our mother and her prayers. Every one of us knew that once Mam really started praying for you, you might as well give up.

~

It seemed the walking stranger had spoken to no one, nor entered any yard. Odd. Anyone who came into dead-end Speedwell always visited someone; there was no place to stay except with a family and no way out, west, north or east, except the south road you had come in on. But a stranger had been seen, and barked at by the farm dogs who charged out of every yard at whatever went by, not even the fiercest brute was ever chained. But the stranger with his red paint pail had passed by without so much as a word shouted at the dogs.

We knew all about fierce brutes. The most direct wagon trail to our new Franka farm led from the main road across the Johann Martenses' yard, between their barn and cattle corral, and their dogs were especially violent. The Martens twins, Abe and Henry, told me, "De Hunj motte fe ons op'pausse." Those dogs have to keep guard for us.

The Martens family of parents and ten children lived in a log house, as we all did, but it was strangely hip-roofed, like the barn picture in a reader with two windows in the gable. Whenever we drove through that yard their dogs rushed us and had to be whipped away from slashing our horses' heels or noses. The dogs followed us anyway, barking and slavering as if berserk. I never understood what they were guarding in that yard that was so special; our black Carlo never behaved so stupidly.

None of us children, especially me at four and five, ever walked through the Martenses' yard. Besides, there was a shorter trail to walk or ride a horse from our Franka place to the church and the Schroeder store; it meandered diagonally south through our bush and across the Otto Dunz and Gottlieb Biech homesteads where there were patches of dust and sand warm as water on your bare summer feet. That trail came out on the main road just north of the church, which stood on the hill above a creek crossed by a culvert whose planks were often cracked or caved in, the road was driven so much. From below, the wide church gable, with its brick chimney straight up against the sky and log walls shingled as smooth as its peaked roof, made the church look even larger. Where over the pulpit every Sunday the mild voice of Präedja, preacher, Jacob Enns pronounced das Wort Gottes, the Word of God.

The graded road cutting up through the crest of the hill beside the church exposed a grey bulge of boulders in a cliff of sand almost as golden as the beaches of Turtle Lake. You could burrow into it as far as your arm could reach, and at your fingertips the sand grew cooler, darker, then changed softly warm in air. And moist, you could shape anything your hands imagined.

But one day, on a boulder exposed by the road in this sand hillside, there appeared words:

BE SURE YOUR SIN WILL FIND YOU OUT

On the largest granite boulder directly below the church. Like a foundational curse.

It must have been the stranger. No one in the community had ever seen such a thing, red words

on a roadside rock, nor knew what to do about it.
I remember seeing them, though I could not have
read that, nor understood it spoken aloud; I'm not
certain I understand it even today. My parents read
the Bible daily, but only in High German and the
only person in our family then who would have
known where to find Numbers 32:23 would have
been Abe, who had already taken a year of Bible
school and so might have tussled with Luther's
translation, which is no clearer than the King
James Version:

> Ihr werdet eurer Sünde innewerden, wenn sie
> euch finden wird.

which in literal English means:

> You will become aware of your sin, when it
> finds you.

There were such red statements burning the
length of the road from Jack Pine to Speedwell, on
rocks large and small, on slab fences and corner post
braces. Every passerby now knew that their personal
sin was a relentless bloodhound smelling them out;
or they were threatened with wrath:

BEWARE THE WRATH TO COME

THE WRATH OF GOD ABIDITH ON YOU

Only miles of barbed wire and slim willow posts defied the stranger's red words.

What a lovely sound: "wra-a-a-th." Your wide mouth, your whole face feels its hiss, its rhythm, its expulsion, and if I had said it then I would have been singing it. As it was, the paint on a rock in the valley below the church, near the creekbed, turned into the first sounds I remember composing. This solitary rock looked like the knuckled fingertip of an enormous hand buried deep in the earth: it could point you in a direction but was too small to reveal a full anathema, and all the stranger could do was print on it a threatening code which would, hopefully, drive you to search out your curse yourself:

JAS. 4:4

Abe must have explained that JAS meant the New Testament Book of James, chapter 4, verse 4. The "fours" fascinated me, not because I knew the sacred number of the Cree people—I didn't yet realize they had lived for millennia on the warm ground I walked barefoot, and lived more or less invisibly around us still—no, it was something about the three short sounds, "James four four," the "four four" repetition. Those sounds . . . and then the literal significations of words reasserted themselves briefly: "James chapter four verse four" . . . but I couldn't like that numb plod, so "chapter" fell away and "verse" rhythmized itself into nonsense and I was chanting:

James four, ver-si-ty four

Da, da, da-da-da, *da*. The meanings of language sounds are always accidental; it is their rhythms that first imprint the memory.

And red words on rock, sung, are ineradicable. This was no gentle Präedja Enns mildly reading a Bible verse: rather, as Jesus once had prophesied, suddenly the very stones were crying out. Here, in our stony country.

~

I was four years, three and a half months old at my parents' silver wedding anniversary, January 19, 1939. The celebration would have taken place in our church on the hill. The Speedwell Mennonite Brethren Church had about eighty adult members by then, which meant at least two hundred people in thirty families, but the entire community in two school districts knew my parents, perhaps three hundred people, and no more than half of them could have crowded into the building, balcony and all. I remember nothing of what took place, but four black-and-white pictures of the day have survived and, inexplicably, two poems from the church service.

The poems were "Glückwünsche," "Good Luck Wishes," also called "Vergissmeinnicht," "Forget Me Not," copied out by hand, read aloud and then presented to the wedding couple. This was a Russian Mennonite custom for publicly honouring parents. The one offered by Dan is a High German "Silberhochzeit," silver wedding, verse in eight rhyming six-line stanzas; the image throughout is that life is a voyage with Jesus at the helm of the boat—of which the couple seem to be the only passengers— and, despite the past "nine thousand days" of being "tossed about in the waves of foaming time," the Saviour will eventually guide them safely into the harbour of ew'ger Lust, "everlasting delight."

Abe's recitation pages have a wreath of apple blossoms glued above his name and dedication. Its title is "Gnade nichts als Gnade," "Grace Nothing but Grace," and like Dan's poem it contains not one actual detail of our parents' lives, how they met, survived years of separation, world war and civil war, revolution, anarchy, plague, starvation, persecution, statelessness and flight that forced them halfway around the world. The only memorable image comes in stanza three, where they are told that today their life's journey together lies before them like a necklace of twenty-five pearls: a rich testimony of God's grace, nothing but Gottes Gnade.

Knowing my parents' profound, humble piety—especially my mother's on memorial occasions—they must have been deeply moved by these verses; and perhaps most by Abe's because it is possible the poem was written for this occasion by "Dijchta" Friesen, as he was called all his life, "Poet, Composer" Heinrich D. Friesen, who with his wife Katherina and ten children tried to farm for several years in the Speedwell district. Years later when we moved to Coaldale, Alberta, I would know him as a short white-bearded ancient, with a startling, direct gaze from under bushy eyebrows, the classic Russian Mennonite village bard who, on the occasion of a wedding, anniversary, dedication or funeral, would be asked to compose a commemoration, and at the appropriate moment he would step forward and declaim with magnificent intensity, eyes closed and head thrown back, the gathered words that could focus the emotions of the community. It was said that often verses came to Dijchta Friesen in dreams by night, and he would rise to write them on the whitewashed plaster of his house walls so he would know them exactly when he awoke in the morning.

Heinrich Friesen's grandson Ed tells me their family left Speedwell in 1937, but my brother's faded ink is, I believe, a Dijchta Friesen original. Abe could have written him a letter, and no Mennonite bard who (as Friesen narrates in his personal memoir) had felt since childhood that he was called of God to poetry would have refused such a request.

A 1939 box camera could take no pictures inside; our four silver wedding pictures show our family in January snow in the Franka yard. One is a vertical close-up of our parents standing apart, with my father's body angled towards my mother and his eyes as usual fixed somewhere in the distance, as if he were about to walk away in front of her, over continents and oceans—back to Russia perhaps. But she is unconcerned; she looks directly at the camera. She is forty-three years old, her folded face fixed in resolve.

We nine children, including Gust and grandson Tony but not baby Eldo, huddle together tightly, almost as if we were being threatened by the huge expanse of snow and sky, the spray of poplars and a bristle of spruce along the horizon spread behind us. We are backed against the rail fence; the decrepit

Franka house is to our left and cannot be seen. Over the garden fence behind us hang frozen bedsheets.

Why would bedsheets be hung out to freeze-dry on a day of celebration? Was someone in our family a bed-wetter? Not likely Liz, almost eight; it could only have been me. Or Helen throwing up sick perhaps; a year later she would begin chronicling all our family illnesses in a tiny notebook, beginning with herself in the third person:

1940. Helen Wiebe got sick 5 of Jan. On her
birthday [her twelfth]. was sick quite a while
had to go to hospital [North Battleford] on 13 of
Jan. got operation the same day 13 Jan. at 5 P.M.

was very sick got water about 15th. got meals
on 16th, then came home on 24 of Jan. still was
very sick then on night about the 26 of Jan got
very sick got heart trouble and stayed in bed
4 months and on Mother's Day [May 12]
Schroeder [with his truck] came over and
brought me too church & after she was well.

That 1940 operation was an appendix removal, but
as an infant Helen already carried those lurking
"heart troubles" with her during our family's flight
to Canada over Moscow. The "troubles" worsened as
she walked to school for miles in every Saskatchewan
weather, and they would end only with her death.

But that spring she could still smile out of our living-room window with little Eldo faintly beside her; and the outside world, where she could not walk, reflected in the glass that protected her.

~

I remember no little-boy bedwetting, nor was I ever teased about it by the family. In winter my parents always had a covered chamber pot under their bed which both they and we smaller children used at night, and before the accidents that would happen to me on the Franka yard, I remember only the church balcony as a place of possible affliction: the murmur of people talking among the benches below after Sunday service and the huge hands of Onkel ("Mister") Aaron Heinrichs.

I cannot recall his face, though sometimes a drift of it, large and open, seems to shimmer unfocused in my searching memory. His daughter Gilda, Abe's wife, gave me a grainy photo of their family surrounding him in his half-open coffin, but even that stirs no certainty. He obviously had the long Heinrichs nose, but he was a tall man and the coffin, tilted sideways, hides his folded hands. His Trajchtmoaka hands, "to-make-correct," healer's hands, had very short, very broad thumbs, which by

some combination of knowledge, goodness and subliminal intuition, over time and with relentless application, wherever they placed themselves and worked
warmth into your body, could soothe and manipulate
it out of painful confusion into perfect order. Like
the village poet and midwife, the Russian Mennonites
had a tradition of Trajchtmoaka that went back
through Prussia to medieval Friesland, and in ages
when doctors were rare—and even they had little
science to make diagnoses—the confident and inexplicable hands of a healer were the mercy of God
upon us. Aaron Heinrichs was a Saskatchewan wilderness shaman—though the people of Speedwell, with
the possible exception of the Metis Naults and
Brieres, would not have called him that. If you broke
a bone or developed an unbearable rotten tooth, you
drove to his homestead; if your body had some persistent problem you could no longer endure, you finally
talked to him after church and then with him you
climbed the open stairs behind the men's pews, up
into the privacy of the balcony. Sunday after Sunday.

Apparently I stuttered. I was four and a half
when Aaron Heinrichs died, unexpectedly and to
everyone's deep sorrow, in April 1939, but it seems
my early speech often sounded, as my siblings have
told me, laughing, "like an empty hayrack clattering
over Speedwell stones." And however long it took for

his great thumbs to reorder those stones in my shoulders, the length of my neck, the roots of my skull, I have no memory of stuttering, ever. Perhaps it was the passing affliction of a quick child pouring out words faster than his larynx could shape them, and the cure was already happening when the silver wedding pictures showed me in my first suit and tie—the jacket a bit tight for my shoulders—but I retain no sensation of my body changing, lengthening under hands I know I saw and felt; no shadow of a huge man bending over me. Only the faint apprehension of three-tiered rows of backless benches in a narrow balcony, two windows with trees flickering in light beyond the sloping porch roof, and those hands, already curved by their indelible thumbs, approaching.

~

When you live by farming, land comes first, house last. The Franka house was no more than three one-room shacks built end to end, logs cobbled together at different times with a closed porch stuck on at the kitchen. The ceilings were so low only three logs lay below and two logs above the single window in each room; from inside, the pole roof rafters were visible outside as level with each window-top. The roof had

a centre peak of barely three feet, and its tarpaper
was so tattered, its slabs so curled and rotting, that
during the first rain we discovered disaster. The only
dry place inside the house was under the oilcloth of
the kitchen table. I have a memory of crouching
there with Liz while Mam and Mary and Helen run
around placing pails, basins, bowls, cups, under the
worst of the steady, or pouring, drips. The twisted
floorboards with their wide cracks in all three rooms
were covered with utensils.

Our mother loved order; her house was always
opp'jiriemt, cleaned up, and she was very unhappy at
having to live and work in such an endless mess. But
she accepted that we had to leave our new, well-built
CPR house, its high upstairs for sleeping under a
watertight roof, for these shacks because of the
Franka fields. There were three, about sixty acres
wrestled clear of the bush; the largest opened east of
the house, upward on a slope tilted into the spring
sun, and beyond a small draw to the north, where
water ran through willows in the spring, lay another
field almost as large. The third bordered the open
farmyard on two sides and part of it was the garden,
convenient and as large as you wanted to plant it
close around the house.

The barn of slim logs hunched even lower than
the house, its roof was flat and covered with sod that

grew bush weeds as high as our grain fields in summer, and leaked long after any rain ended. There was no well on the yard, but a slough good for watering cattle lay a hundred yards beyond the trees behind the barn, and a seepage well dug beside it filtered swamp water that was drinkable—if that was all you had. Pah insisted our Pripps, the roasted, ground barley brew all Mennonites drank instead of unaffordable coffee or tea, for him tasted even better made with water from that well. But it was a very long carry in pails to the house, and cattle heaving themselves through spongy moss to reach open water in sloughs sometimes get stuck; if they sink to their heavy bellies, they may struggle until they disappear in brown water seeping up around them before anyone knows they're in trouble. Certainly no cow can save another from a Saskatchewan slough or muskeg; nor any unharnessed horse.

Pah loved that land. He sits on our eight-foot disk with reins taut, the four horses alert and ready: the matched sorrels Prince and Jerry, which were his pride, hitched on the outside with wide Bell and her white-faced yearling Floss between them. The sod-roofed barn squats in the distance, the poplar trees along the horizon are sprigged without leaves, but he is already disking the big field beside the house, cutting and turning last year's stubble over into a new seedbed. The season is so early he still wears his knee-high winter felt boots inside low rubbers. Surrounded by grey soil and mulched clumps of straw, with only two fist-sized stones visible anywhere. The Franka place, as we always called it even after we had moved away from it too, on the southeast quarter of Section 9, Township 53, Range 17, west of the 3rd meridian.

We lived there from the fall I turned four until the summer before I turned eight. I of course didn't know its legal geographical coordinates, nor saw the surveyor mound already unnoticeable under fallen leaves and young aspen, its black iron rod pounded square with those numbers incised into it, and the warning:

It is unlawful to remove this marker.
Maximum sentence: 7 years imprisonment.

Not red "wrath" from henceforth and forevermore as the stranger had painted, but scary enough; in its cut iron as foreign as sudden words on stone.

Years later Dan found such a corner marker for me. And I certainly felt no implied threat; much more how utterly flimsy the thin pin seemed poked away in this massive, incomprehensible bush; as if, in a flit of surveyor passing quick as the *ping* of its pounding in, the pin's very minuteness could assert possession on this folded earth and force it into deliberate mile grids like the roads built by Roman Empire engineers; as if a single human being with a tiny instrument could, no matter what the land's unalterable physical meanderings, quarter it down smaller than square miles, notch its crested trees with road allowances across long glacial eskers and swamps and dense poplars and thicker spruce, over water and valley straight as the eye could see no matter where the eventual trail would be forced to turn, so that horses driven by people could actually haul loaded wagons down ravines, around bottomless muskegs, up steep hills. And imagine they could declare: This land belongs to me! An iron peg half an inch thick hammered into boreal forest: if you can ever find it to take away, you may have to endure seven years in a six-by-eight-foot cell.

Our father lived his last forty-five years in Canada and laughter was always his best evasion for ugly memory. "Nä, nä, nijch hia!" No no, not here. No police ever pounded on our door in the dead of night. In Speedwell I remember seeing the Royal Canadian Mounted Police once, when I was nine. The two scarlet men turned their crested cruiser slowly into our yard in bright sunlight—we had heard it coming for half a mile—and we all came forward to meet them. They got out and both put on their hats perfectly. A neighbour had applied for citizenship and, after a few questions confirming certain facts, which we children translated both ways, the policemen accepted the hospitality of a glass of cool water from the well, folded themselves back into their car, and drove away.

~

On our new farm I gradually became aware of the powerful differences between my parents. It was not just the miserable house and all the money and time we needed to make this Koht, this hovel, livable—as we did—at five or six you do not think about such things. We lived where we lived, and though this farmyard had no slope to gather speed rolling a discarded wheel down towards the corral where the cows were being milked in a haze of mosquito-smudge smoke, this yard did have more wide, flat space with two tall poplars to centre it and a log laid crooked between their branches from which you could hang ropes for a long swing, or where a dead pig could be hoisted up with a pulley and sliced open. But the family felt different now that the three older children were gone most of the time and our parents had to work more closely together on our growing farm.

Tina and Gust had three preschool children by then and were working a homestead themselves, three bush miles away. Abe and Dan, like most Speedwell young men, "worked out" from early spring to late fall in the beet fields of southern Alberta, earning hard cash for the family; during the winter Abe went to Bible school while Dan went logging for the Lobes. But better weather, good crops on better land as Canada's Depression economy shifted into World War II called for decisions about buying another cow to raise more calves—did we have enough cows to keep our own bull?—or more sows, to sell more pigs, or ways to breed better horses.

Jeld, Jeld schrijcht de gaunse Welt.

Money, money, screams the whole world.

By 1941–42 there was more money, even in our bush world, but, Mam said, our Pah could not always be trusted with it.

~

Money had nothing to do with how they met. In 1897 Russia, in the cemetery of their Orenburg Mennonite Colony village, tiny Katerina Knelsen stood weeping as the coffin of her mother Susanna Knelsen née Loewen, aged twenty-five, was lowered into the muddy ground. And then Abram Wiebe, the Jakob Wiebe boy from the farmstead across the village street from the Knelsens, came beside her and comforted her. She was two years old, he nine.

Exactly a century later I am for the first time in that village, once named Number Eight Romanovka after the Czar. Behind the single long street lined by worn houses, sheds and unpruned orchards and immense trees scruffed with massive raven's nests, the cemetery lies on steppes opening south to a horizon of the gloriously folded Number Eight Hills. Our family beginning here has few explications: did my father pick my mother up, crying hysterically, or did he stand close beside her, perhaps take her hand, warm it between his own in the autumn air? What Mennonite village boy of nine would call such attention to himself, surrounded at a funeral by everyone he knew? Mam was surely too small to remember; Pah must have told her, much later, or the family or community teased her——but then where were all the aunts and cousins, what was my grandfather Daniel Knelsen doing while his smallest child cried? Somewhere here, where these late May lilacs grow dense as purple perfume among sprouts of grass, depressions that reveal only earth enduring collapse, bodies decayed, somewhere under my gaze is the literal century of my grandmother Susanna Knelsen's grave, and I try to balance decades of family story with what happened on this ground a moment before the village young men seized shovels and began to heave the earth down, covering her coffin: of a tiny girl weeping at her mother's grave and the approach of her future husband; of an anticipating warmth and tenderness I do not, in my childhood, remember between my parents.

My mother said to me, cool and distant, "Wie weare je mau tjliene Tjinja." We were just little children.

As if she remembered perfectly well, but it no longer mattered. This coolness did not enter the stories about her father Daniel Knelsen, who remarried within two months of Susanna's death and whose Mennonite patriarchal discipline verged on a brutality she recalled for us all her life with regret and warning. A father from whom she remembered not a single kiss. But that grave—she insisted she had lovely memories of her delicate mother who died when she was barely two, and then little but folk-classic misery with her first stepmother Tina, who favoured her own children Maria and Heinrich (two others died as infants), and who worked my mother as maid and servant to them all. At six she was milking the family cows—traditionally Mennonite women's work, but rarely at that age— caring for babies and working all day in house or garden or barn. She scarcely attended the village school, but she was quick and learned to read and write and do simple arithmetic very well. Her father's unpredictable and endless punishment, for whatever reason he thought she had earned it, was always, she told us, a hard hand or cane or horse-harness strap or rope, often a beating that left her battered, even bleeding.

There is even a family rumour, faint but persistent, that Grandpa Knelsen was a drinker. This was then all too common in Mennonite villages, but anyone who could speak with certainty about my grandfather is no longer alive.

In late 1913, at the age of twenty-five, my father returned to Romanovka from four years of unpaid

Russian national forestry work, which as a baptized Mennonite Brethren Church member he had done in lieu of the compulsory military service then required of all young men in Russia. He immediately began to court my mother, then barely eighteen. Was part of his attraction Mam's dawning hope of getting away from her father and stepmother? Perhaps the memory of her mother's open grave was one they found together; perhaps he told her something she did not know but loved to hear; the weeping girl and his instinctive child comfort, a feeling for her he had never forgotten, or a touch, as he watched her for years growing up across the street. As I saw for myself in 1997, their village farmsteads were almost directly across from each other. Abram Jakob Wiebe was a seventh child, a fifth son, with no land inheritance possible, and unaggressive, dominated by his older brothers Jakob, Klaus, Peter and Franz. He had not seen Katerina Knelsen during four years at Great Anadol near the Black Sea two thousand kilometres away, nothing but men in camps and endless dumb-ox work planting the Czar's forests. But he had not forgotten, and now she was grown up, eighteen, "old enough to get married" as Mennonite wisdom had it.

Mam turned eighteen in September 9, 1913. At the time her youngest half-brother, Heinrich, was three years old and that may have been one more reason why Daniel Knelsen tried to discourage my father: "Ploag die nijch. Met onse Tien loohnt sijch daut aul nijch." Don't bother yourself. With our Tina it [marriage] isn't worth it.

His Tien knew how to work hard, oh yes, but she was always sickly, always complaining about something or other, all her life, why bother marrying someone who would die quick on you anyway?

How many times our father recalled that story of enduring love and ugliness. There Grandpa Knelsen sat, in the one picture we had of him, bald and bearded on a polished chair beside his final, third, wife, Lena Hiebert, less than half his age, both big fists bunched on his thighs and gleaming knee-high leather boots crossed at the ankles—boots he may have made himself because, Dan told me, he probably was a cobbler. And, strangely, there is what seems to be a slim notebook clutched in his left hand while he stares straight as pins into our eyes. For of course my father did "bother" (ploage: literally "to plague yourself") himself with "his Tien." They were married on a steppe winter day, January 15, 1914, and all those years in starvation Russia, war, revolution, Communism, the months of flight via Moscow and trains and refugee shelters and ships and trains again and the endless labour of Canada together and eventually seven children, by 1975 all (except the one who died) married, with twenty-eight grand-children and eighteen great-grandchildren and over sixty-one years of life together, Pah laughed aloud in his final, Alberta, hospital bed:

"Na Tien, some Ploag!"

"Sssshuh," Mam gently, weeping. "All those old stories."

~

When during World War II our father drove to Fairholme to sell a box-load of grain or several fat pigs, perhaps leading a calf behind wagon or sleigh, he always returned with what Mam had listed for him: food staples, clothing, farm or household items. But sometimes he brought a surprise as well. Once I remember a finely stitched double set of horse har-ness, complete with back breeching, of which we already had one set for road driving; they weren't needed for field work. In fact, we had six sets of har-ness, enough for every working horse we owned, but my father said these were extra strong, Storekeeper Rempel had sold them as a special bargain and he'd store them in the granary so they'd be ready when other harnesses broke, as they always did. Yes, my mother said, someday we would need new harness, but now we really needed a harrow! What was he thinking, to pay so much for what we might need someday?

Such arguments live deeper in a child than hearing; the rough strands that lengthen the wide weave of a family. The harness went back; I don't know whether my father eventually drove to Fairholme, whether my mother went with him or if she went with Dan, but their disagreement about our neighbour Johann Martens' cattle was worse. I remember Liz and I, perhaps Helen too, thirteen or fourteen at the time, crying about Martens' perpetually gaunt cattle in our grain field and our father chasing them out again, not confronting Martens and his sons, just accepting the trampled crop, wait and see, it can come back, it's still early in the season. But once the cattle have been in there, those scrubs, they'll just come back! But the Martenses are church members, you can't just go yell at them. Who said yell? Well, that's all that will happen with Martens, you know that. Yes, yes, but . . .

And finally Mam, hoarse from arguing, going with Helen down the trail through the trees to the Martens farm and coming back beaten down and shamed in her anger by Johann Martens who had ut je'brellt, bawled Mam out, horribly Helen said, sobbing aloud: What business had my mother coming to him to say anything, this was men's cattle business and they'd gotten them out as soon as they noticed and if we couldn't keep our rail and wire properly in place then that was our poor farming, they had fenced their share. Which made Mam even more indignant because she was convinced the Martenses had not done their full share; that had been an earlier and much longer argument but once, long ago, Pah had conceded that fine, fine, maybe the Martenses had done their share, so why, Johann Martens now demanded, did souhne Fru, such a woman! come yelling at him? If you know so much, go back where you belong and show your man how to build a fence. Our mother, such a woman!

The fight over Carlo was worse. Our black dog with a white bell of fur at his neck and white-tipped paws. The perfect dog for herding cattle, for playing in brush and yard, hunting gophers, wrestling around the two big trees on the yard, his thick tongue slipping like laughter over his black lips between dazzling teeth. We children were screaming and crying: Carlo had dragged himself home with his leg slashed and throat torn open, we thought we could see right down into his beating heart! Only the two Martens brutes could have done this and Carlo wouldn't back down, never, and Mam told Pah he had to go and say something to Johann Martens about those animals, we had to drive through their yard to get to the road, how could we say nothing and have our good cattle dog torn apart by those vicious beasts? But Pah would not go; dogs were dogs, he would not jacht, fight, with someone who sat on the same church bench every Sunday over a dog. Who said fight? Just go and tell them, explain, look at poor Carlo!

He would not go. It seemed to me then, at no more than six, that my father was hopeless, perhaps even a coward. I had seen Johann Martens' eyes turn into needles behind his glasses, his mouth under its handsome moustache roar in a way I had not heard an adult speak; it was terrifying. Mrs. Martens was slim, bent, and with the incredible ability, it was said, of making Plümemoos, sweet plum soup, for her entire family out of two plums and four raisins, but she never did any family arguing. That was the man's job and stocky Johann Martens did that very well—but not our father. He was quiet, always agreed with whatever anybody yelled and, even worse, expected his family to accept everything as he did. Mam was excessively forgiving, she wanted peace with her neighbours, but it had to be a somehow equal, orderly, mutual peace—not simply suffering silence endured by us. That was not proper behaviour of Christians among themselves; especially for children to learn.

I knew nothing then about the centuries Mennonites had searched to find a peaceful community; particularly among themselves. Nor did I know the long Low German maxim common among our people which might well have been applied to Johann Martens:

If you want to outwit a Jew, you have to get up before breakfast.
If you want to outwit a Mennonite, you better not go to bed at all.

Watching Helen search Carlo's bloody fur for slashes while I held the round Watkins salve tin open for her, I was convinced of one thing: our Pah had no backbone.

Carlo healed fast back to his original toughness, scars hidden under his long fur. Carlo, whom I sat on, whom I tried to ride around the yard before I could climb our heavy farm horses. In a summer photo, probably 1941, the two white socks of one of those horses gleam in the doorway of the weed-overgrown Franka barn, I'm barefoot and in big-buttoned coveralls astride Carlo, clutching his fur for a gallop. But he has braced himself, set his rump solidly on the bare yard, and is waiting in dogged patience for me to get off. He will not move.

And actually, I liked the directness of the Martens family. They hid nothing, what they did was what they were, head on. The Martens twins, Abe and Henry, were five years older than I, not quick in school but always doing fun stuff no one else thought of, crazy stuff I couldn't yet imagine. They climbed trees to grab magpie eggs out of nests while the huge birds dived at them, screaming; they stuck their bare arms down gopher holes we had filled with pails of water, to clutch the gopher as he struggled to come gurgling out and if he curled up and bit them, what's a nip in tough hide, they had him, their hands hard and black-rimmed as iron traps and his tail was worth two cents at Voth's store, cut it off and let him run, he might grow another two cents' worth for next summer.

~

On my first day of school, the Wednesday after Easter, April 16, 1941, Katie Martens sat across from me at the kindergarten table in the back corner of Speedwell School. It may be she knew less English than I but, much like her twin brothers, her unself-conscious words always turned up in a kind of unexpected wonder that easily became a round smile and laughter. Or at recess a teasing tag song:

> Jriepa, Piepa
> Jript mie nijch:
> Ess so fuel
> Enn deit daut nijch.

> Catcher, piper,
> Catch me not:
> He's so lazy,
> And won't do squat.

Except for Jackie Trapp, who lived northeast of the school near the highway and whose father was German from Romania, all seven of us beginning kids came from Low German homes. Our parents understood we needed an English education because Canada had accepted us in our flight from that godless Stalin, but it did not permit living in exclusive, segregated colonies. So we six- and seven-year-olds came to school with our siblings on the day appointed and sat where we were told, on benches at the long table three pine boards wide while the eight grades of regular students found their rows of single desks along the five west windows and surrounded the wood heater forged by Sam Heinrichs from two gasoline drums and protected on three sides by tin sheeting: over thirty desks crowded to the blackboards and the library cupboard against the east wall. All ruled by Mrs. Lucy Bush.

She was an omnipotent blaze of bright hair swirled into shapes we had never before seen, a manifestation inexplicably everywhere in the room with a voice always about to sheer away into space. Though that never quite happened while we seven sat around the table because after "God Save the King" and the Lord's Prayer and roll call we were ordered to leave the school building and walk across the yard, past the girls' two-seater toilet and what remained of the long winter woodpiles, to the teacherage and sit down on the floor around ancient Mr. Bush. Not a single word, silence!

The log teacherage consisted of two tiny rooms, with a neat brick chimney on a shelf above the centre stove going up through the ceiling. The bedroom door was never open, narrow with beautiful grooved boards that left an unforgettable wisp of something sweet on your fingertips; years later, in Vancouver, I would recognize cedar. Mr. Bush sat in an arm-chair beside the table; if he turned his head a little, he could look out the window and down the road leading between pussy willows over the slough and the notch in the trees on the nearest hill, south towards the church and beyond Speedwell into the world. Mr. Bush rolled cigarettes—sinful, our parents told us, but they could do nothing about the war and so few teachers—in a little machine whose handle he turned on the table, and then he cut each in half with a Valet razor blade because, he said, he could only smoke half as much as he had before. He smoked at the ceiling while he asked us questions.

What happened on the Plains of Abraham? (Katie and I knew Abraham was in the Bible, but that wasn't the answer.)

What is the biggest number you can think of? (If someone answered, he wrote that number on a sheet of paper, and then the next, which was always one bigger.)

Why do we say the sun rises in the morning? (No one dared say anything, and when we were outside later Katie said that was a stupid question because you could see it happen every day but of course Mr. Bush had never in his life been awake that early.)

The floor between the outside door, the table and the stove was bright linoleum, very clean because we left our worn footwear on the step outside, with lots of space for all our feet and derrieres. But one of us always lounged against the table under the window; we took turns because on the table stood a row of yellow cans of MacDonald's Fine Cut Tobacco with the oval picture of a young woman wearing, as Mr. Bush explained once or twice a week, a sash of MacDonald tartan, the greatest of the Scottish clans. A Miss Harriet MacDonald, he elaborated at length, had taught at Speedwell School in 1938–1939, the year after Mr. Edward Lachner Diefenbaker whose nephew was Mr. John Diefenbaker, a brilliant lawyer in the city of Prince Albert on the North Saskatchewan River but, Mr. Bush continued, he thought Edward Diefenbaker too elderly and sophisticated for Speedwell. On the other hand, Mrs. Bush was very experienced with farm kids, as any trustee could see instantly and we all knew perfectly well, the very best teacher any one-room Saskatchewan school district could possibly find. And of course we seven agreed.

We took turns standing against the table because on top of the tobacco tins perched balls of chewed gum, sometimes two or even three shining pink in the sunlight on a single lid. Jackie Trapp insisted every ball we borrowed one day and returned the next had lots of flavour left, Mr. Bush—or perhaps Mrs. Bush whenever she wasn't teaching—liked mostly Dentyne but sometimes we suspected it was Wrigley's Spearmint, and Elsie Koehn even recognized Doublemint because, she said, once Mr. Schroeder had given her half a stick at the store, for sure that was Doublemint! But the flavours were too faint for me; I chewed, but I remember better the touch and smell of the closed cedar door, the bedroom behind it must have been so small and Mrs. and Mr. Bush seemed so large to us, how could there be a bed inside big enough for both? Katie laughed, she said they had a room smaller than that where all their five boys slept. Jackie Trapp did not laugh, but smiled so hard his forehead wrinkled and his pale hair lifted, smiled as if he could tell us a few things about his house as well, but he never said a word about that. He was the oldest in his family, I the youngest, but oddly we were the same age; perhaps, I thought then, that's because his parents are Roman Catholic—whatever that was.

~

Speedwell School existed because Trajchtmoaka Aaron Heinrichs, who now "rested" in the Speedwell Cemetery, in early 1930 had applied for a school building grant to the Saskatchewan Department of Education. He filled out the application map of the school district he called Pearl Lake after the small lake less than a mile east of the "Proposed School Site," and by writing the "Name of each Resident Ratepayer" across every quarter section in a nine-square-mile block of land. Then under every name he added the "Number of Children of School Age residing on each Quarter Section." He named twenty-four landowners on his 1930 map, including two Metis Briere families and grizzled bachelor George Stewart half a mile west of the proposed school; all the rest were Mennonite Brethren Church families who had thirty-five children aged seven to fifteen between them. The August Fiedlers and the George Lemkeys each had six children waiting for school; Aaron and Anna Heinrichs had five.

There was no more time to lose. The earliest settlers had filed on Township 53 homesteads in 1925/26 and, with Jack Pine School in Township 52 four to six miles away, five school-less years was more than enough. By the summer of 1930, apparently before they even got the usual $500 provincial grant to start, the Township 53 homesteaders had already dug a full basement, ordered desks and decided they would build with local logs to save money. The regional inspector of schools from Mervin, D. L. Hicks, wrote a peeved letter to Regina concerning what he now called "Speedwell School District No. 4860"—where did that peculiar name come from? Plant books report that small blue flowers called marsh speedwells grow throughout the western boreal forests, but no one ever identified such a plant for us in our district. Mr. Hicks complained:

> . . . all this was done without consulting me . . . I certainly would not recommend a log building, as they need too large a school. . . . I asked the Secretary, Mr. Heinrich, to ascertain how much volunteer labour could be counted on. . . . [But] it is my candid opinion the volunteers would not live up to their promises. The situation is this, there is a very great need for a school in this district as there are between thirty and forty children of school age at present residing there and a considerable number more under school age. There are not more than 500 acres in the whole area under cultivation [out of a possible 5,760], many of the

people are very poor, some almost on the verge of starvation, and they cannot afford to float a very large debenture [to finance a school building]. I am at a loss to know how to solve the problem. . . .

The chief inspector of schools in Regina received this cover-your-ass report on January 3, 1931. But by September of that year Annie Born, a Mennonite young woman from Hepburn, Saskatchewan, had come north to teach thirty-five children in eight grades in the completed log schoolhouse. Trajchtmoaka Heinrichs and his renamed community had, by hard work in the best co-operative pioneer (and Mennonite) tradition, solved the building problem.

"Annie taught in Speedwell one year," Gust tells me in 1995. "And then she married my cousin Albert Lobe, but she had to keep teaching another year till they could find a new one, that was really hard in those days, the Depression."

"Do you remember them building the school?"

"I ripped the logs for it, flat inside and out! I had my steam engineer papers and we ran them through our sawmill, big jack pine, we had them there, forty-foot jack pine."

Magnificent pine trees grew on that glacier-scoured land inhabited until then by sparse generations of hunters; utterly unlike the antediluvian boneyard of warring Europe where, as George Orwell writes, every granule of earth has been soaked with human blood several times. And though today the Speedwell land has for decades been bulldozed bare for cattle pasture, nevertheless those particular sawn and stacked trees remain. The teacherage and the toilets, the school roof, its ceiling, floor, windows, doors, its tall brick chimney are gone, the mud plaster long held in place by buried shingle nails has finally been broken by snow and washed away in rain, but the weathered rectangle of grey jack pine within which I learned to read English remains piled log by log upon the cracked concrete basement, corners beautifully dovetailed, immovable as rock. And every May the leaves of aspen now sprouting close around it gradually dapple the walls into flickering green. Almost as if this man-made extrusion on the long landscape were alive and, like a rabbit or ptarmigan, was once again shifting to summer colours in the spring light.

The board table marked by pencils, crayons, knives and razor blades; Mrs. and Mr. Bush; pink balls of tasteless, re-and-rechewed gum; sheets of paper; a short alphabet that could be arranged into "rudy wiebe" or "jack trapp" with only one r repetition: that was two and a half months of kindergarten at Speedwell School. If red WRATH grew on the road stones leading towards school, I do not remember it; I did not need the threat of God to see, to feel the gathering power of words.

~

Two months of kindergarten remain vivid, yet I remember nothing of an entire year of grade one. The 1941–42 records show our teacher was Mr. Isaac Braun, and that the following year he moved four miles south to teach at Jack Pine School, so he did not leave our area; indeed, he married Doris Heinrichs, Aaron's daughter, in our church where Doris was my Sunday school teacher. I surmise Isaac Braun was so good a teacher that his year at Speedwell simply disappeared into learning everything I loved and wanted; as if I had fallen into enormous Turtle Lake where we drove our horses and wagon once or sometimes twice a summer, seven miles west by bush trail, to play, fish and picnic under the trees above the rocks and hot banks of white, dazzling sand. That year of begun language, reading, writing, numbers, reading, companions, spelling, traumas, anger, impatience, reading farther and farther ahead is an immense void bottomlessly gone. But the residue of first reading remains a lifetime, like breathing.

Words that splashed in my mouth walking home the daily miles from Speedwell School with the crescent moon in the sky opposite the westerly sun, waves of words singing in my head, knowing them by heart:

The Moon's the North Wind's cooky.
He bites it, day by day,
Until there's but a rim of scraps
That crumbles all away.

And I remember the aspen poplar forest, exactly. A mile and a half to school from our house: the trail began behind the snow-covered barn, the east end where in fall Dad and Dan had built a log addition to protect the younger cattle in winter and kept heaping manure higher against the walls to keep in their warmth. It began where that morning's fresh manure steamed off the logs in the dizzying cold, led narrow and deep along the cattle tracks through trees, past the seepage well and pulley and cattle trough hung with ice at the edge of our slough that extended north into Pearl Lake, an oval opening of sky against the winter horizon; the hard, grey world changed into soft, blazing cold. And the school path led west, narrow as our footprints between the trees, gradually bending north.

I'm seven, I'm big, I carry my Rogers syrup pail (five-pound size) of lunch—two slices of Bultje, white bread, spread with jam or syrup if I'm lucky, salty Jreewe'schmolt, crackling lard, if I'm not—and turn off the track Helen and Liz are breaking one behind the other. I thump my own trail between trees alongside a rabbit path run shallow on the snow, tracks spraying everywhere, ending and beginning again in hollows hidden by deadfall down to the dried leaves where the rabbits had perhaps rested or slept, huddled in fear of coyotes, here and there a heap of tiny turds piled so prettily you might pick them up to chew if you didn't know what they were. Rabbits were beautifully neat, not like ugly porcupines plowing through snow and seeding the V of their trail with jelly beans of shit. One rabbit trail ran tight between young poplars, a perfect place for a snare. The Martens twins had told me there were so many rabbits this year they had caught hundreds and even at eight cents a skin that added up, but squirrels were better, fifteen cents to eighteen, and weasels, wow! a weasel could be thirty-seven or even forty-five cents if you skinned and dried a real good one right, that was just about a day's wages for a man before the war. For rabbits all you need is wire, you make a sliding loop like this and they run right into it, see? You just remember how many snares you make and the bush where you set them.

I made and set snares, and when I went back the caught rabbits had thudded down a great circle of snow to the length of the wire. Their white fur riffled softly dark at its roots, their strained bodies were frozen hard and flat as sticks, I could have broken any leg off. The wire was cut too deeply into their necks to undo frozen, you could only untwist it from the two trees. The four-footed track in the snow of a running rabbit was easier to read than a word in a book because it was always the same and told you one thing, or perhaps two, but words . . . words . . . the four shelves of our school library were stacked tight with words, in school our eyes and ears are filled with words and even here under the trees someone a hundred years ago or a thousand could have shouted, a bear stood up and roared and you would be able to feel the air frozen hard with that sound if you had the right fingers— the forest was snow and trees, silence. Only the faintest creak, barely audible, like the memory of a groan heard once, long ago. The great poplar trunks stood everywhere around you, one by one by one and gradually, finally, they became grey poplar and air as far as you could see in every direction; this earth is a ball, wherever you look you are enclosed in a globe.

But . . . if you lay flat on your back in the furry snow staring straight up, the grey columns reached high, they sprayed out over you and their countless fingers moved in a canopy of grey on blue: a blue ocean of continuous, circular rhythm; all the trees over the whole earth were always and continuously moving. They creaked, they groaned, but in summer they would whisper as well. Or shiver. Something too immense to imagine was always breathing over them. That could only be God.

It might be, if you could lie still long enough, you would feel God moving in the air. In the snow.

~

There are elements of myself that have not, in a lifetime, changed much; grown a little perhaps. I did not need stones along the church road screaming at me. Before I was born my mother's blood and breath formed me to know that God is everywhere. Whatever and everything "God" may mean, the presence is.

If I had asked, my brother Abe could have given me some Christian explication concerning God and Eternal Wrath and being born human and soaked in sin from which I needed "saving"; a bit of which I might have, at six or seven, understood. Abe was seventeen years older than I, thirteen when the family arrived in Canada; he received barely three years of education before he had to go "work out" wherever he could: on farms for his keep, for less than a dollar a day at sawmills or laying track for the railroad or, steadiest work of all during the Depression, thinning, hoeing and topping sugar beets—a whole growing season of work—in southern Alberta. But Abe also persisted in learning; he was in the first winter Bible school class in 1937 when the Reverend George Thiessen came from somewhere in the south to teach sixteen young people in the two-room Speedwell cabin where he and his wife also lived. For three winters after that Abe attended Bethany Bible School in Hepburn near Saskatoon, which had over one hundred students. Both schools were taught in High German, but gradually some classes were also taught in English; the Bible was the main text, and it was taught as True: literally, word for word, "God's Word." If some instructors and students, who could read both Luther and King James, discovered a doubleness or, worse, an apparent contradiction in the same texts, they could only attribute it to their lack of understanding and go on to what was indubitably clear, for the Word of God could only be one: it was and is always and forever one and the same.

My experience as a child of this teaching in the Speedwell Mennonite Brethren Church was simple enough: what was read from the Bible, what was preached or sung, that was the way good people who longed to do God's will believed and lived. This experience is focused by the number six, which has shimmered in my head for more than six decades: six was my age that winter—I know it was winter because the coal-oil lamp was lit, its light glinting on the oilcloth of the kitchen table and we had come home from church and I told my mother—there was no one else there—I told her I wanted to be good, I wanted to stop being bad and have Jesus in my heart. She asked me, what had I done bad, and I said I wanted to feel good with Jesus in my heart.

Mam led me to the big room we had built onto the south end of the Franka house. The roof of the entire house was now shingled, no ceiling dripped rain any more, and in this lovely plastered room you could look out the large window and first see the snow melting off the enormous boulder thrust up in the yard where our wagon road bent south up the hill past the root cellar into the trees; it was the room, all whitewashed, where my brothers slept and I slept beside them on a cot when they were at home from working out or Bible school, and where I had once seen the naked breast of a woman sitting on the edge of the bed with her baby in her arms and I asked her what the baby was doing.

She said, "It's drinking."

"What?"

"Milk."

"Where does it come from?"

"Me, out of here, the baby sucks here and it comes out."

And I could see the bubbles where the milk came out of her into the baby's mouth, so I asked her if she was all milk inside. She laughed and said, "No, only in here," and she lifted the baby a little and I saw the full curve of her breast.

In this room my mother knelt down and I knelt too with our hands folded before our faces, my elbows wide on the edge of the bed, and she asked the dearest Lord Jesus to come, come into my heart, and then I said that too. Since before I knew I heard it, I had spoken our evening prayer and now together we prayed that as well, though that evening it felt lightly different:

> Lieber Heiland mach mich fromm,
> Dass ich in den Himmel komm.

> Dearest Saviour, make me pure,
> That I may enter into heaven.

The prayer continues:

> Where I did some harm today,
> See it not, dear God, I pray;
> For your grace and Jesus' blood
> Also makes my evil good.

~

It was said no one had seen the mysterious stranger painting, nor had he spoken to anyone. He left his only words red along the central community road, especially on the rocks below the church, for everyone to see until the coming winter slowly wore them away. And Abe spoke their English aloud to me, explained "Jas. 4:4" so that I could make that rock code into my nonsense rhythm,

James four, ver-si-ty four

He also found the verse for me, and read it out loud from his Scofield Reference Bible, required by Bethany Bible School for its dense, cross-coded index of "all the greater themes of Scripture":

Ye adulterers and adulteresses, know ye not that
the friendship of the world is enmity with God?
Whosoever therefore will be a friend of the
world is the enemy of God.

Too many words, I couldn't sing them; nor understand. Abe said it meant things people did, "adults, older people" but I was too small to have to know about things like that yet.

But I did think of them. "Enemy of God," my head bulged with words, "adulterer, adulteresses," that was almost a singable song, I had "Jesus in my heart" and so I was "saved" though from what I did not know, I was wiedergeboren, born again, though I knew nothing about being born in the first place and Jesus felt good in my heart, as the preachers said so often, come to Jesus and a stone will be rolled from your heart.

"Good," Abe said to me, "good. Dann kaunst du nü frooh senne." Then you can be happy now.

Had I been unhappy? Ever? I could not say, in three languages.

The snow-covered earth held me as gently as falling asleep with my head in my mother's lap while she was knitting. The tall aspen stood over me, great pillars reaching for heaven, every one so thick and hard . . . but I could feel the trunks sway between my hands, against my face . . . under the snow they were rooted deep in the frozen earth and yet they moved; not only their tops were dancing. I untwisted every rabbit snare and never set another.

## 4·

## STUD

~

The best water is wherever you can find it, my father joked. But water on a bush homestead is never for laughing, and on both our CPR and Franka farmyards my brothers searched deep in the earth for it. Holes about four feet square, a good space for a short-handled spade and easy cribbing; one man below filling a bucket and one hauling the clay up to dump on the growing mound. The third person was me, tjleena Schnäatjat, little rascal, five, almost six years old and fondling every clay clump for dampness, which I always found and quickly shouted down into an echo below. Invariably my moisture was mere coldness.

That black, sounding hole, the sharp rim of it, my head edged into a square gap in the earth and I saw only the bent back of my brother in a shaft that day by day narrowed deeper into darkness. I did not dare get lowered in that bucket—not that my brothers would have done it—what would the next stab of the spade uncover? Best would be a burst of water like a dam breaking—the Martens twins told stories like that, but then they would— or even a foot of muddy seepage in the morning. But once I found a harder lump in my hands, that emerged out of reddish clay crumbling into broken angles between my fingers, and inside gleamed sharp, black, like the visiting preachers intoned sadly, "Hidden sin." At my sudden cry Dan glanced over, his hand on the pulley dropping the sticky bucket down, and calmly explained it must be some stray bit of coal, who knew how it got down there, in Coaldale they burned that all the time in their stoves, nothing scary about it.

But if it burned, there was really black fire inside! Dan laughed. "Better than wood, but don't worry, Abe won't find hell down there."

What came up was simple enough; after the first thin layer of earth not even any stones—too bad we couldn't farm underground, my brothers joked, heavy clay but at least no stupid stone picking—and for me the damp clay mouldable into houses, castles, even people and horse shapes that slowly hardened in the sun. Brittle soon, not like warming sand, clay down as deep as you could dig, and one day I thought: I never have felt exactly this fistful before; no one in the world would ever even have seen it deep under our feet as we walked past towards the toilet at the edge of the trees, never if we hadn't decided to dig for water exactly here. Every bit of every single thing was always so *particular*, even if there was endless amounts of it, like ground or trees. Moist, my fingers the first to ever touch and squeeze it, like this. And now exactly *this* ant was feeling its way over my bare toe. If my toe wasn't here, what place would it have to crawl? Maybe be pecked by our rooster crowing near the granary.

If my brothers had not decided the dry hole near the western trees on our yard was hopeless, if they had not already partly filled it back in and the clay mound not been there beside the boards covering the hole, my little nephew Tony, Tina's son, and I would not have been playing there one summer day. And perhaps then he would not have tried to tell me what a man and a woman do between each other's legs when they are alone together.

But as it was, Tony did try. What he told me on the dry clay, what we tried to act out there when I could not understand and he himself did not seem to understand well enough to explain——was it my amazement, his limited information, or language, or simply the incomprehensibly ridiculous act he was trying to describe? It was an astounding moment, and unforgettable; though I don't know what language we spoke.

Do we ever remember how we grow into language? Not specific words, but the immersion of words a baby falls into at birth, of the giants that surround you laying a sheen of seeming order over endless confusion by making sounds with their mouths? I came to English through my child's comprehension of family Low German and, to a lesser extent, through the more formal and careful High German——it was the language of the Bible and therefore of God——and it may be that learning to hear, to understand, to speak and to read English more or less at the same time was the reason I have not the faintest memory of learning any of the three. For a child, language may be less a learning than it is a ceaseless circulation of blood through flesh and brain and bone, caught like an apprehension, perhaps an instinct that develops all the more powerfully before you are conscious of it. Caught especially, and most intensely, from other children.

As Marilynne Robinson says it: "I don't know how the mind learns. I mean, language comes before any self-consciousness really."

What I do remember is discovering individual words. Once when we boys were building a fort of leafy poplar in the bush corner of the schoolyard, someone yelled, "Drag them branches over here!" and that word caught in my breath:

Drag!

Apparently we were doing that, so I drawled the word into sound again, "Dra-a-ag," felt it push out along the top of my tongue and stub against my lower teeth, harsh, almost ugly, but it felt oddly good as well, every sound that was a word for some reason felt good in my mouth, my whole face flexing to make it.

"We're dra-a-gging them!" I yelled back, and we did, the rustle and weight of the branches dra-a-gging through brush behind me like an echo, and later when the bell clanged for classes, I ran in beside Katie coming from some girl direction and I told her, "We dragged branches, for a fort." She looked at me, uncomprehending, and laughed.

"Oh, you," she said, "you dictionary."

I had discovered how a dictionary worked when our school visited neighbouring Jack Pine School. Troy Fehr, who though two years older would later become my best friend because of the friendship between our sisters Helen and Isola, noticed me turning pages in their school's huge dictionary, the heaviest book I had ever seen, and he said with a quick twist of derision, "Don't you know how to find anything?"

I blurted out, "This one's so big!"

And he took pity on naive me. After I understood the simple sequence of alphabet, a further realization hit me: "But what if I can't spell it?"

"Then you ask somebody smart!"

So *drag* was easy to find, easier than its fourteen different meanings; the first was all I wanted: "to pull along with great difficulty." I didn't notice the etymological Old Norse *draga* at the end, but in repetition I heard the echo of Low German *droage*, which in English meant "carry," which in High German became *tragen*—neither meaning "necessarily physically difficult" but they could be; and I began to notice how words in sound and meaning slid closely over each other, though slightly changed, like wind over an oatfield, through the tops of trees. Fun.

~

The three languages I lived played between themselves, especially in the long church services where possible games in a hymn—hymns mostly High German, but an occasional "special song" sung in

English by a small group of young people on the pulpit platform—could easily carry me the length of the Reverend Jacob Enns's slow, meandering sermon, always full of being good and loving God who was always so loving to us, but he rarely told a story to imagine. With the other little boys I dangled my feet off the front bench directly below his benign eye, and of course there was Pah two benches behind me and Mam's everlasting attention from the women's half of the church across the aisle to my right, but certain hymns could play games with my mouth and then my mind; not even the sharp edge under my thighs made me squirm while our log church filled with magnificent four-part harmony, four verses of "Er Bedeckt Mich" ("He Will Hide Me"; literally, "He blankets me"):

Wenn des Lebens Wogen brausen,
Wenn der Stärkste kaum held Stand,
Will ich ganz getrost mich bergen,
In dem Schatten seiner Hand.

When life's billows roar and thunder,
When the strong can scarcely stand,
I will confidently hide me,
In the shadow of His hand.

In the chorus the deep men's voices repeated the women's rising "Er bedeckt mich" after three beats like the crests of waves foaming in to shore, and the High German *Wogen* was like Low German *Woage*, which was English *wagon*—but how could wagons *braus*—roar and smash like whitecaps on the rocks around Indian Point at Turtle Lake—or was there a different meaning in one of the three? *Berg-en* must mean many *Bergs*, which was *Boajch* in Low German, *hill* like big Peeta "Boajch," Peter Berg, thumping bass behind me, whose daughter Julia was in my grade and sitting across from us on the girls' church bench with her hair like mist flowing about her face; she laughed so easily, or cried, when she was asked something in school, no, Julia was no *Berg* in that way, no English *mountain*—but mountain couldn't mean "hide," well, maybe *berg* in English could be like *ice-berg*, could God hide you, "berg" you in ice, shelter you from the roaring ocean?—but berged and buried in ice you'd freeze, and then you would really stand firm and strong, frozen stiff, buried and stone dead all right—the song couldn't mean that, it ended with "in His hand"!

But *Schatten—Schaute—shadow*, and *Hand—Haund—hand* were so alike, you didn't even need God's actual hand. Everyone was singing, the tremendous lilt and harmony resounded from the plaster walls, off the timber ceiling, and tripled this amazing image of refuge into incredible, hierophantic power: to be completely blanketed, protected, you needed no more than the shadow of God's outstretched hand— no hurt or hit in that hand, only goodness and shelter you could feel folding over you—and then if you stepped out into His sunshine—why would you need to be protected there, in warm loving sunshine? My multiplied imagination, unhoned by biblical desert heat, staggered: God was forever high in His bright heaven and only the towering clouds or occasional hawks or the great black ravens rowing themselves *whiff! whiff! whiff! whiff!* through air shifted light shadows, passed over me soft as breathing . . . and now in church gentle Präedja Enns's devotional voice was lowering itself into his usual murmur of closing prayer.

Ve Präedjasch Sähns enn dolle Bolles saul eena op'pausse.

Around preachers' sons and raging bulls, be careful.

Präedja and Mrs. Enns had four sons. Abe Enns, my own brother Abe's best friend, and Jake and Henry and little Johnny in short pants on the bench beside me. Henry, three grades older, wore a strange shoe with a layered, three-inch sole on his shorter left leg, and limped a little on that side—I liked the Enns boys, all of them.

"Amen," Präedja Enns said. His head was bowed, but sitting directly below the pulpit I knew his eyes were quite undevotionally wide open. Already ready for after-church Low German.

~

The joys of Speedwell Church services were powerful four-part hymn-singing and story-filled preaching, but the highest drama was Gebetstunde, the so-called prayer hour, which might easily extend to fifteen or twenty minutes because anyone in the church could pray aloud for as long as they were moved to do so. When Präedja Enns said, "Jetzt wollen wir Zeit nehmen zum Gebet," now we want to take time for prayer, the entire congregation rose, turned around and knelt down on the floor, bent into the benches they had been sitting on.

Since the benches had only a narrow top back support, you faced directly into the backsides of the row behind you. A completely different view of your church community: shiny trousers worn thin almost to the point of seeing underwear, frayed cuffs, cracked and broken shoe bottoms, even holes in socks became visible, which Mam would never have allowed her family to wear to church—she would rather have spent half a night darning. And the smells; feet wrapped in foot clothes inside felt boots all week do not change their yeasty, over-powering odors for Sunday.

But sight and smell could not compare to the sound of the prayers rolling through the church. The person praying stood, speaking out to God over the kneeling congregation, and the prayers of the women especially, able now to speak their need aloud in the church, moved everyone with their thankful praise, their pleading with God, often in profound weeping, for healing in sickness, for a loved one still disappeared in Russia, for children wandering and lost "in the ways of sin." O God help, O Lord be merciful. Prayer after prayer, this became utterance beyond words, beyond persons. I remember the whispers, the cries passing over us as we knelt on that board floor often moved even us little boys, bent over the front bench, to tears.

~

In church Gust and Tina always sent little Tony forward to sit beside me on the front bench with the other small boys. Our early family pictures invariably show us two together, beginning at the CPR home-stead where Tony is dressed in baby white and laugh-ing in the lap of a neighbour girl while I, in tan shorts buttoned onto my shirt, am twisted as if to walk away grumpy, annoyed at his receiving so much baby attention. A year or so later we're both in tan summer shorts on the homestead Gust already owned before our family arrived in Speedwell: standing at the corner of the house he built of logs sawn square in his sawmill, the corners neatly dovetailed. Tony is looking aside as we stand close together, but we are holding hands as if to prevent either of us from run-ning. We played endlessly together, our yards were huge to hide in and scare each other from behind machinery, among the haystacks of the corral or tan-gled willows in the bush. My sister Mary often watched us; she preferred trailing us about the yard to washing those eternal dishes in a grubby basin.

She had us motionless, tight on her arms among the spring aspen: just back from Sunday church, she knew for the moment where we were.

So of the three languages in our world, which did Tony and I speak? We had our own, fourth, child language, to exclude everyone else, one of gesture and body more than specific sounds. He and I simply learned the three adult languages simultaneously, from my parents, from his Fiedler grandparents who

spoke only High German in their family, from my
sisters telling us both English school stories and
then, when we two played together, we used whatever words in whatever language occurred to us and
concocted our own as we wanted. An orality now as
vanished as our childhood.

For me Low German remained fixed, and always the easiest; a phrase, a comment, a quip on my lips all my life and spoken even while I thought it. The clearest way to speak, no worry about grammar or vocabulary and always a direct act of making yourself understood face to face. A language that could not be written down, nor corrected by being made visible.

Nothing to be found years later, to hold in your hand and see. Everything my parents and I told each other in the first twelve years of my life, gone. So unlike the wonder of Helen's neat English still here on the paper of her tiny notebook with its delicate circles over every "i", coverless now on my desk and string binding lost, outlining our sequence of family sickness in a revelation beyond memory. On the first fold of a page:

> Mrs Wiebe got sick on Friday afternoon. Lay in bed for quite a while then had to go to the hospitale on 5 of aprial. got aperaichon on the 8 of aprial. was very bad first week then came home. 20 april was pretty good

On the second and third folds:

> Helen Wiebe got sick 5 of Jan. On her birthday was sick quite a while. . . . etc.

And on and on until:

> Dan Wiebe got sick on Fri 9 P. M. November 1
> was very sick taken to hospital 2 nov. got opera-
> tion [appendix] . . . Mom went to visit him on
> 19th he was very well then. Then the same day
> mom went to the doctor about her fals teeth and
> got them on Monday . . . Dan came home on
> Christmas eve . . . etc.

A cryptic litany of "got sick" that eventually includes me:

> Rudy Wiebe got sick on Sat July 22 about [num-
> ber indistinct; could be] 5 whent to the Doc on
> the same day and he was not home so to the
> nurse and she was not home either so they came
> home in the night. was very sick for first weeks.

Beyond all odds in my older sisters' relentless opp'rieme, cleaning up, after our mother died, Helen's notebooks have survived, though not so much as a letter in High German—which my mother wrote very well, my father never—exists from before the 1950s. It may well be these notebook words exist because they were Helen's; her life was so short and we had so little to remember her by; and she lived such a continuous illness that the repeated litany became her solitary solace. In our horse-and-wagon world so far from medical care, she timed our life by sicknesses, like a family heart beating. Her own "heart troubles" written down on pulp paper, but in durable ink.

Helen's little notebooks actually record "Rudy Wiebe got sick" twice, but they are exactly the same words and there is a contradiction in the dates. One note says it was "1940" and "Sat July 22," the other "1939" and the day "Sat July 27." But these dates are reversed: in 1939 Saturday fell on July 22, and in 1940 on July 27 and therefore both dates are wrong. So, which year was I sick once? Was I almost five or almost six years old when I was dragged uselessly from "Doc" to "nurse" to be brought back "home in the night" and be "very sick for first weeks"?

If only my sweet sister, now sixty years gone, had left a single descriptive word about my sickness. I remember being seriously ill as a child only once, and it happened because of what Tony told me, the inexplicable story he tried to act out on the clay by the dry hole of our well.

~

Our best, most powerful farmhorse at the time was a broad sorrel mare named Bell, and the summer after she foaled I discovered a game with her. Whenever she stood in the yard, waiting to be hitched up or ridden, I would duck down and run through between her front and back legs, under her belly.

For me, farm animal babies simply were there: calves, colts, chicks, kittens, squirmy piglets. As a child I never saw any being born—there are certain things Mennonite children are kept from seeing—but I saw them tiny, saw them growing larger, and also saw our big animals, in the monotony of their continual eating, drinking, shitting and pissing do some ludicrous things. Sometimes a cow would heave itself up onto another and stagger along on two legs, holding on tight and trying to keep up with the mounted, then drop aside, only to have others inflict that leaping again and again on the same suffering beast. When a bull was let loose in the herd, the ridiculous mounting heaved itself through the herd, violent attempts to ride one another despite their huge bellies and stubby, straining back legs. It was what cattle did to each other, like one calf head-bumping another between its back legs and trying to nurse where there were no teats.

So a child asks why, and a cryptic answer is easily caught; an adult evasion is always more intriguing than relaxed information. Farmyard chickens for Mennonites are housewife concerns: she feeds them and in summer, when they graze for food, their clucks and squawks and chortling float over the yard like wild bird songs from the trees and the children must keep watch so that when the chickens are counted in the evening, none has wandered away, and also search for their eggs wherever they try to hide and lay them under the granaries or among the haystacks or even under the low willows at the edges of the bush. Eggs were not eaten: Mr. Schroeder would buy them, eight or nine cents a dozen against our running bill at the store—good money when a man might earn a dollar a day if he found work with a CPR track crew, or mom and kids forty to fifty cents a day for dried seneca roots if they found a good patch to dig in spring—so we watched every chicken closely. And of course one day I asked why the rooster sidled with lowered wings against a scratching hen, who would either edge away and leave him to his silly posturing or, inexplicably, squat at his feet and let him leap onto her, his immense claws trampling her wings and his beak clamped onto the back of her head, and he'd hunch his body tight around her, mashing her against the ground, until in a flurry of awkward balancing and flapping feathers he uncoiled and hopped off. And after this grotesque attack, the hen would lift herself out of the dust, give a shudder that shook her feathers back into place, and continue her calm search for food. But the rooster would rear his head high, stare about as if he had certainly been missed while not strutting about the yard, and his neck would arch, his beak gape and he would crow; a tiny animal in a wide yard screaming into the sky.

I asked, "Why does he do that?" The oblivious hen was pecking the earth, singing as before.

Mam said, "He's just saying hello to her."

Hello? Clawing himself onto her, squashing her down and biting her head? The hen was near him all morning.

On the other hand, horses belonged to the world of men. I was not allowed to see what happened after the studhorse man drove his buggy into our yard with his enormous animal tied behind it and whinnying, all arched neck and bulging muscles, but within two years I learned how to disappear behind the barns before I was sent into the house, to peer around a shed corner and be astounded at what I saw. And become aware of my own body inexplicably shivering at that violence; like a fever, but almost, faintly, pleasant. At six I could not imagine where Floss came from, how she could be a lighter, more beautiful sorrel than Bell, have a white left hind stocking and a wide white blaze down her face from ears to nostrils. Even Floss's lips were white, and she would walk alongside, tilt, thrust her head under Bell's belly between her huge thighs and suck at her black udder. Bell's udder was tiny, her teats stubby compared to our cows, but there seemed to be enough milk for Floss, she grew fast, her hide slick when I ran my hands over her flanks warm as white baked Bultje. She nuzzled my armpit with her soft lips, but I had nothing there she wanted. Floss and I were small together in a world filled with giants, and perhaps it was her smooth movement of going alongside her mother, of her sleek head gliding down and open mouth reaching while Bell stood motionless, waiting for her lips, probably that began my game of running under.

Farm animals are for work, not play. If a family adult had seen me do anything so uselessly stupid as running under a horse, I would have been yelled at, whacked once for emphasis and sent howling. Tony and I were alone in the yard when he tried to explain what men and women did, and I knew nothing to tell him—absolutely nothing astounding like that—and I leaped up, I had to show him something I knew he wouldn't dare do after me, he was nearly five but I was way bigger, almost six and I'd never be scared like he was, of anything, I would always have nerve and know first. Bell was loose in the yard near the granary and this is what I can do, Tony, just watch me.

Bell stood with her long head stretched down, cropping the yard grass in a tight semicircle as horses do; I ducked and ran under her. But at that instant she moved—was she reaching for more grass or did I brush her full udder?—she moved a step forward, she knocked me down and her huge hind hoof landed on my stomach, the full weight of her next step.

~

Thank God it was not my back, but at the moment no one thought of that.

It was obvious I would die. There was no bleeding, no bones seemed broken, I was simply crushed and dying in dreadful pain. Any homestead family hours from any possible medical care would recognize that, especially Mennonites from a Russian steppe village:

children live, children die, who understands the inexplicable ways of God? I had been named Rudy for a six-year-old Speedwell boy who died on the operating table in North Battleford Hospital when he finally arrived there after a week of stomach agony and swelling: when the doctor made the first incision, his brother Paul Poetker told me years later, pus spurted across the room. He was bloated from the infection of a ruptured appendix. Who could anticipate or prevent that?

The will of uns leewa Gott, our loving God. Bell had crushed me and Trajchtmoaka Aaron Heinrichs, whose hands would have felt and known everything, was two years in the graveyard. And yet my family cried and prayed, I was always so thoughtless, so impulsive, oh God have mercy.

I curled into a ball, not even my mother should so much as touch me—Loht mie toch, leave me alone! But she washed my face with water, she kept me awake and screaming, and someone galloped to the store for John Schroeder, who came immediately with his truck—or was it his car—and there is a shadow moving like trees upside down in the thick window of a vehicle, I am coiled in the soft, useless warmth of my mother's lap and we are bumping into the yard of the Reverend George Thiessen south of the railway tracks in Fairholme—what good could he and his sobbing wife do?—and then driving somewhere east but we find no one who can help beyond weeping, there is a yard with a slavering dog where they send us away, and another, and I have no idea why they can't find Doc Coghlan in Glaslyn—is he away fishing?—but we do grind over all the bush trails and gravel that far, until it is finally summer dark and we are home again in the north room of our house, I am twisted in my parents' bed and who knows how "very sick" I am for the "first weeks," but I never do see the doctor about it, particular pain rarely leaves a memory beyond screaming, and it would seem after time I recover completely.

After all, I'm not yet quite six. Running around the yard and bush and animals and barns every sunny day at that age I will do stupid things and accidents have to happen. God in his mercy was there with his Schitzenjel, guardian angel: it was only the stomach and not my back or head.

Five years later a surgeon in North Battleford would find my appendix unnaturally grown onto my stomach. Bell's hoof had apparently rearranged my stomach cavity, and my immediate experience of that was nausea. I began throwing up in the back seats of cars the rare times I was in them, just climbing in made acid nudge up in my throat but in our almost carless world no child ever rode in front; the best I could ever do was sit beside the back door and, at the critical moment, stick my head out the window and try to project far enough not to splatter the car. Which for me wasn't at all difficult. A crowded bus to North Battleford was worse, and years later the ultimate adult body humilation in propeller-driven planes. But my mother, who endured much lifelong body misery herself, had a sentence for all uncontrollable physical voidings, no matter where they caught and shamed you:

Bäta enne wiede Welt auss emm enjen Buck.

Better in the wide world than in the tight stomach.

My childhood nausea was not limited to extremely rare rides in cars or buses; it also churned my stomach in winter when we drove in our horse-drawn caboose, a sleigh enclosed in canvas with a tiny wood heater to warm us on long trips in the cold. By the time I was eight I learned it was often better to get out and walk behind in the sleigh tracks, or balance on the runners when the horses trotted, clutching the canvas. I preferred frigid air, the immense frozen trees and fields to the thick warmth in the caboose, everyone knee to knee and talking, breathing. The open cold clamped onto your bare face, licked up your nose like ice and you knew every bit of your body was working inside your hooded parka and underwear and wool pants and felt boots and double leather-and-knitted mitts, you were strong, alive, the bitterest arctic could never hurt you. Mam would open the caboose door a crack, "Na?" but I'd wave her off, running.

I was riding the left iron runner one winter Sunday, coming home fifteen miles on cross-country trails from Livelong where my sister Mary and her husband Emmanuel Fiedler served a mission church, when Emmanuel got out of the caboose and walked in the right sleigh track and told me more about what Tony had started.

"The Bible calls it 'the way of a man with a maid,'" he said, talking King James English. Winter twilight shone gold over the snow between the pale stems of the poplars, the wind and sun circles hollowed at their base. "Even the wisest man in the Bible can't explain it, it's so wonderful."

Wonderful? Little Tony had told me two years ago that men stuck their pissers into women and I still thought that stupid. Why would they do that? Where? And Tony had not really answered those questions with his simple: "Because they want to, and women have a big hole and they like it." I refused to believe anything so abominable; pee was poison, my mother said, and since before I could think I had been taught to take my Schwenjeltje, little handle, out only in private, to pee in our chamber pot or toilet or behind something where no one was looking; at the very least to take a few steps like a big man and turn my back. So how could a grown woman be so crazy, to let a man do that?

Tony had spoken with more confidence then, he knew this: because men make them lie down, I'll show you—a man lies down to piss? Whatever language we were speaking, we were using one word because all three languages have the same possible structure: "piss" as both noun and verb. So Tony lay down and spread his little legs wide in the air, come on, he said, women have nothing to aim but you have—aim?—sure, the woman has a hole and the man gets down on top of her and sticks his pisser in it, you want me to piss into you? no I haven't got a hole there, sure boys have a hole too you have one, that's too small but women have another one . . .

Tony lay against the clay mound by the dry hole where my brothers tried to find water, on the side hidden from the house. His bare legs and feet waving a little, inviting me. We couldn't actually do much of it: he wore his summer shorts, but he wanted me to open my overalls and pull out my little handle, he wanted to show me as much as possible, the woman flat on her back and the man between her legs, that's what they really like to do, he said. That was when I ran away, across the yard and under Bell's belly and she stepped on me.

~

I knew the world, even on our bush farm, was as full of differences as I could endlessly discover. And I knew my sisters had no penis like me, but I never suspected they might have a large opening. When they stepped into the washtub to bathe after me, what I saw was barely a fold. As for bulls, the bags between their hind legs grew bigger, but cows' bags got way bigger, and bulls' hung differently, they never grew teats like cows to get milk out of them. By the age of seven I knew all about the heat of cows against the side of my face and shoulder, the swollen warmth of their four teats alternating in the rhythm of my small fists that soon ached but grew stronger and stronger squeezing them; my work was milking the two easiest milkers morning and evening, they needed only a last stripping from Mam to make sure they were completely empty.

Cows were huge, but with Carlo helping you could easily yell them into a herd and even a small boy could warm his bare fingers in a winter barn milking, you could squirt milk into your mouth and swallow as much as you wanted while the cats climbed down from the barn beams where they slept and sat in the aisle begging for a turn, meowed please! But a bull was useless, what did he do? He had nothing you would want to touch or hold, a big hanging sack and always spraying himself dirty in the middle of his stall, not like the cows hunched properly over the gutter behind them. And horses rubbled you with their noses, soft as fingers, but studs—a stud must be something out of nightmares. That was the word for a female horse, mare, and nightmares could be terrifying, I knew.

~

My beautiful blonde sister Mary married Gust's brother, Emmanuel Fiedler, when she was eighteen. As Helen wrote in her tiny notes:

> Emmanel and Mary got engaged 18 October
> 1942—there marriage was held in church 25th
> Oct. 6:30 P. M. and drove away 9 of Nov. to
> Stump Lake for mission work.

But before the marriage this had already happened: Troy Fehr and I had stood in the aisle of the Fehrs' barn staring at the massive, dappled-grey hindquarters of a Percheron stud. The great rear fold of the horse was covered by a short, docked tail, but his huge stockinged feet and legs were spread wide and inside the heavy notch of his thighs, just where the double bulge of his testicles nestled, hung the unbelievable length and thickness of his penis spiralled grey and white and purple to its knotted head. He had finished urinating, a yellow stream that smashed on the stall floor and splattered his legs and the plank wall. Troy leaned forward to get a better look, and I could not resist doing so too: that huge column of meat always there, hidden inside the stud's body. It was like a long beast curled and dangling around the Tree in the Garden of Eden as the travelling preachers declared, now fully revealed in the hot stench of the stall: the rimmed purple head with its slit mouth dripping poison, thicker than my leg and swinging under that immense belly, waving hello. Frightening to watch . . . and impossible not to.

Troy grinned sideways at me bent forward, staring. He had once explained the ways of the dictionary to me and now he was full of much more astounding information.

"What he does to mares," Troy said in his familiar dirty-secret voice, "with that schlong—you know Emmanuel wants to do to your sister."

From around a barn corner, where I was not supposed to be, I had seen this massive beast mount our mare Bell, his yellow teeth clamped onto her neck and haunches pounding against her as though he would hammer her into the ground while she braced herself, every hoof gouging in. Was that what they meant by "screwing," the stud's "schlong" screwing itself into the mare's hole while he tried to screw her whole body into the ground like a massive four-legged screwdriver—Emmanuel, and Mary? She'd never put up with it!

"That's stupid! What're you talking about?"

Troy laughed out loud at me. "Squirt, you don't know nothing. They want to do it in bed, all the time."

"They're gonna get married!"

"Well yeah, and that's how you make babies! Where'd you think they come from?"

I hadn't thought about it much. Mam said they came from God, okay, but what did people babies have to do with this thick club sliding back into its hiding? The horse shifted, immensely, his haunches adjusted themselves as he dropped his enormous head to the hay in his crib. Our family didn't stand around watching animals urinate—though we had to see it often enough on long trips when our horses would trundle to a stop, no shouting helped, and the gelding would hose down onto the road or the mare pour out right over the wagon hitch—no more than we stared after people when they went into the bush. There was something unspoken, an aura of both privacy and indecency about acts of elimination. Beyond the obvious foulness of what came out of your body, there floated a smell inexplicable as sin: your body did these dirty things, yes, but you did them alone and as quick as possible as though they never happened, you just closed or pulled up your pants and wiped your hands if you could and your body was contained again, clothed and clean, nothing had happened. But like any child, I also knew it wasn't that simple: voiding felt good, in your body, felt good somehow beyond the relief of it, and especially around the parts you covered most carefully. To urinate properly a boy has to hold his penis and sometimes mine started to change shape even as I held and emptied it, I felt it thicken a little in my hand and then something more, like a touch whispering through my body until I knew my bare toes had curled; as if they all wanted to clutch the earth, harder.

Vaguely I may already have sensed that in life "fair and foul are near of kin," but that love should "pitch his mansion in the place of excrement" was beyond me; and far beyond Troy to explain, other than the crudest snickering mechanics of it. A stud's dangling penis, a mare's anus or multifoliate vagina—both of which I had seen under uplifted tails in all shapes and functions—surely that could not explain what would happen in bed between my beautiful, irascible sister and her husband, the gentlest, most exuberant man in my short life.

But. That massive, doubled-horse screwing I had been forbidden to watch; the "schlong" disappearing between the stud's legs as if loading his immense body for its next assault into another mare: my own penis briefly stiffening. Where had that come from? Sometimes in the morning when I awoke it was so erect I could barely bend it down to urinate. Why? Was it like that wherever I was when sleeping, so hard I couldn't forget it once I noticed? In the land of sleep did everyone go around stiff like that? And a boy couldn't even hide it, like any stud.

It came to me then that perhaps that was why people did do it in bed, in the dark at night—and from behind too, like animals. Little Tony got it wrong, I thought, lying there facing me. If people did that, they surely wouldn't want to look at each other and feel even more ashamed.

But the winter when I was nine, Emmanuel laughed in the cold while riding the iron runners of the caboose with me during that drive home from Livelong. He cracked jokes, and explained that "the way of a man with a maid" was a lot more complicated than John Vallentgoed bringing his stud into the yard once or twice a year and letting him jump a few mares. And more beautiful. Mary was a high-strung woman, he said, and whatever he meant I knew she had the quickest tongue and sharpest temper of any of us, and he loved her so much, he said, he wanted to live with her forever. That was what happened between people; they loved each other, truly love without end, because that was the way God had made us: to love each other.

I had heard that all my life: God and love without end. Mam kissing you with a long cuddle, Pah's smile and big hand on your shoulder—but apparently when you got older, love started to change its shape. As far as I could imagine, now, it got downright brutal.

~

During the later thirties and the first years of World War II a number of families, including the store owners William Voth and John Schroeder, left Speedwell.

The world seemed to be emptying, trickling away south nearer the circle of the sun where the weather was obviously warmer. And then August and Pauline Fiedler with their four sons and one daughter still unmarried moved to Vancouver; they had helped Pah find Speedwell, given us a house to live in for the first year, they were our in-laws twice over and Mam and Pah's best friends. How could we go to Turtle Lake for our annual summer picnic without them?

Mrs. Fiedler knew how to clean and fry jackfish perfectly on a fire between stones, and her sons knew where to catch them by the boatload. Even Mam's wonderful potato salad and Schnetje, layered biscuits made with thick cream, without Mrs. Fiedler's fish would be like trying to celebrate Christmas without a candy.

Then, in spring 1942, our family itself began to separate. Helen recorded it in her first notes that did not begin with "got sick."

> Gust and Tina drove away the 30th of Aprail
> 12:30 A.M. were a week at home yet

Like his father, Gust had given up on Speedwell farming for the lure of another place: Coaldale, Alberta. He acquired a 1927 Graham truck by trades and barter and, as Helen notes, they spent a last week with us carefully loading it.

We took pictures with our box camera, family or couples lined up alongside the truck being loaded, my sisters about to cry holding the new baby, Carol, wrapped to her tiny nose in blankets with Annie or Eldo or Tony peering up beside them. We loved them, they were us and they were leaving. Everyone, even Gust, wept, but inevitably the packed truck slowly ground itself through the ruts and washouts up the hill south past the root cellar and disappeared between the grey April trees.

We stood in the yard, listening. That stupid truck. Past the empty Dunz yard, past the Biech place, like smoke drifting away they were gone . . . no! they were climbing the church hill . . . and then they were gone. Gone.

Life without Tony couldn't be imagined. After a week of carrying Annie and baby Carol, suddenly Helen and Liz had no babies to play with; they cried abruptly and disappeared somewhere. My sisters had never been much fun in the sandpile anyway, but what was there for me to do alone? Chase Carlo, try to grab a cat, run through cowpies, splat!

~

Nonetheless bright spring came: blue sky and hot sun turned the grey world green with a wedding. Helen laconically records:

Abe Wiebe and Gilda Heinrichs [Aaron's daughter] got engaged the 15th of February and 1942 Abe went to Pierceland and stayed there

till May 1st, and on 24 of May was their marriage
then went to Hepburn they stayed there a while

Pierceland was an isolated village in the boreal forest
beyond Meadow Lake; Abe and Gilda would pastor a
Mennonite Brethren mission church there for the
next eight years.

I remember their wedding only as one black-
and-white photo: Gilda in her amazing (to small me)
long dress and tiara veil and Abe in dark-striped suit
coming out onto the Speedwell Church steps crowded
with everyone in the community. Later a studio portrait was made of them in Saskatoon, posed again in
the same clothes, but that May Sunday must have
been dazzling. The trees, the road and the small
clearings of the hill and valley below the church
where the creek ran through willows and poplars
shimmered golden green as if the heavens and the
earth had just been spoken into existence. In God's
seven twenty-four-hour days, as Abe preached Genesis
all his life. "And, behold, it was very good."

The crops were excellent that year I turned
eight, and to save the expense and to keep the bundles dry until the threshing machine appeared, Dad
and Dan hauled our early barley and oat bundles
from the fields and stacked them in the yard. Bundle
stacks were different from the long, breadloaf

haystacks behind the barn; they were temporarily piled round as beehives near the granary for easy pitching into the thresher, and I discovered a new game to play between them. Gust had given me a worn-out tire for playing which I hoisted and rolled endlessly around the yard, down the small hill from the root cellar, jumped it over logs and bumped into trees, fence posts, even slammed it against the barn door when no one was listening. Then I found an iron machinery wheel with spokes. If I stuck a stick through the axle hole, I could bend down and, holding the stick with one hand on either side, my arms were just long enough to keep it clear of my face as I rolled it around the yard. Not like rolling a heavy tire and watching it crash wherever—this was a wheel I could control and I bent low over it, roaring, wheeling figure eights between the round stacks like the Fiedler or Lobe brothers who always had everything interesting like guns and bucking horses and a motorcycle like a little colt to follow their big car, the first anyone had ever seen in Speedwell—head down, running as fast as I could, I was spinning circles on my single-axle motorcycle around the stacks and across the yard, bbrrrrrrmmmm!

I forgot about the four-wire fence strung across the yard to keep the cattle away from the bundle stacks. Bent close over the wheel, roaring around the stacks and sprinting for the house, I drove headlong into the barbed-wire fence and ripped my face.

Screaming again. My sisters and mother came running, and this time there was blood enough to make it look frightful. But blood can be wiped away, Mam knew there was lots of it under my tanned summer hide. So, no desperate evening search for neat doctor stitches, just her tight bandages torn from sheets wrapped criss-cross over my face. Such wild running around! "Etj woa die aunbinje mett'n korten Strang," I'll tie you [to a post] with a short rope, she told my mummied head. She also knew I healed quickly, and when school finally began that year, there were no bandages left for our new teacher, Miss Hingston, to ask about.

But the body remembers, and some remembering is redrawn on your changing skin for as long as you live, visible to anyone close up and loving: the flat, disordered gnarl of an operation that begins under your ribs and vanishes in your crotch hair; the faint, white writing of barbed wire on your face, one line slanted across the bridge of your nose and a longer, deeper, couplet below your right eye, What's that? A story that grows warmer the more intimately you desire to tell it.

~

For lack of a teacher, Speedwell School began late in 1942, on October 19. That was the Monday after the engagement of Mary Wiebe to Emmanuel Fiedler was announced in the Speedwell Mennonite Brethren Church. I know these exact dates because of Helen's notebook. The engagement was announced on October 18 and the wedding held next Sunday evening at 6:30 p.m., October 25, in the middle of milking and chores, when fall darkness had already settled in and the two kerosene mantle lamps would need to be lit in church—why the sudden rush?

Not for the usual quick-wedding reason. In 1942, after Gust and Tina left and Abe and Gilda were married, our family moved our farm operation from the Franka land on Section 9 to Gust's homestead on the southwest quarter of Section 5. Gust's fields were as good and the house much better than the Franka place, and his well was known as the best in the entire Speedwell–Jack Pine area. I remember nothing of that move, but the October wedding picture of our reunited family is taken in front of the house Gust had built. He and Tina returned from Coaldale for this marriage of her sister and his brother.

The wedding photo shows baby Carol is old enough to sit erect on Tina's arm and peek over Emmanuel's shoulder. Our entire family is in the picture except for Dan, who is taking it. Wind and

rain have washed the plaster coating off the logs to above the window sills and nothing has been done to prepare the house properly for a wedding—was that also because of the rush?—leave alone for winter, but Helen and Liz and little Anne pose in their bare-arm dresses. No one, not the bride, the groom, or even us little kids, looks particularly happy. My sister Liz insists that Mary cried all day.

As Proverbs has it, "The way of a man with a maid" was "too wonderful" for Agur of Massa to understand. It may be that Solomon the son of David, king of Israel, added Agur's lines to his collected wisdom for very personal reasons; it certainly makes sense to me that with each new wife he added to the hundreds he is recorded to have had, Solomon might very well have understood less and less the delicate mystery that can be inspired, or embodied, between a woman and a man.

Understood, understand; I do not believe Emmanuel could, or tried to, make me understand anything that darkening afternoon as we ran behind the caboose inside which our family sat warm and patient for home. On either side of us leaned the walls of boreal forest, with stars brilliant as ice gradually appearing one by one in the narrow sky, but the winding trail led us true and with winter wilderness like cold steel in our nostrils, we might well ponder mystery and contradiction. I knew a mist of sadness drifted through our family talk: Mary was not happy at having married Emmanuel. The man she really wanted—the helpless, uncontrollable expression of "falling in love" does not exist in either Low or High German—was one of his John Lobe cousins. I was never sure which, there were several single sons, all tall and handsome and carrying themselves as if they knew everything worth knowing in the world and they would do it too, whenever they felt like it. But the Lobes had also left Speedwell—for Cold Lake, Alberta, where the Lobe sawmills were expanding as the war demanded more and more production—and something had happened, or hadn't happened that should have, and Mary suddenly agreed, on the rebound as it might have been whispered, to marry Emmanuel who had tried to woo her for a long time and whom she just teased, laughing. She liked certain ways of laughter, very much, and he was forever telling jokes—not really witty or ironic, more folksy sayings or long, slow build-up stories that were sometimes okay but at other times she would simply snort her disdain and walk away, her lovely lips curled. But nothing discouraged Emmanuel Fiedler; he was irrepressible, not tall but we all thought him very handsome, and not cutting with words like the Lobes could be in their erect confidence: rather, he was unfailingly gentle, a considerate man of whom my mother was particularly fond because, she said, he was soo trü'hoatijch, so genuine, literally so true-hearted, a Christian. Moody, asp-tongued Mary would never find a better man. Which was probably true, but such a truth could not necessarily make Mary happy. Ever.

It was typical of Emmanuel that he would leave the warm caboose to keep me company, running in the snow. The summer before I had briefly lived with them at their mission in Livelong near the south end of Turtle Lake, and during a week of daily vacation Bible school with him I had memorized all the names of the books in both the Old and New Testaments. I can recite them to this day, the Major and Minor Prophets a delightful ramble of galloping Hebrew names. On that winter day we ran together, talking, travelling a wilderness trail that would eventually find our farm clearing. I had never lived in or even seen any other place on earth: this was home. The syncopated "hoo hoo hoo—hoo hoo" of a hunting owl floated over us as we passed a small glade bright with the moonlight, and Emmanuel said, "God made everything good, anything a man and a woman want to do together is very good."

The horse bells and harness rang, the runners creaked over the snow and a hymn circled its rising music in my head,

> Lord Jesus, I long to be perfectly whole;
> I want Thee forever to live in my soul . . .

to the chorus with its indelible contradiction of Jesus's warm, cleansing blood,

> Now wash me and I shall be whiter than snow.
> Whiter than snow, yes whiter . . .

The Lord Jesus already for me the lifelong hunter, always circling, relentless, always there pouring out his blood—here, wash—that's not enough—as long as you live it may never feel enough—here, wash cleaner.

Emmanuel talked on. What stallions did to mares with their massive bodies, what bulls and dogs and boars and calves and roosters did was the way the Creator had created them. And it was the same for people, but even more so because God had shaped people out of the mud of this earth with his own hands, in his very own image, every single bit and part of them. So when people loved each other, whatever they did or wanted to do together, spirit and mind and body, that was good, he said, it was very good.

What if they don't love each other?

Only with love.

~

My brothers did eventually find some water in the deep hole at the Franka place beside which little Tony tried to act out that, at the time unbelievable, story. But the water did not taste good, nor was there much of it, and one major reason we moved to Gust and Tina's land when they left was because it had such a marvellous well. Only twenty feet deep, it tapped a spring and so the level in it remained at eight feet of water no matter how much you hauled out. Always fresh, a living spring inside the earth.

During winter, of course, a good well was not quite so urgent. Your horses could eat snow easily enough if you fed them well and under the deepest slough ice there was always water; if you chopped a hole and kept it open every day, water rose to the rim so all your animals could trail out from their sod-and-snow covered barns, both morning and evening, to drink. As for people, the world was thick with trees; we could simply build larger fires inside the big stoves we needed to cook food and warm our houses anyway, and melt snow.

And there was my job, now I had turned eight and was in grade two: bringing in firewood every day. The wood had been sawn to stove/heater length, we had split and stacked it across the yard, long rows piled high for good drying, and now it waited for me under the snow. When I had dragged enough loads to the door with my sled, I gathered up an armful and went in, toed off the rubbers covering my felt boots and began stacking it behind the heater in the living room and beside the stove in the kitchen. I had to open and close the outside door fast so as little heat as possible would escape. Mam would be cooking supper, Helen assembling the milk separator parts together for that evening's milk, Liz setting the table, and when I had piled up enough wood for the night I would sluff to the stove while they worked and talked around me and raise the front firebox lid with the coiled-steel lifter and push in a triangled piece of split wood. On the bright bed of coals its pale edges leaped into light, before my eyes the frozen wood was transformed into running flames, into thin smoke curled towards the draw of the flue, into flakes of ashes.

The warmth of people living in our home shrouded under boreal winter; the hot water always singing in the steel kettle ready for Pripps or tea; the warm water in the attached stove reservoir from which we scooped one dipperful each into the washbasin to warm and clean our hands and faces; the oven where Mam baked golden Tweeback, our ancestral double-decker buns carried for centuries across three continents; the huge pot of borscht simmering on the back of the stove, a superb soup the Ukrainians had taught us to love and which, with Groffbroot en Jreewe'schmolt, coarse brown bread and crackling lard, constituted an entire meal for a winter day—though we preferred it made with Mennonite cabbage rather than Ukrainian beets—in the open firebox I was forced to see that Hell itself lived in the wood I carried.

The fires of Hell, though hidden, stood thick around us in the Speedwell forest I loved. Like the eternal, looming Word of God coiled black in our German Bible lying closed, so innocently on top the pedal organ beside the rocker in the living room. Always there, ready to flame out. And yet, inside our heater, inside our house stove around which we sat eating, laughing, dozing, reading, arguing, playing Chinese checkers, visiting with neighbour families every Sunday afternoon and often in the long winter evenings as well, always talking—inside stove and heater, fire was so strangely, so marvellously, good. Life, happiness, the *gentillesse* of family and community were impossible without it.

5.

# STALIN

~

DAILY REGISTER

FOR

RECORDING THE ATTENDANCE

OF

PUPILS IN

SPEEDWELL S. D. NO. 4860

FOR THE YEAR BEGINNING JULY 1, 1942,

AND ENDING JUNE 30, 1943

Over sixty years ago the Speedwell mice found our school register in Miss Hingston's desk drawer sweet chewing. They gnawed away the bottom of it, I recognize now, into a pattern like the west-central Arctic Ocean coastline of Canada. On the left spine of the register the pattern begins high at the Baillie Islands of the Amundsen Sea (71 degrees North) and flips down and up and meanders east and south over the Perry Peninsula, along the coast of the Melville Hills down to Coronation Gulf and finally falls off the right bottom corner into the depths of Bathurst Inlet near the Arctic Circle (66.5 degrees North). I was marked north early, long before I knew it.

The mice are the reason I have a complete copy of that register: the regional inspector of schools refused to accept the gnawed one; how could he send a mouse nest to the Department of Education in Regina? He made our teacher Miss Hingston recopy the entire register—two days of meticulous work, she told me, kept after that in a tin box—and so she still had the damaged one to show me in 1971 when we met again, both of us laughing then at the compulsive ways of mice and of men.

Thirty-two students in eight grades are recorded in that register, including the Wiebe family children: Helen in grade seven, Elsie (Liz) in grade five and Rudy in grade two. We knew nothing about Miss Hingston's other names as recorded there, Elizabeth Frances Georgina, or that she had a temporary student teacher certificate from normal school in Saskatoon and that her "Length of teaching experience" was "1st. yr." The world had been at war for over two years and teachers for the thousands of one-room schools in Saskatchewan were almost impossible to find for a "Present annual rate of salary—$800." In October 1942, Trustees Sam Heinrichs, Chairman, Peter Berg and Big John Dick knew a mere seven weeks' delay in beginning school meant we were very lucky. Especially, as I discovered for myself, with a teacher like Miss Hingston.

War, Tjrijch, the very word hissed. Our parents said it was like the Communist Revolution in Russia, men killing each other, as many as they possibly could to see who had the most dead first; then that one lost. I could not understand. I was born into a world where I saw countless animals killed quick for eating, like chickens and large pigs, and was taken to funerals where dead people dressed in their best clothes lay in coffins and were prayed over in church before being carried, surrounded by sadly singing people, out to the churchyard where they were shovelled under the ground while everyone wept. But groups of men attacking, killing other men, I could only think of the Martens dogs and Carlo, naked teeth . . . I could not imagine it. Don't try, my mother said, don't think about it.

That was, of course, impossible. The war stared at us every minute we were in school. When we entered the door, hung our outdoor clothing on the hooks—boys left, girls right—and stood at attention beside our desks, the war faced us on the front blackboards: the Union Jack flag, the world map, the picture. After we had honoured both God and King by reciting aloud the Lord's Prayer and singing "God Save the King" together, we sat down to say "Present" at roll call, and it was the picture that focused the war like a flash of light.

Not a large portrait of King George VI as there once had been, Helen said. Rather, at the top corner of the blackboard beside the western windows, a framed picture under glass of the King standing in naval uniform with Queen Elizabeth all in white at his left and Winston Churchill in a black suit beside her, short and stocky, his heavy face fixed like stone into inexpressible courage. We had been told that on June 4, 1940, a month after he became Prime Minister and thirty-six days before the Battle of Britain began, Mr. Churchill had made the first of his greatest speeches:

> We shall go on to the end, we shall fight in France, we shall fight on the seas and oceans . . . we shall defend our Island whatever the cost may be, we

shall fight on the beaches, we shall fight on the
landing grounds, we shall fight in the fields and
the streets, we shall fight in the hills; we shall
never surrender. . . .

Mennonites did not "go to war to kill people," my
father said. But what if war came to them, as the
teacher said it had to King George and Queen
Elizabeth and Mr. Churchill?

Mr. Churchill, it was said, had the face of a bulldog. I had never seen a bulldog; I sat in the front
desk in the second row, between the west windows
and Miss Hingston's desk, and the picture was
directly in front of me. Mr. Churchill's face was the
face of war.

No one in Speedwell, neither parents nor teacher
and certainly not any pupil, could know that by late
October 1942 the tide of World War II had almost
reached its turning point in Europe. We knew very
little about Japan—it was there on the world map,
curved like a scimitar to slit the bulge of China, but
the massive blue Pacific was too scrambled with
islands for us to understand what was happening
even if we Wiebes had had a radio—which as yet we
did not—though the worst disasters did eventually
reach us via the *Free Press Weekly Prairie Farmer*,
which Mrs. Lucille Handley, who ran the Speedwell

post office, received from Winnipeg, and the news of the fall of never heard-of countries like Indonesia and Burma to the Japanese soldiers was frightening in some incomprehensible way, those brown men with eyes like slashes and screaming mouths on posters Mrs. Handley kept adding to her post office walls. Two of the English Handley boys, Archie and Charlie, were already gone in the Canadian Army, shipped overseas with guns to England and, it was said, young George, only sixteen, could hardly wait to join too.

But the lightning advance of the German army into the Soviet Union raised fearful awe in the hearts of Mennonites who had so recently escaped Communist Russia. Magnificent St. Petersburg, now Leningrad, was enjetjätelt, literally "kettled in," besieged, and Moscow almost surrounded, the Mennonite settlements of Ukraine were overrun to the western banks of the Volga: how could unstoppable Hitler be stopped? And should he be? Why? Stalin himself, that worse-than-devil, certainly deserved Hitler, if only the poor Russian people . . . and with all our relatives still there. But no one had received a letter in four years. Outside the post office—they didn't want to get Joe Handley talking England—at Harder's store, or after church when the men hitched up their horses at the church barns, bits of rumour were exchanged as everyone worried about all those relatives we all still had in Russia, whom everyone had prayed for for years, that they might somehow live despite revolution and collectivization and starvation and purges and secret police and no preachers or church but Siberian labour camps, ach, and now invasion by millions of soldiers killing with guns and tanks, and bombs exploding out of the clear sky—would there never be an end to the world getting worse?

And we Mennonite Canadians, far away and safe from that Land of Terror for no reason except God's inexplicable mercy, would eventually hear about those events; decades later, personally from the few aunts and uncles and cousins and friends who had endured it all and yet survived, somehow. Though often with their bodies, and minds, torn beyond fathoming.

~

In our home, not in public, Pah said, "Those Germans better watch out, Stalin has lots of practice, he knows how to kill anybody."

"Such talk," our mother chided him. She tried never to speak of suffering or killing; only in her long prayers in the evening before we went to bed did we overhear her endless fears.

"And your brother Heinrich, if he's still in Stalin's army, they better watch out even more!" Pah laughed, but not as if it was funny.

Mam said nothing; she turned away to the pan of Kottletten, flattened meat balls, deep-frying on the stove; next to raw sliced potatoes fried brown my favourite food. In our cardboard box of family pictures was a portrait of Heinrich Knelsen in a Red Army uniform, complete with the Red Star on his pointed military cap. He had a handsome fringe of moustache over his full lips. I thought of him somewhere in the Russia that spread across half the school's world map like a long bloated monster, a soldier certainly bravest of the brave with a big rifle fighting Germans, though I could not visualize how. What did soldiers in a big army do when they fought? What happened when a bullet hit them, did they explode, their head break open even if they wore a uniform? I had never seen a man in uniform, only pictures, not even the Handley brothers—though Dan worked all winter with Bill Handley for Lobes at Cold Lake, we never visited the Handleys and they never visited us— and when Abe Fehr brought his .22 and shot our big pig for butchering, only a tiny hole happened on the pig's forehead. Though it fell over and Pah could dagger its throat, thick blood pouring out like a spilled pail, but in war shooting people would be much more horrible, bullets bigger, bodies would explode. Maybe there was a picture in a book at school of armies fighting, but Helen said no no, there was something quite terrible about Onkel Heinrich's picture too. What, with such a nice, sad face? Well, how could he wear such a uniform for that Stalin? And also, Onkel Heinrich had written on the back with a very fine pen, in perfectly shaped German,

As Red Army officer . . . with artelistic greetings, your brother, brother-in-law and uncle, Romanovka, x, xi, 1931

"What's that, 'artelistic'?"

"A Communist word, Mam will never say."

I studied the beautifully swirled, indecipherable signature of my uncle Heinrich; the Communist words "Rotarmist," "Artelistengrüss." But "Onkel" was written there as well, the word as warm as Preacher Onkel Jacob Enns smiling over the pulpit. And if Onkel Heinrich was with Stalin he would be fighting against Hitler now, and maybe Hitler and Stalin would kill each other and everyone could go home happy. You don't understand yet, Helen said, and there's Onkel Johann too.

"What about Onkel Johann? Is he a Rotarmist?" I asked.

"No no, he's older," Helen told me. "He was in the First World War, a medical orderly."

"What's 'medical orderly'?"

"He helped wounded soldiers get to hospitals from the war, but now Stalin dragged him to Siberia, to prison."

"Why, if he helped soldiers?"

"That's the way Stalin is," Helen said. "Onkel Johann was a teacher, but now he's chained like a dog, freezing in a camp."

"Siberia is on the big map, where in Siberia?"

"Onkel Johann is maybe dead. You can't understand yet."

Yet! The youngest in the family so I had to learn everything from everybody, and always yets! But I would know, sometime, soon I'd know everything I wanted, know so much I could forget half of it and still know more than I had to tell anyone, maybe even as much as Mr. War Churchill if I wanted to, glowering in that small picture at the corner of the long blackboard that stretched across the entire north front of the school and halfway down the east side, right to the library cupboard below the small window; the picture beside the two large, rectangular Neilson Chocolate maps, one of Canada and one of The World with the Communists, including Siberia, in green—I thought, though I never asked anyone—and the British Empire scattered everywhere on the blue oceans in obvious red because Canada was that too, the sun never setting on it, not yet. And it never would, Miss Hingston told us. I'd know everything by then, exactly what had gone so badly wrong between my mother's brothers Heinrich and Johann in Russia.

~

The five large western windows let the light fall on our desks from the left. This was standard prairie school design, since everyone had to write and draw right-handed; those born naturally left-handed were, by Department of Education fiat enforced by the school inspector, simply forced to write with their right hands. In spring and early fall when most of us came to school barefoot we played at writing with our toes in the dust, or with sticks held between them. We discovered our feet had skills parallel to our hands.

It may have been Wesley Dunz in grade two who said, "See, I can write better with my left foot than my right hand."

Someone told me his last name in English meant "stupid."

"Don't say that," Helen said. "He's just a hard learner."

Like my brother Dan, as our family said, though I think now it was mostly his erratic, quickly ended Canadian schooling; in any case he was an excellent, hardworking farmer, managing our farm with Mam better than when Pah was home from working out. Dan was nineteen and, like Abe and Emmanuel, had to report to the government in North Battleford. I knew our church and family did not believe in guns; the only time our father would allow a small rifle on the yard was when we butchered pig, not even a gun for hunting. And though the Fiedlers and the Lobes had big rifles and hunted deer and ate them every fall season, none of them believed in killing people either, not even when the Canadian government decided it was good, they'd send you over the ocean where you were supposed to kill Germans, the Mounted Police wouldn't put you in jail if you did that, rather you'd become a hero and meet the King so he could pin a medal on your chest. There were pictures like that in the *Free Press Prairie Farmer* quite often.

Our family had no soldiers during the war years. Gust was too old with four children, Abe and Emmanuel were pastors in mission churches in small towns in Saskatchewan bush: Abe and Gilda north in Pierceland, Emmanuel and Mary in Livelong, then Sandy Lake, and Dan was excused for essential farm work. We did not have much more grain, our land on Gust's homestead as Speedwell stony as any- where else, but we did have more cattle, both milk cows for cream and steers for sale as beef, and pigs for pork. With war food prices rising, in 1942 our family finally paid off the last $100 of its Reiseschuld, the travel debt almost all Mennonites owed the CPR for bringing them from Europe to Canada on credit in the 1920s.

Pah had our family's exact travel route and dates stamped all over a long four-page yellow form issued to him by the Prenzlau, Germany, Police Authority on 7 Feb. 1930:

Personalausweis Nr. 157, Identity Card No. 157
Passersatz, Passport Substitute

which declared him a staatlos, stateless, person who had left Russia on 1.12.1929 with a present temporary address at the refugee camp in Prenzlau, Germany. On Mam's long yellow Passersatz, Nr. 158, just above and to the right of her name were the names of their five children listed by order of birth. In the picture our mother, thirty-four years old, is gaunt and large-eyed; it may be she has never known how to smile.

Sometimes on a winter Sunday afternoon my father would take de Papiere as he called them, the papers, out of the box on the short shelf above the clothes hanging in a corner of the bedroom and bring them to the kitchen table. I would kneel on the bench so I could lean into the lamplight beside him and look at, even touch the strange heavy documents long as foolscap in school but thicker, so yellow, doubled with broken edges and incomprehensible words. The names were clear enough, delicate pen-and-ink names that were certainly my parents and sisters and

Gültig bis zum 6. *Februar* 192*1*

-7. Feb. 193*

Polizei-Verwaltung Prenzlau den 192

(Ausstellende Behörde)

# Personalausweis Nr. *1582*

Paßersatz:

Kinder:

| | |
|---|---|
| Katharina | – 25. 10. 1914 |
| Abraham | – 23. 5. 1917 |
| Daniel | – 26. 1. 1920 |
| Maria | – 28. 3. 1924 |
| Helene | – 5. 1. 1928 |

Familienname: *Wiebe*

Vorname: *Katharina*

Staatsangehörigkeit: *staatlos*

frühere: *Rußland*

bis wann: *1. 12. 1929*

Beruf: *Ehefrau*

Ständiger Wohnsitz mit Anschrift:

Gegenwärtiger Aufenthaltsort mit Anschrift: *Flüchtlingslager Prenzlau*

Geburtsort: *Romanowka, Orenburg*

Gestalt: *mittel* Haar: *schwarz* Augn: *braun* Gesichtsform:

Besondere Kennzeichen: *keine*

Es wird hiermit bescheinigt, daß der Inhaber die durch nebenstehendes Lichtbild dargestellte Person ist und die darunter befindliche Unterschrift eigenhändig vollzogen hat.

Unterschrift: *Im Auftrag*
*Hoffmann*

Unterschrift des Inhabers:
*Katharina Wiebe*

Nr. 3 54. Berlin, Reichsdruckerei (7. 26).

brothers, but with so many stamps pounded blue everywhere in the spaces and the long blank pages: round Prenzlau Police and the absolutely critical "Department of Health Canada 10 Feb. 1930," the rectangular blocks of "Government of Canada Civil Inspection Hamburg" and "Immigration Officer Grimsby," to the miraculous tiny oval of "Immigration Canada St. John N. B. Feb 24 1930." And just below that, the last indispensable stamp in high capitals: C. P. R., followed by a handwritten "# 19622."

The Passersatz, passport substitute, had a small black-and-white picture attached to the front page, stamped on its top corners by both the Prenzlau Police and Canadian Immigration Hamburg. My father's stamped picture seems barely possible: a man in a high black turtleneck, trimmed moustache and tight cropped hair staring straight ahead so wide-eyed and frozen he appears on the verge of terror. Even in Germany, well beyond Stalin's clutches.

In Speedwell, Saskatchewan, fourteen years later my father sat with his head between his hands, his elbows on the kitchen oilcloth, musing over de Papiere as he did his Bible; saying nothing. Staring at his gaunt family backed against a board wall in Moscow, November 1929. At Baby Helen crooked tight in Mam's arm, her face already blurring before life's iron reality.

And Germany had been so good to us, had welcomed us fleeing the Communists in winter with barely our summer clothes, fed us, given us papers so the CPR could bring us to Canada on credit because they knew Mennonites always paid their debts . . . what land is Canada, what will we do there penniless with all our children? A total of seven hundred and twenty dollars Reiseschuld, travel debt: seven people by train from Prenzlau to Hamburg, ship to English Grimsby, train to Liverpool, CPR ship SS *Metagama* to Canadian Saint John, train to Montreal and Calgary and finally the small station in a prairie town with "Didsbury" painted on its mansard roof; almost a month of travel, February 8 to March 4, 1930. And now, in 1942, our Abe and Dan were supposed to help Canada shoot Germans?

According to reliable statistics, during World War II about 12,000 men who identified themselves as Mennonite registered with the Canadian government. Of these, 4,500 served in the military forces and 7,500 did alternative service as registered conscientious objectors. In Speedwell three sons of Mennonite families joined the Canadian military: Abe Koop, who served in the medical corps, Henry Koehn, a son of our Speedwell Church deacon, and Orville Fehr, the oldest brother of Isola and of Troy, with whom I was now becoming friends. One summer Sunday Orville came

to church in a belted khaki uniform and I studied him
as he talked to a circle of young people in his confident "I've-seen-pretty-much-everything-there-is-to-
see" manner. All those badges on his jacket, and a big
"G S" sewn on his sleeve at the wrist. I was confused,
I dared not ask a question, but later I whispered to
Troy, "That 'G S,' is Orville really a German Soldier?"

Troy laughed out loud at my usual ignorance.
"You stupid, that's who we're fighting! It means
'General Service.'"

The great miracle of Canada, as great as enough
food and always some work and seeing a policeman
only once in twelve years and giving him a drink of
water, was that my brothers were forced to shoot no
one; not in the name of Canada, not for Great Britain,
not for anyone else. Even in the throes of war, in this
country their personal conscience was respected.
They could individually register as conscientious
objectors and work at acceptable public-benefit jobs
for fifty cents a day while making monthly donations
to the Red Cross on terms that were negotiated
between historic peace church leaders (Mennonite,
Quaker, Brethren in Christ) and the government of
Prime Minister Mackenzie King. There was some
writing in the *Free Press* about this, but in Speedwell
no one said a word, not even Joe Handley, and in 1944
our next teacher, Miss Klassen, showed us a picture

of Mr. King and Mr. Churchill and Mr. Roosevelt sitting close together with the stone walls of Quebec City behind them. But we never saw Mr. King beside King George and Queen Elizabeth, and so the Quebec picture was never hung at the top of the blackboard. Mackenzie King had no war face.

~

Any number, any word, could be written white on the big blackboard, any picture drawn. The longest number in the world, or those less than zero, or all the words in the English language. I leafed through the school dictionary and looked at the blackboard: since Speedwell School began—in grade two I had no idea that was barely twelve years before, the school might well have existed forever—numberless words had been written and erased there. Thin as chalk marks were, perhaps if they had not been cleaned off with the felt ERASER—what a beautiful word, fast and abrupt as a SWIP over the board and it was BLANK—if the words had been written over and over on top of each other, perhaps the latest chalk words Miss Hingston wrote would stick out thick enough to drip dust onto her desk! Writing on the blackboard was like talking, more and more words could follow each other, you could write and see and say them in endless arrangements, write or speak and erase and forget them as long as you wished, they were there an instant and gone. But books were different.

Books always said exactly the same thing; if you had the book in your hands the words were there to see, they could not be erased, changed or forgotten. When you opened *Highroads to Reading*, Book Three to page 224—Book Three was none of your business but you looked across the aisle at Wilfred Heinrichs' grade three reader anyway—you saw:

SILVER
Slowly, silently, now the moon
Walks the night in her silver shoon . . .

"What's a 'shoon'?"

"How should I know," said Wilfred.

"It's a very old word for shoes," Miss Hingston had materialized at my shoulder, "so old it isn't used any more, it's dead."

Words could die? Why did it die, it felt better than "shoes," it didn't end hissing; so, books could say words even after they were dead—

"Rudy! Read what I told you," Miss Hingston said in the air over me.

I already had, seven times. But I flipped back in *Highroads to Reading*, Book Two, to page 229: to the last section, called "More Enjoyment (For Good Readers)" where I always saw "4. The Fisherman and his Wife." On page 230 was the picture of the bare-foot fisherman hauling a huge fish onto the beach, the black diagonal of the fishing line between his right hand and the fish's gaping mouth cutting through the tiny thatched hut far away up the sand. And the fish exclaiming, hook in mouth:

"Oh, do not eat me. Put me back into the sea,
and you shall have whatever you wish."
　　The fisherman quickly threw the fish back
into the sea.
　　　"Who would want to eat a talking fish?"
he said.

True enough. But when he gets home his wife calls him a goose! and sends him back to make a wish. Reluctantly the fisherman obeys; he walks slowly along the sea and sings a song I have always remembered, word for word:

Oh, Man of the Sea,
Come listen to me,
For Ilsa, my wife,
The plague of my life,
Hath sent me to ask a gift of thee.

Her first desire is for a "pretty little cottage," but one wish fulfilled can never be enough for the woman: the next is for a big stone castle; then she gives up on houses and asks to become queen of all the land; the fish grants even that, but as her fourth wish approaches the sea is black under rolling thunder. When the now fearful fisherman shouts his song into the roaring surf,

> The fish rose to the top of a wave.
>
> The fisherman said, "My wife wishes the power to make the sun and moon rise and set whenever she chooses."
>
> "Go to your little old house," said the fish. "Remain there, and be content."
>
> And there you will find the fisherman and his wife to this very day.

I knew it would end like that. Again. I flipped back to the fisherman's poem:

> For Ilsa, my wife,
> The plague of my life . . .

Plague. Like Pah said my grandfather had told him when he wanted to marry Mam: "Ploag die nijch met ahr," don't plague yourself with her. I realize now that this word is a translation shift; the lines of the song in the Grimm Brothers collection are, literally, "My wife, Ilsebill, does not want what I want," a disagreement that grows from her wanting to be Queen, then Emperor and even the Pope, and finally shatters at her demanding to be God. But I was learning English, this was the penultimate story in Book Two, and I read that in four fast demands a wife could become so greedy as to be, for her husband, a "virulent, pandemic disease?" Something here, as Miss Hingston sometimes said, was really fishy.

I remember grade two so well because of Miss Hingston: she very much wanted us poor Speed-wellers with our weathered log-and-plaster school—Jack Pine four miles away now had beautiful board siding painted creamy yellow with brown trim around door and windows—to be proud of ourselves. So she took individual pictures of every class, and when we told her we had never won a softball game against Jack Pine, she drilled us every noon and after school for the annual sports day and that spring, 1943, with the Martens twins alternately pitching and catching, we won both games, first on our school diamond and then on theirs. In 1971, when CBC television was making a documentary about my childhood, she came from North Battleford and we leaned out one of the school window spaces together—the building had been unused for fifteen years, but the walls, roof and floor were still in place—and she gave me a copy of the mouse-eaten school register. But the library cupboard, which always stood below the high window on the opposite wall, was gone; and so were all the books.

~

I studied the mouth of the huge jackfish Dan hauled hand over hand out of Turtle Lake into our rowboat.

I was in the bow to bail the seeping water out with a tomato can; the summer sun blazed blue to the bristle of spruce on the far shore and in the heat of rowing Dan had taken off his shirt. I watched his enormous hand, already thickened by endless heavy work, clamp on the neck of that jack writhing, pounding itself against the boards of the boat, saw it tighten, and then his other hand lifted our farm hammer and hit the fish once, exactly, on the flat of its slick bone head. Crunch. The jack had hit the trolling hook so hard Dan had to slash the lower jaw open to get it out, use pliers to reach in past those spiked teeth. His quick cut ruined the fish's mouth: how could a fish, even though it had teeth like a saw, speak to me with its lower jaw split?

But I watched it, Dan rowing back to the beach at Indian Point where Mam already had a fire burning in a ring of stones to fry it. The Fiedlers were gone, there was no picnic of fresh fish and potato salad to spread out for all of us families; only a few children, Liz and Helen and our neighbour Herta Klassen, who was no fun at all, played on the golden sandbars where the lake stretched so thin it seemed they ran on bright water. No Tony, no little Eldo and Annie to tease and bury. I had to sit in the heat and bail water in this leaky creaky lumber; watch this shining fish die. Slick as a finned bullet; its torn jaws kept moving slightly, there were fish words, fish stories to be told from the black depths of the lake, stories stranger than castles and popes if only I had the right kind of ears to hear. How many stories there must be here in Turtle Lake—no one, they said, had ever been able to measure how deep it was—and how many more beyond the spruce that disappeared everywhere west over the Thunderchild Hills into sky.

Years later I would hear that people in Livelong at the south end of the lake still tell of a monster that someone they know has seen, once, and which may appear again out of the depths of the lake, at any time; also, the Cree people of the Thunderchild Reserve west of the lake know why it was called "Turtle," the animal on whose back, their stories tell them, the entire continent rests. But I knew nothing of this then, my school and the books in it told me nothing about my place on the earth. I was where I was, here, a solitary child seated on a few boards between air and water, rocked in a numinous world as immense as any unknown ocean.

What I saw, so close I could have touched it: Dan rowing with his brown back to me and the shore: his bend and pull, his long arms reaching and then his blond head heaving back made the muscles of his back flicker under his tanned skin.

For me, my big brother was the biggest, strongest man in Speedwell, his shoulders as wide as any bull, and I saw against the blazing lake an enormous bull's head of tight black hair anchored by two shining horns—he was the Minotaur! If he opened his mouth and bellowed as he reared back, the world would shiver.

Our hammer and the skinning knife lay in the water gathering around the fish. Dan's foot splashed. "Hey! Get that can going!"

Theseus fighting the Minotaur, with one hammer-smash on the head and one knife-stab between the shoulder blades he'd be dead in the boat before he could say another word, he'd never devour another young maiden, not one!

A story in a book in the school library. The low winter sun picked out the small book almost hidden between readers on the shelf, a book as blue as *Highroads to Reading* but the stories were longer, more complicated, Greek heroes, and Theseus was the greatest. He followed a ball of string like my mother's ball of knitting wool into the labyrinth of the Minotaur and tore the beast apart with his bare hands, no hammer or knife needed. But at night in bed under the roof with Dan breathing in sleep beside me, it was Theseus's meeting with Procrustes that kept me awake: was Procrustes' iron bed like

Dan's and mine upstairs under the rafters, a spindly coiled iron bedstead with a straw pad on bedsprings so hollowed towards the middle that Dan shoved me away without either of us waking up? Slowly the peaked rafters darkened above me, and I pulled the sheet over my face. Dan's thick smell, sleeping. He would be too long, and I would certainly be too short. Procrustes would hack Dan off top and bottom, the chopping would be quick as the swing of an axe, but I would be roped tight by neck and ankles, drawn out straight as a log and slowly, slowly I was being stretched creak by creak until the pain of longer and longer became unbearable, I stuffed the sheet into my mouth to catch my scream.

How long was Procrustes' bed? Only one man had ever fit it perfectly; a little longer and I'd be that man, the perfect size—what did it matter if you lived only to be Procrustes' slave forever? You could run away, in Speedwell that was quick and easy as the nearest bush, in the muskeg only an Indian could track you, it was said. Indian wagons sometimes drove past on the road allowance but they never stopped at our place, but all the sheltering trees . . . I was already asleep.

"Good-for-nothing," Dan said, folding up the oars. We were on shore, I seemed to be sitting on a board of water. "Get out before you drown."

I never liked fishing. A fish was too beautiful to torture, to drag up out of the lake and kill. And yet, and yet, spiny jack that it was, after Mrs. Fiedler or Mam had fried it, you tasted again that you could never imagine how delicious it would be.

~

As I grew aware of the world beyond family Speedwell, there was war, only war. That was de groote Welt, the big, the great world, my parents said, and it fit right in with the brutal, starving stories I heard our visiting neighbours tell again on Sunday afternoons or winter evenings about the Russia we had all, by God's mercy, been able to flee. And even here, hidden deep in Canada's silent boreal forest, we could not escape the worst century human beings had ever violated themselves to endure: it roared into a reality we heard and saw, from out of the sky.

It seemed that isolated Speedwell School was a point on the training grid for war pilots. The planes of the British Commonwealth Air Training Plan, based at an airfield near Battleford, thundered up from the southern horizon of trees and low over our school as if the tiny goggled heads inside that contraption hammering itself through the air had somehow planned to glare down on us children scattered frozen and staring from the softball diamond at recess. This happened numerous times, and the smallest of us were terrified, running inside to hide under our wooden desks. No one ever waved; to me, such a machine controlled by men going where they pleased in air seemed less likely than a Minotaur.

Bullets or bombs, suddenly, out of nowhere in the clear blue sky: those were the most terrifying of all machines made to kill people. "De groote Welt," our mother was almost weeping, "so es daut"—that's the way it is.

Nevertheless, my nearest memory of flying is not those training planes, nor the horror of what they were trained for; rather, it concerns seeing and feeling a new pair of royal blue pants with the sharpest creases I had ever worn. One spring day, perhaps early May, I walked to the boys' outhouse past what remained of the stacked woodpile after a long winter burning in the school heater; and I contemplated my new pants as I sat on the planks worn so smooth by years of boy derrieres. I had asked to be excused in the standard, silent way by raising my hand with both first and middle fingers extended—a signal Mr. Churchill made famous as a victory salute, but for us it still necessarily meant "Number Two, quickly please!"—and therefore I had legitimate extra time to pause and hum, as I walked back, "Hmmm-

hmmm Pilot." It was not so much the sharp crease of the pants as the golden label sewed over their left pocket: FUTURE PILOT.

I was singing that, walking back, and I don't know why "future" had sound-shifted into "hmmm hmmm," perhaps it was merely the rhythm of the hum that allowed me to sing at any pitch, high or low, and repeat myself as feeling demanded, but it was PILOT that carried all the meaning even as I had no concept of what pilots actually did in war, they "flew planes" and that was more than enough, they could go anywhere in air faster than a hawk, sit there and streak over farms and fields and bush and in a minute they'd be over Turtle Lake, "Hmmm-hmmm Pilot."

In 1942–43 our family received a High German church weekly, *Mennonitische Rundschau* ("Mennonite Observer"), which always carried one brief column of "world" news, but within the year Dan would subscribe to the *Free Press Weekly Prairie Farmer* and bring home a battery radio because he wanted to know what was happening in the war. Perhaps Miss Hingston explained some facts about the air devastation of the Battle of Britain, but I am certain Miss Anne Klassen, who arrived to teach us in January 1944, could not have told us anything about Canada's RCAF Bomber Group which was

sending great fleets of four-engined Stirling and
Lancaster and Halifax bombers across the English
Channel every evening in massive night bombing of
German cities. In any case, few Canadian civilians
knew that they carried not only explosive bombs, but
also the far more deadly fire bombs newly developed
for total destruction by saturation burning. No men
from the Speedwell or Jack Pine school districts were
in those planes, but no civilian could then know that
more than 10,000 Canadians would die in those
raids—pilots, navigators, bombardiers, tail gun-
ners—and even if no gravesite existed, each individual name would be listed in government records and
would eventually be engraved on community honour
memorials, as was proper. On the other hand, no one
would ever know the number of children—say those
my age at the time, eight or nine or ten—who were
killed by burning or explosion or flood or crushing
when those fleets of relentless planes dropped their
"eggs" on a terrified city; to say nothing of knowing
their names.

As for me, I walked to school in my creased blue
pants humming "Hmmm-hmmm Pilot" for a few
days, and the isolated bush world I knew continued
its cycle of day and night and work and inevitable
weather as it always had. Slow spring was coming at
last, the drab poplars bristled leaf-tips and the sunny

sides of hills sprouted grass until one morning the world had rolled over into bright green to the music of frogs singing between the rushes of every flooded slough. The creeks ran loud as ducks gabbling under the plank culverts, and before I was aware of it my creased pants were crumpled from not having been rolled up far enough when I waded in the mossy, sinking slough, muddy and slimed with frogs' eggs. After my mother's powerful arms had drubbed them through tub and washboard, and I had crunched them through the wringer turning the handle, they never regained that first, so essential, military crease. But the golden label shone: FUTURE PILOT.

I did not know it then, but I could never have been a pilot; my recognition of red and green variations was slow at best, sometimes lost completely in the finer shades of either, with green sometimes edging towards blue. How does a person actually see colour? No colour-literate person has ever usefully described it. For me yellow was marvellous, my favourite because it was absolutely recognizable; goldfinches remain the loveliest of birds.

"These are the reds," Katie Martens would say with not a second's hesitation and of course there they would be, in her hand and offered to me while I had been doing a comparative search by spreading out the twenty-eight wax crayons over the table and studying at least seven other possibilities: yellow and black and white and dark purple were obvious enough but some of those—what were they? Why weren't the colours named, printed on the paper wrappers to see and read, then I'd know for sure!

~

With over thirty students in eight grades, and several taking provincial correspondence courses for grade nine, Miss Hingston did not notice my colour problems. I was too busy reading, scribbling, colouring maps in whatever colours—I could recognize difference perfectly well even if I couldn't name it—of possible worlds to need much help. And she could not teach in Speedwell a second year; she had promised to go to a school nearer North Battleford, though Samuel Heinrichs, the Speedwell board chairman begged her to come back; he knew a fine Christian teacher when he had one.

Sam Heinrichs was also our community's blacksmith, a tall man beaked forward from a lifetime of hard work and listening carefully to people shorter than himself. Liz and I cut across their land and home yard every day to walk to school, and the Heinrichs kids, Esther who was in grade eight, Louise and Wilfred, walked with us the last mile and a half. The log blacksmith shop at the south corner of their yard had the widest, blackest chimney I had ever seen, and I had often been inside its double doors where the forge fire glowed under a tin canopy to catch the smoke. There was no split wood in his open tray, but coal, big black lumps of it hard as stone, not crumbly like the bit Abe found in our Franka well.

"This comes from deep mines," Sam Heinrichs explained in Low German. "Men work in the dark all day, breaking it into pieces, shovelling it."

He showed me how to turn the bellows, and slowly I whirred the coal piled in the centre of the forge into solid chunks of fire; no flame, my fists circling the handle of Sam Heinrichs' mysterious forge revealed coal for what it was: intense light that burned in my eyes until I could see nothing, only light that blazed bright even behind my clenched eyelids. Not at all like wood fire, which flickered, ran, burst in unpredictable and leaping colours anywhere it pleased, and back again: this fire coiled black inside coal released itself more and more fiercely, gradually changing the dull plowshare thrust into it into the same blazing intensity; as if transforming the steel into itself.

And then, without warning, he lifted the share out of the forge with tongs onto his anvil and began to hammer it. The huge hammer in his right fist pounding the bright share back into the glowing blackness of the original coal, the sound of steel on hot steel on steel ringing like an iron bell. I had never heard a church bell ring. The Roman Catholic church in Fairholme had a bell tower with a bell donated by the Canadian National Railway, but we were never there on Sunday to hear it ring and no Mennonite church, since their first persecution in the sixteenth century, had had bells to announce their prayers and gathering—I thought a church bell in a tower must sound like Sam Heinrichs hammering a plowshare on his anvil. A sound like molten, hardening steel, shivering the poplars and your body too.

In Sam Heinrichs, with his long ridged nose and leather apron hunched over and running sweat in that smoke of iron heat, I gradually recognized Hephaestus, the Greek god of fire and the forge. And I read the story again in the blue book and understood why laughing, golden Aphrodite, the irresistible goddess of love and beauty, born of foam out of the wine-dark sea, could love someone as bent and blackened as Hephaestus: with his hammer he could shape anything imaginable from glowing steel.

In August 2004, Frances Hingston Cotcher, now eighty-eight years old and living in North Battleford, tells me, "In spring 1943 Sam Heinrichs begged me to come back in the fall. He was already ill then." And in the Speedwell Church Cemetery list I find his name in the men's row of graves, the second last from the north:

SAMUEL HEINRICHS

Dec. 3 1900–Sept. 9 1943

Parallel to his grave, four feet east in the women's row, my sister Helen is buried.

Perhaps the remaining two men on the school board could not find another teacher before his death; perhaps, as some former Speedwellers think they remember, a young woman named Friesen was hired from somewhere in the south who "did not work out." It might be that the Christmas concert went wrong, something happened between a soldier on leave and the teacher, in the barn, while Santa Claus was handing out Christmas bags to us little kids—that may well be a shadow incarnation of the ending of my first novel—but the fact is I can remember neither teacher nor problem; nor if we had any school whatever from September to December in 1943. I do remember Sam Heinrichs lying in his coffin like his elder brother Aaron, the man who brought Speedwell School into existence and whose legacy Sam and then his youngest brother Dave carried on. Sam, the last man in Speedwell who knew the mysteries of fire and steel. After his death we had to drive ten miles to Fairholme where stood a false-fronted building with the name "A Tanguay" painted on it and below that the words, blocked out in letters made of three rows of beer-bottle caps:

BLACKSMITH

FAIRHOLME • SASK

Mam would not enter a place that flaunted such evidence of drunken sin, but luckily, she never had to; Pah or Dan got our plowshares sharpened.

Somehow the school board found Anne Klassen, and she came to be our teacher in early January 1944. Fifty-five years later, at a Saskatoon reception after I have given a fiction reading, we meet again. Her gentle face widens in a smile as she greets me emphatically with: "You were a naughty boy!"

Everyone standing crowded about, listening, laughs with me. It seems it was I, not mice, who got her into trouble with the all-powerful inspector of schools. I always did classwork very fast and since, she explains, I had already read all the books in the library, I had time for mischief. Nothing serious of course, such a nicely behaved little boy (more laughter), so when she returned for a second year of Speedwell, she simply kept giving me more assignments; by June 1945 I had finished all the work of both grades four and five and she promoted me into grade six. The inspector declared that no one skipped grades in his jurisdiction, he wouldn't allow it, but when Miss Klassen proved to him that I hadn't skipped anything, that I'd really done two years' work in one, he grudgingly accepted. But he didn't like it, and said so in his report.

All I can say to her in 1999 is, "He should have got you more books for the library."

Though I remember that "skipping" very well; it moved me into a class where the only other pupil was Nettie Enns, the quiet eighth child of our church minister, who if she didn't already know everything necessary, certainly knew how and where to find it. Three years in classes with her, only two of us, and I was never first again. With time I could only comfort myself with the thought that Nettie would always come out ahead just because she was so schratj'lich je'neiw, dreadfully neat.

~

Except for the five German Trapp and the three Russian Sahar children—by my time the Metis

Brieres had none of school age—all of us in the Speedwell School district were Russian Mennonite and attended the Mennonite Brethren Church. That included the Speedwell teachers Isaac Braun, Anne Klassen and later Sarah Siemens. Community dances were sometimes held in Jack Pine School, which had a larger, more mixed population—including the English school board chairman Joe Handley, whose youngest son one summer burned down the school on a dare or, as rumour had it, so there would be no school for him to be forced to attend—but it seems nothing so ungodly as dances with their inevitable drinking and fights and fornications ever took place in Speedwell School building. Rather, the Mennonite Brethren congregation, established in 1926, met there from 1930 until 1933, when the log church was completed; after that, the school Christmas program and an occasional bazaar or taxpayers' meeting were the only community events that took place in the school, and the church was the centre for all other happenings.

Our families taught us we were Mennonites, and that meant we were hard-working, quiet and simple people who should do almost anything to live peacefully together and go to church several times a week to pray, study the Bible, listen to sermons and sing, sing, sing. Always full harmony, the small church

bulging with harmony you could hear across the hilly forests for miles if the windows were open. And visit. The only community recreation, every Sunday and sometimes two or three evenings a week, especially during the long winters, was family visiting.

To visit meant eating, laughing, drinking Pripps— no church Mennonite in Speedwell drank alcohol; true, a bottle of Alpenkräuter had a higher alcohol content than any wine, but it was advertised in the weekly *Rundschau* as an excellent medicine "to cleanse all body systems," and two tablespoons every evening before bed was perfectly acceptable to my mother for her ever-unsettled stomach. Above all, visiting meant Resse'riete.

Like so many Low German expressions, the subtleties of "Resse'riete" are difficult to translate. The two words do not simply mean storytelling; they carry an alliterative aura of communal comprehension, and earthiness; the very sounds spring a taste in your mouth. The noun "Ress" means both a "well-deserved whipping" and a "trick," a "prank"; the verb "riete" means "to pull, tug, tear," very much like an ache in the body (the noun "Rieting" means rheumatism), and so Resse'riete could be paraphrased in English as whipping out or tearing off some good stories that will make you ache, or sting, with laughter, sentiment, even tears. For Russian Mennonites who don't drink or dance, storytelling is the heart's core of visiting and my generation, the first born in Canada, was imprinted with story in our mothers' wombs.

Stories of the magnificent Ukrainian and Russian steppes, the lovely Mennonite villages where everyone lived, not isolated and scattered, lost somewhere in bush like Canada, but together, sheltered in a deep, sometimes steep valley where a stream of clear water always flowed, where the great village farmsteads faced each other across the single street and the window gables of the high-raftered houses kept watch over each other through the leafy branches of mulberry trees. Trees you planted exactly where you wanted them—you never had to chop them down in their thousands to create a field, never had to laboriously hack down and uproot even a single tree— and every morning the men drove their horses and machines out to their big fields sloping up from the village onto the horizon of the steppes and children walked to school at the village crossroads opposite the church and in the evening the Ukrainian or Bashkir herdsman brought the village cattle herd back from the communal pasture and every cow with her calf would turn in at their home gate, where the mother was waiting with her pail, ready to milk her.

I sat on the floor in the heater corner or under the kitchen table and listened to this, a world I did not know and would never see. I would lay my head on my arms folded across my drawn-up knees, and I would feel as if I were looking at one of those pictures of tiny thatch-roofed houses almost hidden against hills beside a stream that were background to the German Bible mottos that hung in every Speedwell living room, ours too: "The Lord is my Shepherd, I shall not want." As real as my leg muscles' ache when I plowed my felt boots through snowdrifts to the woodpile.

But then the stories changed. The First World War came, bringing Forstei duty for the men, and long hospital trains where Mennonite men and women served as medical orderlies or nurses for thousands of horribly torn soldiers who died of their wounds in the train cars and were carried off at sidings—who knew who was shovelled under, or where—and then, worst of all, the Communists and their violent, unending Revolutions. Speedwellers had lived in Russian Mennonite colonies thousands of kilometres apart; they had escaped to Canada in many different ways between 1923 and 1930, but they all had stories to tell that were stunning in their own way: of starvation, cholera, murderous bandit raids, beatings, fire and theft, vicious Red and White Army battles of advance and retreat and again advance; of torture, sons forced at gunpoint to torture their fathers, the slaughter in villages of every male over fifteen with not a shot fired, sabres only, and every woman—

No one ever said the word "rape." I knew the word jewaultijch, which meant God, All-powerful and Great and Capable of Anything, but never did I hear the word vejewaultje—to be overpowered, or forced, as in sexually violated. No Mennonite child in Canada needed to hear that such a word existed, oh God have mercy.

And in our small family, a story stretching thin between the two pictures from Russia that my mother sometimes held in her hands, crying as she prayed: of her two brothers, Heinrich and Johann, the Red Army soldier and the conscientious-objector medical orderly. My parents never spoke of them while visiting neighbours, and only decades later, from my cousins in Paraguay and those who resettled in Germany from the Soviet Union after 1982, would I hear more about the tragic Stalin-Communist fates of my two Knelsen uncles.

~

The August Fiedlers, who had helped our family so much and whom we visited most often, seemed not to have such stories about their past, and neither did their close relatives the Lobes, the Dunzes, the Biechs and the Leischners. Their older children were born in the United States, the younger ones in Canada and they spoke only English among themselves and there was nothing about Orenburg or Molotschna or Neu-Samara or Chortiza for them to tell: their stories were from the isolated plains of North Dakota or, for the parents, Bessarabia on the Moldavian plateau—wherever that was, I was never certain—where they had lived in German villages as well, though even old August, who had married Pauline Lobe there, could barely remember them. Nor did he appear to want to; he had been forced to serve the Czar three years in the Russo-Japanese War and when he finally got home again to his Pauline and tiny Olga in 1906, they packed up and left for the United States as fast as they could. Eighteen years later they hauled themselves north into Saskatchewan, where they chopped and burned and plowed a homestead out of bush and got their six sons on their feet—husbands would take care of Elsie and Ruth. That was enough for old August to think about, forget that slave past of Europe where every little big shot could tell you what to do, what good was it talking about that now? Now was Canada, here, and he'd had enough of Speedwell too, they were moving again, to find a warm place by the ocean to die.

Mrs. Fiedler rarely smiled; her lips seemed too thin for it. She was always busy sliding deep bowls of boiled potatoes and sausage and very strong sauerkraut onto the oilcloth of their kitchen table around which sixteen or seventeen people could sit, easily.

When my sister Mary married Emmanuel Fiedler I became aware not only of the possible sexual behaviour of human beings, but also that Fiedler life was not as straightforward as patriarch August implied. It seemed that one of the six Fiedler sons was perhaps not a son at all; perhaps a grandson. His mother, they said, was the Fiedler's oldest daughter, Olga, who was married to Gustav Racho after, with whom she had five other children; they lived on the ramshackle farm just over our sledding hill north of Speedwell School. As if by family and communal osmosis I came to understand that God sometimes gave a girl a child before she was married and then she had to leave it with her parents, maybe forever. Maybe that explained Mrs. Racho's face: her features were handsome like all the Fiedlers, but her facial expression was often fierce, scowling, and her left eye peered out from under a dark growth round and hard as a marble poised on her eyebrow. And then, when Troy in the Fehr barn shoved me into knowing what a man forced on a woman in sex, I thought that might explain it: her anger had solidified into that growth and now she had to stare out from under her sin forever.

~

Well. Such things happened in the United States, or Bessarabia perhaps, but not to Mennonites who fled Russia to escape de Kommuniste. So I thought then. And, our parents repeated, it was Germany that said to them in December 1929, Come, come to us out of that Stalin hell. Germany gave them refuge, fed them for three months, made them healthy enough to pass the Canadian doctor tests every time till the CPR could bring them here . . . but now Germany was so horrible, and Churchill and Roosevelt were calling Stalin their friend, his devil's Schnur'boat, moustache, smiled on the front page of the *Free Press Prairie Farmer* with them. And the Americans had even built a highway thousands of miles long across Canada to Alaska and were hauling guns and food to help him—what had happened? In a few years?

"It's the war," Mam said. "War turns everything good upside down. Suddenly in war good is evil, evil good."

Dan said, "Hitler never got us into Germany."

"Was it Mr. Churchill?" I asked.

Pah guffawed, without amusement. "Huh! Aul de groote Manna," he said. "Wann' et doa'ropp aun tjemmt, saje dee bloss, 'Itj sie fe Dootscheeten.'" Huh! all those big men! When it comes right down to it, all they ever say is, "I'm for shooting them all dead."

But what if Stalin had converted and was now, really, good? God could do anything, the Bible said that He could even change a heart of stone—so steel would be easy, just heat it a little like Sam Heinrichs. And Stalin was fighting Hitler, who they said had started this latest of world wars. So, had the worst Communist in the world been saved?

There was a late summer evening, after the mosquito season, when I brought our small cattle herd home from their slough pasture, and I looked beyond them to the barbed-wire gate that opened our yard to the road allowance, there between the young poplars always sprouting along the fenceline with the muskeg spruce black, spiky across the road behind them; almost as though they were a great wall, hiding us from the Big World of Groote Manna forever killing poor people in some new, more horrible way. I watched our scrubby cows—I knew every one clear as a photograph, the warts on every leg, the twist of each horn or dolloped ear—trail to the water trough I'd laboriously filled by hauling the long bucket up out of our well over and over. Beyond the eastern trees the Thiessen dog was barking half a mile away, and farther still the Enns rooster crowed once and then again, faintly. The late summer twilight was levelling down into shadow.

And it came to me: okay, war and Big Men twist the world upside down, so what if a big touring car suddenly appeared and turned in at our gate, a long car with the top down, all yellow with black trim and Stalin sitting in it. And he would stop in our yard beside the buggy and from under his moustache offer my father his land in Orenburg again, if he wanted it back. I knew my father was forty-one years old when they fled Russia and that he had never owned land there; my parents had always been landless, they worked for their parents or older brothers who inherited the family lands, but Communism taught that everyone should share equally, so if Stalin— What would Pah answer? It struck me he would laugh, incredulously; wordless as he often was.

Or say he would think about it, the way he tried to avoid direct decisions and ask Mam when they were alone, what is to be done? Or maybe he'd just smile a little, and mention that perhaps Stalin had a lot of people on his famous memory, what about them?

But my mother would know instantly, absolutely: "Niemols. Wie komme nie tridj." Never. We're never coming back.

And since she had Stalin right there, smiling in her yard, face to face, she'd lay it on him: "Now you tell me, Joseph Vissarionovich, where is my brother? Johann Knelsen, the teacher in Orenburg, Number Eight Romanovka. Woa hast du dem omm'jebroght? Where did you murder him?"

And Stalin's smile would slowly freeze into the steel of his name. For he would certainly know Johann Knelsen. They said Stalin never had to write anything down, he remembered everything his Bolsheviks did and to whom, every single name. God gave him that living hell, my mother said, to be able never to forget, anything.

There were moments when my parents' stories, and the distant explosions of the Great World that I heard about at school or saw in the *Free Press*, settled my bare feet into the grassy muck of our yard splotched with cow and chicken shit—every summer evening we washed our crusted feet clean in a basin before we went to bed, that cleansed feeling of my hard, tough feet as comforting as the eleven-word prayer I ripped off to Lieber Heiland, my Dearest Saviour, while curled under the blankets— my bare feet on bare earth made me feel as if I knew, that my body already remembered what happened everywhere on the globe, and that someday I would understand it too; that what I was aware of had some meaning and that by believing in Jesus as the Son of God—as I surely did, as I hoped and trusted and believed with all my heart I absolutely did—I would someday comprehend what that meaning was. As clearly and directly as I knew that, in a moment, I would chase these cows into the corral and start milking.

Over years of daily repetition, milking a cow is an intense intimacy; a warmth you comprehend even decades after you have stopped doing it. The corral is drifting with good, acrid smoke from the smudge you have lit to drive off the evening mosquitoes, you have balanced your small butt on a one-legged stump stool and now you lean your head and right shoulder tight against the cow's flank and belly. The milk pail stands on the ground (your legs are too short to hold it between them, like Mam or Dan does) directly under her heavy udder and you clamp your left hand onto the nearest front teat, your right reaches across to the other, and you are surrounded by warmth, and anchored: your hands can begin to grip and release and grip the heat of her teats into rhythm and the warm milk will jet out in a thick stream ringing in the pail. Every milking is a reincarnation of your own infancy, your hands your tiny mouth at your mother's nipples, you will not smell or feel such comfort move everywhere within the skin of your body until you lay your face between your sweetheart's breasts and she enfolds you.

I did not know enough, had endured too little hard facticity in my nine years to comprehend what I experienced watering cows. As I tipped the pail into the trough, the water crashing out, what I saw was scrubby animals stretching their necks down, their hides bumped by warblefly larvae about to hatch; I did not know I knew even less about my Mennonite forebears than about the barbaric war killing people half the world away; such knowledge came only with years and reading and many books, the stories of Jesus's followers martyred as Anabaptists—"rebaptizers" as they were derisively called—for their beliefs during two centuries of European Reformation, their flight from Friesland, Holland and Flanders to find a generous refuge in Roman Catholic Poland from the Spanish Inquisition, their further flight to Imperial Russia's Ukrainian steppes two hundred years later from Prussian militarism, and their flight again from Communism to North and South America in the twentieth century. Neither my parents nor my community could tell me this massive burden of stories; what they knew were their own, particular, small narratives: so obvious, so usual in our circles they were almost unnecessary to relate.

Certainly no one in Speedwell could have told me of a genius named Wybe Adams, or Adam Wiebe, the Frisian ancestor of all Russian Mennonite Wiebes, who in 1616 sailed from Harlingen on invitation by the Free City of Danzig to become its water engineer, and who protected Danzig from the ravages of the Thirty Years War, which between 1618 and 1648 destroyed more than half the population and nearly all the civilization of Europe, by building a high, thick wall of earth around the entire city which was impenetrable by cannon balls. He moved all that earth in the walls from the hill across the Raduane River by inventing the cable car: buckets hung from an endless rope running over wheels on poles that circulated over the river, carrying the earth down and returning the empty buckets back up again.

That's a long and complex heritage story. For a bush homestead boy doing his evening chores, a bucket on a rope running over a pulley was simply water down the well, it had to be dipped full before it came up, and there was Liz coming from the house past the firewood piled along the fence to pull the butter and cream for supper out of the coolness of the well, and behind her smoke rising from our summer kitchen—Joseph Stalin in his touring car already gone like momentary mist. A red-and-black rooster was following a hen across the yard,

> Kjemma die nijch omm de Eia dee noch nijch
> jelajt senn.

> Don't concern yourself about eggs that haven't
> been laid yet.

an unnecessary animal after summer who would be supper soup tomorrow; but he padded across the yard placing one claw foot and then the other so precisely, his head cocked and twitching at each step as if he could stare the world into living forever.

~

While I gnawed my way happily through grade school, Helen did not. Miss Hingston's register in October 1942 lists her as "Age 14, Grade 7, Distance from School 3 miles," but her attendance days throughout October, November and December are simply marked "S"—sick. Her fifteenth birthday was on January 5, 1943; the school began on Wednesday, January 6, and her line of attendance for the rest of the year is blank: she never returned to any school.

She was the gentlest sister. In her tiny pulp-paper notebook she always recorded the dates of her life in the third person:

Helen Wiebe got baptized August 10, 1941,
11 A.M. at Turtle Lake

I remember a grey picture, now lost: a blank sky and water horizon with a line of seven slender girls, unrecognizable at that distance but all holding hands, coming out of the lake curling waves at the hems of their white dresses. A man, it must be

Reverend Jacob Enns, wades beside them in shirt, tie and trousers.

And a notebook hint of something else:

Nov. 18, 1943 John Koehn got an operation

John was the fourth child of George and Liese Koehn, a year older than Helen. What had happened—or not happened—between them that she should mention him? What could happen, with Helen so much in bed, barely able to step outside the house for a brief picture? Pencil dreams in a tiny notebook. One blank line later, on the same page, she adds the only other words that do not refer directly to our family:

Koehns moved away March 15th 1944 from
Speedwell to Swift Current

In fact, by 1944 more people had moved away from Speedwell than remained. Adult church membership in 1936 was 114 but by 1944 it was less than sixty. And that year my sister, again after the fact, wrote her longest personal entry:

Helen Wiebe took sick in April 1944 with heart
trouble then had to go to the hospital on the 26th
of April and stay there till May 19th 44/with

Mr. Harder [Did the storekeeper take her there
in his truck?]. Was at home for a month and was
not feeling very good. Had to go and see the doc
in Battleford on the 21. Had to stay home a
whole month and on 21 June went to see the doc.

At dawn, June 6, 1944 the Allied invasion of
Normandy began. By then Dan had insisted on
bringing home a radio; it sat on its heavy battery
under our living-room window beside Helen's bed,
the aerial leading out through a window crack to a
high wire he had strung between white insulators
from the peak of the roof to a tall lodgepole post
beside the garden. When he twisted the black but-
ton, *snap!* instantly voices spoke English. It seemed
that even over our cul-de-sac homestead the empty
air was filled with endless human voices, and a bare
wire could find them. When I peered at the back of
the radio I saw glass fingers—tubes, Dan called
them—each with a tiny spark glowing inside it:
words in air, I thought, are infinitesimal lights this
small machine can translate into sound.

I was allowed to hear only certain broadcasts, and
the "News" was one. I remember hearing the deep,
doom voice of Lorne Greene announce the Normandy
landings on "CBK, Watrous, Saskatchewan," and
then, "This is Matthew Halton of the CBC" reporting

directly, his voice said, from Juno Beach with the Canadian soldiers, his precise, crackling words almost lost in the roar of war, of weapons and men screaming around him.

Helen was certainly there on her living-room cot where she lay for nine months, listening as intensely as I. Later, in 1945 when the radio was sent away on January 24 "to be fixed," she notes in her diary, "I miss it very much." She particularly missed the daily "Dominion Observatory official time signal . . . the beginning of the long dash, following ten seconds of silence, indicates exactly eleven o'clock, Mountain Standard Time." But I have no memory of her listening with me to the invasion of Normandy, nor is there any picture of her in bed.

The remaining pages of Helen's tiny notebook are blank, except for the numbers of our family wartime food ration cards. The list begins with "A.J. Wiebe—SN-102949" and ends with "Rudy Wiebe—SN-102954." Mine adds up to 21 and ends in 4, perfect numbers for a Saskatchewan refugee bush kid: Christian 7 x 3, Aboriginal 4. And because of Canada, neither Liz nor I can say we were ever hungry; unlike the rest of our family.

6.

# MANSIONS

~

Daut halpt tjeen Mül spetze, daut mott jepiept
woare.

It doesn't help pursing your lips, you have
to whistle.

Low German in the daily spoken life of Speedwell
could be as sardonic or friendly or hilarious as
any vernacular on earth, and as I grew older I found
rolling that sense of oral comic over into English
could be as flip as opening my mouth; I knew intu-
itively how words fashion easy group laughter. There

came a time when my friends expected to laugh whenever I paused—I expected it myself—but, when in my late teens I began to write stories, I discovered they were rarely funny. It seemed that stories carefully worked on over and over, alone, searching within your self, stories as words on paper were not a passing moment of convivial wit, repartee, outrageous extrapolations, punch lines or throwaways. "We read to know we are not alone," C. S. Lewis once said, and it may well be that a writer writes for the same reason.

In any case, for me stories truly well written were stories seen, were stories heard in your head through your eyes, exactly. They must be worthy of contemplation and pondering, echoing in the imagination; at best "a work too hard for the teeth of time."

I always associated this concept, even before I read it in Sir Thomas Browne's unforgettable phrase, with profoundly serious matters. Why "serious matters" should for me only rarely include the gossip and laughter that rumbled everywhere in our community, especially during our neighbour visits which were continuous throughout our years in Speedwell, I still do not understand.

Though clearly the Bible carried some of that heavy weight. The Bible, as I heard its stories told and was taught to read it, at home and in Sunday school and in church, was not funny. The Bible is God's Word, and the only book my mother ever gave me, other than the Bible, was *Hurlbut's Story of the Bible* which she ordered for me from Eaton's when in grade two I began to read so endlessly: "The Complete Bible Story . . . Told in the Simple Language of To-day, for YOUNG AND OLD / One Hundred and Sixty-eight Stories . . . Forming a Connected Narrative of the Holy Scripture." The first story begins so beautifully, but within a few minutes the lovely garden and its four rivers are gone, and immediately after that Cain kills his brother Abel, and then there are cities, floods and endless family fights and wanderings in the wilderness until Moses comes down the mountain with the Ten Commandments chiselled into slabs of stone: God Almighty, the judge of the quick and the dead: that's no joke. And not even Jesus, who can transform any human situation into brilliant story, ever really tells an outright joke. Life is serious, especially for Mennonites having fled a world destroyed by Communism; God's divine revelation only underscores the heavy, mostly murderous, history of mankind.

And if my father tended to grasp the ironies and ignore the inexplicable brutalities of his past, as he often did, my mother had their lifetime of hard memories of which to remind him and cut his laughter, his defensive anger quick. Years of suffering rarely make people gentle comics; beyond irony or gallows humour, their defence can often only be sorrow or forgetting. There was much in her hard life my mother could never forget, nor, in fact, could my father, and with age he came to weep as easily as he had ever laughed.

> Äwrem Hund send wie aul; nue mott wie bloss
> noch äwrem Zoagel.

> We've gotten over the dog, now we just have to
> get over the tail.

So, despite all the happiness and laughter and good work and play in my childhood, for me nothing could be more serious than life itself; as ultimately every death declared.

Death is part of daily life on a bush homestead. From the regular, on-demand axe-decapitation of chickens—whose headless bodies pound themselves against the chopping block as if refusing to die and, if you don't hang on tight, will hurl themselves across the yard in reflex spasms of spraying blood— to the pig you've fed for months which is one fall morning shot, its throat cut and blood caught in a pail, hung from a log between two trees and slit open so its viscera spill out in a fall of pink, coiled organs steaming in the cold air, death lives with you. By evening you are grinding tender, aromatic flesh between your teeth with no more sentiment for it than for the cabbage you hacked off its stalk, peeled and boiled.

"Ein Mensch ist wass er isst," August Fiedler would laugh, a person is what he eats, his wide mouth full of meat and belly shaking, an excellent butcher who often helped us slaughter our animals and would then eat a gargantuan meal to complete the day before he drove home. But since in spoken High German "is" and "eat" are a pun, the joke was that he could also mean "A person is what he is," or again, "A person eats what he is." The latter is how I first understood him: a homestead child in 1940s Canada saw and felt and smelled exactly all the stages of what he was; there was no supermarket Saran wrap to delude him.

Life and death and every possible variation of health or damage between them were not confined to plants and animals. Births, accidents, weddings, celebrations, parties, deaths: everyone in Speedwell knew what happened to anyone. On January 5, 1945, on Helen's seventeenth birthday, she got up from her bed, put on her best dress and came out of the house briefly to have her picture taken on the steps with

Liz and me; her birthday present was a five-year
diary, bound in faux leather with a small clasp and
rudimentary lock and key. She wrote of the Eaton's
catalogue delay:

> Sat'day January 20: I recieved this diary today,
> it was a belated birthday present. I had always
> wished for one, and I will be Thankful many
> years after.

My sweet sister, carefully levering ink from the squat little Waterman's bottle up into her fountain pen. Afflicted with sickness all her life, she had already spent the previous six months in bed, but her hope for "many years" did not falter.

~

After she received it, Helen filled in what had happened during the first nineteen days of 1945. The vicious blizzard that lasted through New Year's Day brought this entry:

> Tuesday January 2: We heard Mr. Stuirt was
> dead. Mr. D. Heinrichs came and told us. All
> I did was set puzzels together all day long.

George Stewart was for us a bleiwet Wunda, a blue wonder. Where had he come from? Why to dead-end Speedwell? Who was he? Aaron Heinrichs' 1930 district map already marked his homestead half a mile west of the proposed school. In the centre of our Mennonite community of large, related and intermarried families, on the east–west road behind a coppice of gangling pine, there stood his log shack surrounded by the junk he collected walking the district roads with his small, hairless dog, his own grizzled hair and whiskers spraying from under his cap, a sack on binder twine hung over his shoulder. A man who spoke English clear as any teacher through his decaying teeth was both a bachelor and a gentle, uninsistent beggar. When he wandered into a yard, our mothers gave him food while his dog cowered between his feet for terror at our enraged, barking brutes; and at the same time we children watched him closely, especially when he bent over yard bushes where foolish hens tried to hide their eggs. George Stewart, no family, always hungry, always alone . . . strange. And English. Why didn't Joe Handley from Jack Pine help him?

When Liz, I and Sam Heinrichs' kids walked to school, we often followed the trail across Dave Heinrichs' and onto the road allowance directly opposite Old Stewart's clump of pine. His one field, which Dave farmed, lay open to the sky over the long northern esker that ran out as our sliding hill behind the school; we could not see his cabin though sometimes the smoke from his stovepipe was visible. One spring afternoon as I started home from school alone, I came up on the rise where that long hill branched across the east–west road and I glanced back: an animal trotted there, following me. I had walked home alone hundreds of times—but that could be a wolf, its long nose lifted so strangely it seemed to be running slanted, coming closer—coming after me.

No one had ever seen a wolf in Speedwell, but like a body explosion that shattered all reason I was terrified. I scrambled into the brush behind the stone pile along David Lobe's field; if it attacked I could hurl stones, I would barricade myself, I'd dig down . . . the animal trotted by on the worn wagon track without a twitch: Old Stewart's miserable dog. It had looked so huge chasing me!—its hide rubbed raw in spots from its endless fight with fleas.

The dog lay on the bed of gunny sacks the only time I was inside George Stewart's cabin. One summer Sunday afternoon three of us boys somehow dared to walk in from the road, around the trees, and he saw us through the open door—it had no screen—and beckoned that we should come in. Henry Enns, the minister's son who limped a little on his elevated shoe, was the tallest of us and the old man asked him the question,

"You've taken history, haven't you?"

As if "history" were a single pill swallowed at will. When Henry quickly nodded, old Stewart continued,

"History says the Stewarts were once kings of England, right? And I'm a Stewart, right? My name is George Stewart and that means I have the right to be king, eh, maybe more right than George Windsor because I'm George *Stewart*, eh?"

It had never entered my mind. But then I knew nothing about Stewarts once being kings of England, leave alone George the Sixth's family name—did kings have to have one? Henry, who apparently knew, nodded, but for a moment I was so startled that I might be in the presence of a king whose clothes and skin were seamed with dirt that I backed against a trunk near the door and knocked a horse harness tug to the floor, its chain clanging. The log shack buzzed with huge Modeschietasch, as we called them, maggot-shitting flies, and so crammed small with stuff I can't remember any of it; only the clang of torn harness and the small dog—completely useless for cattle—heaving up on the dirty sacks of the bed and scratching himself furiously with one hind leg.

Stewart continued talking as if to himself, the way he always did: "Now I'm not saying nothing against King George, I wouldn't do that, but I don't think he's running the war right, look at what Hitler's doing to the poor buggers. I'm not against George, but if he came up from England and said to me, 'Stewart, will you come and take over?' well, I wouldn't refuse him. First I'd stop the war and I'd say to Hitler, 'Listen here, we've got to talk this over!'"

To talk things over rather than shooting made perfect sense to me—but King George coming to see Old Stewart? Living in this filth and walking the roads with his gunny sack, to whom my mother often gave a heel of bread and some sausage? And what about Mr. Churchill? He made all the war speeches, wouldn't he have to come too? When we got back to the road none of us could believe it and, as we discovered, most adults in Speedwell had already laughed at that story many times.

"If all the George Stewarts in the world were kings of England," my brother-in-law Emmanuel said, "they'd fill the cow pasture with thrones."

Then on January 2, 1945, Dave Heinrichs came to tell us Old Stewart was dead: apparently frozen to death during the four-day snowstorm before New Year's. Dan got the RCMP in to his place, our team and sleigh breaking through the heavy drifts. They must have brought the body out past our yard but Helen notes nothing about that, nor do I remember. His poor dog had frozen to death as well.

Nevertheless, such a dream; such a human death alone in the wilderness of this world. Ten years later the first story I wrote for my university writing class was about George Stewart, and it didn't make him funny or ludicrous as it easily might have. Rather, it tried to grapple with a boy's inchoate sense of "the fleeting stuff of human majesty." And F. M. Salter, my writing professor at the University of Alberta, who years before had mentored W. O. Mitchell to his first publication in the *Atlantic Monthly*, found my effort "a very remarkable picture . . . indeed, when polished up, publishable." And so it was, about a decade later as "Tudor King"; several years after that the National Film Board made an eleven-minute film of it.

~

The seriousness—one might well say deadly seriousness—of my early attempts at writing fiction continued. My first published short story, in *Liberty magazine*, Toronto, September 1956, was about my sister Helen.

It was also a story I had written for Salter's university course the winter before. At the time I couldn't look through Helen's five-year diary, but when Liz showed it to me years later, the many tiny details in it that corroborated my story only strengthened my trust in memories I had that were not recorded there. The diary provided five lines of space for each day, and Helen wrote her last entry in early March 1945. Throughout February she had often noted how her illness was growing, how she could do nothing, "just lie and think." Then, her last diary words:

> March 5, Monday: Today I feel better, so good
> I had to spill ink on Jan. 31. That will stay
> there as long as the book exists.

And it has, a shapeless blot with a strong stroke tilted right, fading for sixty years.

March 6 to 28, 1945, are blank. Helen's final written words are on a torn bit of paper when she could no longer speak, her neat writing collapsed to a slanted sprawl:

> I want to go to bed
> lets all pray
> I can have more
> breath and sleep

She must have been sitting up, held in someone's arms in an attempt to help her breathe.
Someone has written "March 27th" below the first
line, and across the bottom of the paper is Liz's
handwriting:

Helens last writing on March 28. 2.00 oclock P. M.

Those are the same words with which Liz's thirteen-
year-old handwriting continues the five-year diary:

March 28 Wedensday: Sister Helen died on 28
of March. Her heart tore off she had an easy
death though died March 28, 1945 2.00 P. M.

Dates, times, contradictions. Visible words that fix
memory despite decades of forgetting and impossible
recall.

~

How to tell such a story. Sing? I can't compose
music . . . I've never learned to dance nor wanted
to . . . I'm too colour "challenged," as they say it
now, to paint a picture—but I once did try to hum
a song into existence. The first morning I rode
Prince to school after Helen's death. I was alone.

I never wrote down a word of it but I know them, I can yodel, bump them together without a thought:

> Old Dan Tucker in the grand old days
> Swept the floor in the bachelor ways
> He could knock the stuffing out of any guy
> With one big slug of his double-jointed sigh

—what is this nonsense branded in my brain? I imagine "sigh" means "scythe," because that's the way we pronounced it at the time. Obviously a hillbilly radio riff about "Old Dan Tucker" was banjoing through me as Prince plodded along trails he knew so well he needed no rein, my mind flipping, looping around words, sounds: "one big slug of his double-jointed scythe"? Well, it's ridiculous, almost scat, but under certain farming circumstances "double-jointed scythe" might be as funny as "died of a toothache in his heel." That morning any rhythmic sound that floated me away in the sunlight, the winter poplars barely tipped with buds, was good.

Memory is whatever you find in it, a rhythm, a wisp; Theodore Roethke says it perfectly, though in a slightly different context:

> Love is not love until love's vulnerable. . . .
> All who remember, doubt.

So I will lay out this particular, for me a lifelong, doubt in the way I first tried to order it at age twenty-one, eleven years after Helen died. Not the story as published, but my first fumbled draft, a stained holograph barely decipherable now, scribbled and crossed out in a notebook written on both sides of the page sometime during January 1956.

### Eight and the Present

In the darkness under the rafters he awoke to the screaming.

It seemed he had heard it a long time, as if it reached back endlessly into his sleep, even as if he had heard it forever——the swift crescendo, the high plateau of sound and then the moaning fall of it down to a whimper. It was like the dream he had of being crushed by a huge tree and when he forced himself awake his brother's big arm had been on him, inert and heavy in sleep. Only now he had had no dream, only felt this endlessly before he awoke, and heard it.

It had been quiet for a moment as he felt these things and suddenly he knew that his brother was not beside him on the straw tick. Fear seized him. He rolled under the cover over into the other hollow and it was warm from the big body. He noticed as he moved that the stovepipe seemed surrounded by light, and he sat up in bed, forgetting the darkness, and saw the light from downstairs coming through the hole around the stovepipe. He could hear movement. Were they all up, with the light burning?

Then, inhumanly, the screaming came again. It was like a pointed . . . he could hear and feel nothing, just the searing scream, as if he and it were the sole inhabitants of a universe. It drowned his brain until he could not hear it for the sound, and then it fell horribly, as if stretched beyond itself, down to a burbling moan.

He jerked the quilt up and over himself, but the warm darkness was not enough. He wanted to go downstairs to the warmth of his mother. His small bare feet were cold on the rough boards as, huddled against the darkness, he felt for the top of the ladder-like stairs near the oblong shade of grey that showed light below. Then he felt them and slipped down, feet quick on the familiar steps. The moaning had almost died, and he could hear movements beyond the curtain of the living room. He crept over and pulled it aside.

He did not know what he saw, for a long moment. It wasn't that lamplight was too strong for his sleep-roused eyes, but rather that his sister, who had lain in bed in the corner of the sitting room for months because of an enlarged heart, was now in the middle of the night sitting up so stiffly nailed to a chair and his father and brother seemed to be holding her down. He had never seen her face like that before. It didn't look like a face, more like the Hallowe'en mask he had once made. Her black hair hung in damp strings over her forehead as his mother wiped her face with a cloth, and then he saw the clothes pin stuck in her mouth and the blood trickling down her chin from her lips where she had bit herself. In the wonder of it, he stared and suddenly the sound within her seemed to rip loose and he heard that scream again, saw it torn from her throat and he saw how the muscles in the men's arms bulged and knotted as they tried to hold her on the pillowed chair.

He was suddenly afraid. He looked here and there as the sound seared him and he was relieved beyond measure when his sister Toots, four years older than himself, who was sitting crying by the door, reached up and clutched him to her.

The scream was not as long, and he looked up as his father, face beaded with sweat and tears, said desperately, "Mother, we have to do something, we can't stand this," and his brother Dan, maddened by his own impotence and love for his sister, hissing fiercely,

"Do something! We can't stand this! How can she stand it? What're you thinking about us for? She's burning up."

And his mother, wiping the tortured face again, saying, "Dan, don't, that doesn't help. She bites herself so much, if we could only stop the fire in her . . . maybe we should get the Thiessens. . . ."

"Mrs. Thiessen would know something—do something. Get Rudy up to ride and get her."

They noticed him then where he huddled with his sobbing sister, not knowing whether to cry or not. He didn't want to, here in front of his big brother, crying was sissy, so he was relieved when Dan said, "Rudy, get on Prince and ride to the Thiessens, quick."

His mother, tear-stained, bent over him. "I have to leave this house, I can't stand to see her like this, Toots, get some colder water and wipe her face, I'll take the lantern and go to the barn with him."

In a rush he was dressed and out in the coolness where the spring frogs croaked through the morning darkness. Near the barn they heard the scream again, but it seemed far away and unattached to him, almost like a coyote howl when he was in bed at night. He jerked at the barn door and the warmth from the horses wrapped him in its living smell. Straining, he reached up and looped the bridle off its peg. His mother wept silently as she stood in the open door holding the lantern.

"Whoa," he said softly. "Easy there, Prince old boy," as he touched the black object in the single stall. Prince moved over, waking up, and he went into the narrow stall murmuring quiet words as Dan had taught him to do in the dark to animals. He had some difficulty in getting the bridle bit into the soft but resistant mouth, so he scrambled up on the manger and strained over to force it in, then slipped the bridle over the soft ears, snapped the strap, unsnapped the halter shank and, grabbing the long mane, half swung, half jumped to the bare back. Prince began to back out and he said,

"OK, Mom, get out of the road."

He saw the lantern light swing away and he backed the horse out of the stall, then wheeled it sharply and rode out the low door, hanging over on the left side, right arm and leg curled and clinging.

"What shall I say, Mom?" he asked.

Her voice was half choked, "Tell them Helen's dying—to come quick, to help."

Somehow her expression of these few words made him feel her sudden need for someone to share this horrible night with them—he didn't know how he'd ever get them up, but he knew that he was supposed to do something and he kicked Prince sharply, and as the horse began to move he could hear her say, "Be careful, my little Sonny," and then how her voice fell into a moaning prayer even as she started away from the barn. He was so busy getting Prince into a gallop that he didn't hear the scream again as he swung through the gate and out on the road.

The clouds raced across the moon, its light flicked over the landscape as if whipped by fierce winds, but down among the trees all was still as he heard and felt the rhythmic clop of hooves carry up through him and into the night. He didn't like the spruce at night, they were solidly purple and grasping, and he kicked the horse to get him past the muskeg faster. When the moonlight flickered spasmodically, the black gobs of shadows seemed to leap up and at him and pour around him, and when it did not, the darkness was over all. The last bit was an opaque tunnel, with the horse's withers rocking up at him, solid and living, in the choking fear that wrapped him. Just at the end the scream seemed to ring in his ears out of the blackness of the trees, and he was terrified, and then he galloped around the corner, out of the forest, to where poplars bordered the road on one side and the level blackness of the Thiessen field stretched out against the lighter blackness of the moving sky.

With the lighter darkness about him, his thoughts raced on with the galloping horse. This was like he had sometimes dreamed, racing through the night for help—all by himself, just as he had read in *Black Beauty*. Not many boys, not even most men had ever done this—ride alone to the rescue, Helen must really be sick if she screamed like that, Thiessens would sure help, and he'd get them.

There was a patch of trees now, then the wooden bridge over a rushing spring creek between two sloughs where frogs croaked with self-inflated importance. The hooves clunked hollow twice, then he was over and in an instant saw the outline of the Thiessen gate. Prince turned there and he rode up the lane. The farmyard lay dark and mysteriously violet and grey.

The dogs barked raucously out of their sleep as he banged on the door. "Mr. Thiessen!" If it had not been for the noisy dogs, he couldn't have opened his mouth against the night. Finally footsteps came and the door creaked curiously.

"Mr. Thiessen—" then he saw the long night dress "—Mrs. Thiessen . . . Helen's awful sick, Mom says you're to come and help."

"What's the matter?"

"She's—she—" he did not know how to say it, "she bites herself, sitting in a chair. . . ."

"Ride home quick, tell them we'll come right away. George . . ." she turned to her husband who had now appeared behind her in the little porch.

In a trice he led Prince close to the wagon in the yard, climbed up, jumped to his back, and was heading home. He was colder now as the excitement waned and the eastern treetops just tipped in gold foil. Prince knew the way home and galloped with a will, so he closed his eyes to it all and hung on. The clippety-clop seemed endless, the horse seemed to run hard and he felt shaken apart and terribly sleepy. He did not see the spruce now.

His mother was waiting in the yard. "They're coming right away," he said. She met him as he came out of the barn and she took his hand.

"I went in once, but it's so terrible—oh my Sonny, she's burning up, and I can't do anything. It came just like that—so quick—and she's burning up. Oh Lord, Lord, be merciful."

They were near the woodpile and she dropped to her knees beside the blocks, and he could feel her desperate clasp on his small body as she wept and prayed. He tried to say something, "Aw Mom, she'll get better . . ." but he did not know what to say. What was there to say? He was terrified—he had never known his mother like this, she who could do everything. Then his crying rose and fell with hers, at the great unknowing fear and the helplessness he felt from her. The scream, as he heard it through his tears, was very weak and did not come again for a long time.

Suddenly he heard the jingle of harness, and in a moment the Thiessens were there. As Mr. Thiessen tied the horses, Mrs. Thiessen came over to his mother standing near the woodpile and put her arm around her. His mother, still holding his hand, sobbed, "She was getting so much better, and suddenly, in the night . . ."

"We brought a bit of laudanum, perhaps it will help."

They went towards the house. Sleep kept pulling his head over, even as he walked, and he did not know what happened after they got to the house.

In the late morning when he awoke and came downstairs, his mother told him Helen was dead.

The house did not smell right, and everyone seemed as if struck dumb, and cried unexpectedly. He could not find Dan anywhere. He did not want to go into the living room, and he could not think of anyone as dead. "Mom," he said, "I want to go to school."

His mother made no answer, did not seem to hear him in fact. After she had told him she turned away and was washing dishes, unhearing and wrapped in her grief for the girl she had nursed for months.

He went out, and the early spring sunshine was fresh and good. No one noticed him as he sneaked into the barn, bridled Prince, and rode off.

Yet, somehow, school was not right either. When he got there he did not want to tell about his ride, or even why he arrived during recess. He sat in his little desk in the one-room school and the teacher said, "Take out your Healthy Foods scrap books."

He opened his desk and there it lay, the book he and Helen had made for Health in school. Actually Helen had done all the work: he had just watched. That was why his book had been first in class. There on the cover was the round red tomato she had cut from one of her tomato juice labels, and there was the kink she had made when he bumped her because he was leaning so close as she sat in bed cutting it out. Then he said, half aloud, "She's dead." And he knew that "dead" was like the sticks of rabbits he found in his snares.

And suddenly he began to cry. Everyone stared, but he could not stop.

~

When a written story ends, others are always continuing. What did our neighbours Elizabeth and George Thiessen actually bring, what did they do when they came to our house that harrowing night? What was I doing all of Wednesday, until Helen finally passed beyond her pain at two in the afternoon? Did I ride Prince to school the last morning while she was still alive, humming those Old Dan Tucker words, or did that happen on Thursday, or several days after the Sunday funeral? I have no idea. But there is one memory of Helen's dying not in the story: a memory of my oldest brother, Abe, who had come home from distant Pierceland when Helen's illness grew worse in March. He was also in that room that night; a memory I sorted through only fifty years later, and spoke for the first time as Abe's obituary:

It is the middle of the night . . . the lamps are lit and we are crowded around Helen in her narrow cot in the living room: my sister Elizabeth and I, Mom and Dad; my brother Dan sits on the cot behind Helen, holding her upright in his arms as she struggles for breath between gasps, between cries of pain. And Abe kneels before her: he holds her hands so tightly between his and he is speaking calmly, steadily into the weeping that overwhelms us all, speaking the words of Jesus:

"Let not your hearts be troubled; you believe in God, believe also in me. In my Father's house are many mansions . . . I go to prepare a place for you. And I will come again, and receive you unto myself, so that where I am, there you may be also."

The words that have comforted Christians for two millennia, which also reflect Helen's feelings:

February 28: I feel just as bad today as ever. And did a bit of crying about it too. Between 4–5

I got terribly sick I really thought I was
going HOME. And longed for it too.
March 1: . . . Had a few heart attacks again.

She died on March 28, 1945, the day the German
Army collapsed on the western front; her funeral
took place on Easter Sunday, April 1, the day the US
Marines landed again on the beaches of Okinawa.
I'm certain we did not notice these "great" world
events, as no one beyond our tiny community noticed
our single death. Towards the end of the war Dr.
Coghlan's practice was so enormous, distant country
calls for his help were endless; then, after Christmas
1944, Helen became too weak for her to be taken to
the North Battleford hospital in Harder's truck, and
though Dan may have brought the doctor to our
house several times in our cutter from the highway,
with his huge buffalo coat and black satchel, I don't
know whether they tried to have him come during
that last month of hard winter. It seems a kind of
peasant Christian fatalism had settled over our family: Helen had been sickly, sometimes gravely ill,
from the day of her birth; the Lord gives, yes, but
there also, always, comes a time when the Lord takes
away, especially after years of giving notice—so
finally what could a doctor do, even wonderful Doc
Coghlan? Blessed be the name of the Lord.

The community did what it always did. On Thursday, March 29, Anna Heinrichs, who with her daughters and oldest son had run their bush homestead as efficiently as any man since Aaron Heinrichs died eight years before, came over with her daughter Rosella Poetker, as did Elizabeth Thiessen again. They helped my mother prepare the body, clothe it in a new white dress Helen's best friend Isola Fehr gave them, a dress Isola had just received by mail order and not yet worn, and then they carried the body into the cold March air and laid it out on boards in the granary. No one worked on Good Friday, March 30, but there was a church service and neighbours came by; the yard was full of sleighs. On Saturday, March 31, Dave Heinrichs and Abe Fehr, Isola's father, came to help Dad make the coffin, while the women hand-sewed its black cloth covering and Anna Heinrichs the padded, ruffled interior. The painted silver coffin handles used at every funeral were brought from the church, while in the iron ground of the cemetery just south of the church barns other men were chopping, digging out a grave down to the unfrozen earth below the snow. And Abe and Dan drove to North Battleford, probably in Gustav Biech's car, for whom Dan was working that winter, to register Helen's death and telegraph Mary and Emmanuel in Mayfair again.

~

The granary in which Helen's body lay was built against the east end of our sod-roofed cow barn. The granary walls were log, its roof rough-cut boards and tarpaper. When you opened the barn door in winter with your lantern and pails for milking, the mousing cats were coiled in the warmth under the roof, waiting on the low beam for you to get yourself settled between the cows, to wipe Nelly's udder and teats clean, and when they heard the first spurts of milk ring in the pail, they'd come down the posts quick as weasels, come seat themselves close in the aisle and meow at you, tails twitching. Their tiny mouths opened in such delicate plaints, a sound threading into the blackness where the larger animals moved in the thick, vivid heat of their bodies, their slab-like teeth gnawing at hay or the wooden manger beams. You could walk along behind them and touch each one, their tough hides always exactly there, huge as their great bones beyond the lantern-light, the smaller calves nuzzling over their pen to try and suck your fingers as you fumbled for their curly heads—but the cats were crying, they would break your heart, and you pulled Nelly's udder around, aimed her right teat with your right hand and clenched and clenched: the cats leaped at the white beam of milk, it splashed into their mouths, washed their faces with hot, fat milk and for an instant you streamed it straight into the yellow cat's gaping gullet and then it dropped, knocked down by too much—there, you got it, lick yourself clean and be happy—and you tipped forward again tight against Nelly, grappling to clutch both of her teats, the bulge of her great belly gurgling comfort along your arm and shoulder, the whole side of your head so warm, so good.

The barn granary had no cats and no window; only the open door let in the grey winter light. Helen was here. In motionless cold. Covered by a sheet that reached almost to the earth floor. The low bin with oats was behind her, the wheat and barley sacks, the white dust of chop swept into the corners. She was cold, hard, as rock. I seem to be alone in the granary, touching her shoulder perhaps. Not holding our barn lantern, that's impossible, I couldn't have opened that door alone in the dark; her body must have been inside the lumber box to protect it from the mice until they finished the coffin. But I saw her laid out, draped under a single sheet the length of her body and her face uncovered to her halo of long black hair, so perfectly black as my mother said hers had once been. My mind, though unconscious of it then, gathering the mass of indelible knowing that would seep through my life. In school Miss Klassen was letting me wander past grade four into five, keeping my mouth shut by stuffing my mind with words, numbers, maps, pictures, ideas and every day I knew that at home Helen lay all day on her cot with her feet near the wood heater whose tin pipes passed up through the ceiling and the peaked space under the roof, beside the sheet that separated Dan's and my bed from the space where Liz now slept alone. And each day when I got home and did my chores and brought in all the stove and heater wood, Helen would sit in her bed and we could set puzzles together; me doing the edges and easy shapes and often, when I came from school next day, she had already ordered the shifting colours I could barely recognize, showing me where to place them. Each day she was there. On January 7 she wrote in her diary:

> It's three months I have been in bed today. Biechs were over today. In the evening Rudy read stories to me. Got a dozen oranges from Mrs. Biech.

Over the weeks we read *Rock of Decision* and *Tom Sawyer*, and then *Mystery at High Hedges*

> out loud . . . till I came to a place where the Heel Woman walks, then I made a short stop (boo!).

What an obvious book *High Hedges* is now when I look for it in a used book store: a wealthy heroine exactly Helen's age whose life is filled with abrupt disasters always resolved so happily by amazing— often money—coincidences. But there is one chapter title I have never forgotten: "The Heel Woman Walks." And Helen—perhaps she dreamed of a life chauffeured about between estates in big cars, lying on beaches and never, not even for an instant, feeling sick.

> Saturday, Feb. 3: I started to knit the other sock
> while mom and dad went to school to wash
> floor. I helped Rudy make a scrap book on food
> in the evening.

> Sunday, Feb. 4: Today nobody was over, and
> Rudy helped me learn the ten Bible verses by
> heart, which was terribly hard, He also stayed
> home with me at night for there was church.

Helen, much like Dan, had difficulty memorizing; sounds that aligned themselves as easy as swallowing in my mind seemed for her to evaporate, no matter how often they were spoken.

> Wednesday, Feb. 21: Did some embroidery today,
> after school Rudy and I played crokinole and
> had lots of fun.

And the last mention:

> Tuesday, Feb. 27: Felt pretty blue today. Never
> did much talking. Bill's letter came today cheered
> me a little. In the evening Rudy showed me how
> to divide.

Who was Bill? No one who came to the funeral as far as I know, and Helen's letters no longer exist.

It is impossible that her body lay on bare boards covered by a sheet. But that is what I remember in the granary. Cold like frozen steel, it skins you at a touch.

Liz, not quite thirteen, wrote in the diary what she heard said about Helen's death: "Her heart tore off." But why she would add "she had an easy death though" I cannot imagine. Were we all trying somehow to comfort ourselves? Mam always said that Helen's medical condition, beyond her infant illnesses brought from Russia, was rheumatic fever, which affected her heart; bed rest was basically all Dr. Coghlan could recommend. And the entire community knew where her rheumatic fever started: with the frilly crepe-paper dresses the little girls wore for the Jack Pine School Christmas program in 1937 when we still lived on the CPR homestead. The school was packed with stage and audience; the only place the little girls could change into their cute fairy costumes was Miss Ferguson's teacherage, then they ran through snow in the darkness and climbed up a ladder into the school window behind the stage curtain. Their wand and piano dance was so beautiful, everyone said, but Mam never called it daunce, dance, always "Soohn dommet e'romm'jeran," such stupid running around—but that sprint through the fierce night cold dressed in nothing but underclothes and paper, my mother said, their arms and legs completely naked and running back they were sweaty as well, that was where our Helen, nine years old, caught her rheumatic fever.

~

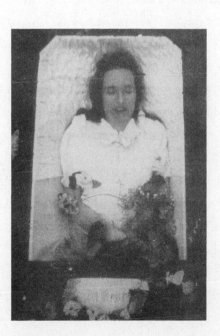

When the pallbearers carried the coffin out of the church on Easter Sunday, April 1, 1945, they set it at the foot of the church steps and opened it for the last time. Our family stood around it, our community surrounded us. Helen's long hair lay about her shoulders, her lips slightly open to her perfect teeth, arms crossed among the few bright roses and ferns my brothers could only have brought from North Battleford.

Es geht nach Haus, zum Vater Haus,
Wer weiss, vielleicht schon morgen

We're going home, to our Father's home,
Who knows, perhaps tomorrow.

We sang that plaintive song following Helen's coffin to the cemetery in long procession. Abe and Dan and four neighbours carried it; Emmanuel was not there, nor Gust, and I was too small.

At the grave Abe Fehr unscrewed the handles and then the black coffin with the white declaration still fastened to its lid—

SAFE

IN THE ARMS

OF JESUS

sank into the hole, down so slowly on ropes in the silence you could hear them creak, the coffin bumped and settled into the box waiting at the bottom for it. Arms lowered someone down, the box lid was tipped shut, pale straw thrown over it and as Reverend Jacob Enns prayed the young men seized the shovels and the rumble of earth falling began, passing spades swiftly from one to the other, frozen clods pounding hollow, fill it quickly, quickly, the sheltering earth, beyond pain, safe in the arms, at home, at last. I stood tight against my mother, but that was no help.

Three days later, on Wednesday evening, Mary and Emmanuel with Gracie and their new baby Gerald drove into our yard in their Model T. They had had not the faintest hint that Helen died on Mary's twenty-first birthday, that she had been buried on Easter Sunday; not one of all the messages and telegrams we sent had reached them at their isolated mission near Mayfair, Saskatchewan, and they had simply come for a regular visit, praying to find Helen improved. Mary's shock, her frantic, wailing despair was as harrowing as another funeral.

When I add up the distances now on a provincial map, Mayfair is no more than a hundred kilometres from Speedwell as the raven flies. Why could they not be reached? Tina and Gust, who had moved from Alberta over the mountains to Vancouver, received our telegram within hours of its being sent. But to penetrate the lakes and boreal forest of Saskatchewan during the last months of a world war—who can be blamed? What cannot be changed, must be endured.

Anne Klassen, our Speedwell teacher, was at the funeral; fifty-eight years later she tells me that she remembered Helen very well, such a "lovely, lively young girl." And also, that after Helen's death I "became troublesome" in school, so she took me alone into the teacherage. "I talked gently to you," she says, and on the telephone her voice at eighty-eight is so gentle still I feel my whole body shiver. "And you burst into tears."

I see in the diary Liz continued that on the day after the funeral, Easter Monday, April 2,

> Rudy was sick & didn't go the church, but we
> went to the Heinrichs in afternoon. Had a good
> time singing etc.

She notes I wasn't well enough to go to school on Tuesday either. I was ten years and six months old, and my loving sister who had read and told me stories until I could read them back and forth with her—what was she doing in heaven? She'd be without pain, and the Bible said they sang praises there forever and ever, as we did in church and at home, hymns that ran through my mind in an endless echo:

> How beautiful heaven must be (must be),
> Sweet home of the happy and free (and free),
> Fair haven of rest for the we-e-eary,
> How beautiful heaven must be.

Helen loved to sing, smiling even when she could not breathe well enough to join in with Isola on her guitar or Mary pumping our brown organ. And singing with angels and harps, that would be even better—but all the time? She liked stories, would God let them tell stories, not just sing, in the Bible Jesus told lots of stories, would he do that in heaven too?

The first week of April 1945 was so cold that on Friday Liz records "Didn't go to school today [on ac]count of the weather . . . Got a letter from Tina." Even with Mary and Emmanuel there, our small house was empty. I remember we sat in the lamplight around the kitchen table, looking at the worn oilcloth.

~

April greyness dragged into brighter, thawing spring, and a sharp physical ache suddenly hit me. At gradually increasing intervals, a swift punch in the stomach that hung there like a rock growing longer and sharper until it slowly dematerialized. And an hour or a day later, without warning, it punched me again in the same place. Soon I could sense it all the time hovering like a shadow about to shift into solid agony.

This was much harder than the frequent gut pains I already knew about. For my nausea, vomiting was simple relief, and as for doing "Number Two," as we laughed about it in school, I remember telling Liz, who was forever trying to improve me,

"I can hold it, I don't have to go to the toilet for three or four days."

"You're stupid, that's why it hurts."

"It doesn't hurt there, this is here," I fingered my lower right side gingerly, "But that—if I don't really want to, I don't go."

I had worked it out: if my bowels tried to move, I'd go if it was convenient, sure, like going for a slow stroll in the fresh air to the boys' toilet, but if not I'd just hunch up tight and soon the feeling would vanish and I wouldn't have to; especially not during the long evenings in winter, all the way to the frozen toilet across the garden among the trees near the icehouse.

"You're so dumb." Liz was disgusted, I knew, even to be talking about that. "You'll get sick worse if you don't . . . go . . . every day."

"Go-o—go-o—go-o," I chanted. Since the vivid English word was ultra-boorish and forbidden in any case, as swearing, I rocked all the more on the pale euphemism, "go-o-o, in the ice and sno-o-ow!" and then, to give her a dig with my boorishness, I sang the German rhyme Pah would repeat when he saw a woman mincing along on high heels, someone, as he said, laughing, who really "meant herself something"—"Yeah, yeah, you Fraulein, von hinten, scheisst ka-ka-rinten!" Lady, from the rear, [you] shit cu-cu-currants.

"Rudy, you be still," Mam was worried. "Dit es tjeen Sposs." This is no joke.

And it wasn't. Though I now "went" whenever my body demanded, the sharp pain came more often. Then on May 2 the radios of the world announced that Adolf Hitler was dead; on May 7 and 8 the last German forces surrendered unconditionally to the Allies. I must have heard some of these announcements on the CBC news because I remember thinking, Now the World War is over, there will be no more news to broadcast; no more Big Ben tolling "This Is London Calling," or Matthew Halton talking while Germans shoot at him, the only thing left would be Elton Britt yodelling once again, "Wave to me, my lady, as I roll on down the line." If the war was over, all the news was over. But according to Liz's diary:

> Friday, May 4: Ma went to Battleford with Rudy today he stayed to have an operation.

And I know that as soon as I got to North Battleford, where Dr. Coghlan had sent me fast from Glaslyn, I was on the operating table and doctors were looking for my appendix. They finally found it, one of them told me some days later on his morning round, rearranged and grown against my stomach where it had no business being, and that was one reason my incision was so big; they had done a thorough abdominal search and found it among the confused organs just before it ruptured. Why had I waited so long, in pain?

Doc Coghlan was a country doctor and no hospital surgeon, but had known our family for ten years; by 1945 he was a legend far beyond his love of fishing, and today a room in the Glaslyn CNR Station Museum is filled with his memorabilia, including the huge buffalo coat he wore as he climbed out of the cutter when Dan brought him from the highway where he left his car in winter, and the black satchel of doctor mysteries he always carried, including I suppose scalpels he might have used in a desperate emergency to open and explore me. Though he could not save Helen, among hundreds of others he certainly saved Dan's life, and Mam's and mine, and Isola Fehr's as well, so she could marry Dan in 1947 and they could raise a family of five and love each other for over fifty years.

The hospital doctor in North Battleford tried cracking jokes about my wandering appendix; he and the nursing sister laughed, but I was thirsty. I was dying of thirst, water was all I wanted—I didn't care where I vomited or if the sisters in their stiff grey and white shoved bedpans under me somewhere or took them away or offered me a long-necked pisspot or noodles on a plate or taped a new bandage over my stomach that looked worse than trying to sew a butchered pig back together. Mam could have sewed stitches far neater and not such thick string either. "I want a drink!"

"Just be thankful," the sister said, "you didn't need clamps and buttons to hold you together."

And the doctor, who in a hospital controls the world and everything in it, told me, "It's the ether. When you're over the ether you can drink all you want. Just wait a little, it won't be long."

An hour was a day! The spring hours dragged on forever and finally I got tiny sips, not even a decent swallow, a sip through a paper straw! A bent grey man in a white hospital gown kept walking past in the corridor, back and forth, the sister told me he had cancer, poor man, and I asked her if he could drink water and she said of course he could. I told her I wanted to have cancer, then I could drink and walk around bent. She gave me another sip and I was burning up. Just wait she said, you'll heal perfect, all healed up.

After mother returned home I had visitors, including Abe and a Bible school friend who grinned without stopping and told funny stories, but I clearly remember only the old man with cancer and my thirst. And also the room: not anything inside it, but the brick outside because Dan brought me a postcard of Notre Dame Hospital, North Battleford, and pointed out my room window to the left of the main entrance on the second floor. A beautiful three-storey brick hospital with what looked like an iron grating up its right side; I knew nothing about fire escapes, I asked why did they have what looked like shelves there and Dan told me, that's right, they were shelves for storage, that's where those Catholic sisters put all the sick stuff the doctors cut off or out of people, the legs, the fingers, the gall bladders, the appendixes. So my hospital window remains unforgettable: it was half the brick building away from where they stored the body parts.

~

Tina arrived in North Battleford by train from Vancouver. She brought little Anne and Carol and baby Rose, born a month before Helen died, with her, and she got me at the hospital and all together we took the Greyhound bus north on Highway 4. On Wednesday, May 16, Liz admitted to her diary,

> We went to Fehrs to see if Rudy + Tina came + sure enough they did boy was I glad too.

My stitches were out, I was healing fast, but it took a while for me to recover. During late May and June our entire scattered family came to Speedwell, except for Gust who had to work, and Tony and Eldo who were in school. We were all still grieving: Tina who could not come to the funeral, Mary and Emmanuel who had so tragically not known about it, and all of us who had been there, especially our mother for whom Helen had prayed so much, often ill herself with Helen lying there for months, helpless to help.

The first picture taken inside our house shows what we did together: Gilda and Mary could not sit motionless quite long enough not to blur, but Dan and Tina, especially Tina, mother of five, are as focused as Abe reading from his preacher's leather Bible. Above Abe's head on the organ tilts a mail-order dress box full of the family photos they have been telling each other stories about, and on the left hangs the small oval picture of a high tropical waterfall which I remember contemplating often. BE OF GOOD COURAGE it stated with biblical conviction—but why, I wondered, would you need courage when facing such beauty?

At some point I returned to school, where Nettie Enns had carried on perfectly well alone in grade five. The annual school picture had been taken without me, but I did receive a copy of it. The tiny snapshot—twenty-seven kids whose every name I still know clustered together against the grey bush, the boys in overalls and the girls in skirts and blouses—is autographed on the back in wide, black pen

> To: Rudy Wiebe
> From: Miss A. Klassen
> your teacher

Liz played with Gracie and Tina and Mary's new babies Rosie and Gerald; Anne and Carol and I chased the spring calves around the hay corral; Tina and Mam planted the garden; we took pictures of each other, either in the yard or under the spruce across the road, of us and our friends and our family in variable combinations. One shows our mother seated in our rocking chair in front of the house with her grandchildren Gerald and Rosie wrapped in blankets in her arms; she is smiling, but sadly. Behind her tiny Grace hugs a blanket to her face while I'm on the porch beside the house door, chewing my fingernails as usual.

From Eaton's catalogue we ordered a white marker for Helen, the first gravestone rather than the usual wooden grave fences in the Speedwell Mennonite Brethren Church cemetery. Sixty years later it is there still in the clearing of thirty graves hemmed in closely by brush and deadfall, small and weathered but indelible, with a tiny angel face surrounded by wings worn into the centre top, and below that

HELEN WIEBE

1928–1945

FOREVER WITH THE LORD

Also, plans were made. That fall, after the district threshing was over between squalls of snow and all the vegetables had been stored and canned and shelved in the cellar below the kitchen, after two months with a new teacher at Speedwell School— Liz was in grade eight and I in grade six—we were back in North Battleford again. We drove past the hospital, laughed at Dan's fire escape story and continued down the long hill to the sprawling station of the Canadian National Railroad that overlooks the panoramic North Saskatchewan and Battle River valley. There Mam, Pah, Liz and I would board the daily passenger train west for Vancouver, the enormous city across the Rocky Mountains on the Pacific Ocean where Tony lived and where, he wrote me, winter never came.

Hey, I told Mam, I won't even need a jacket there! But she laughed and bought me one anyway in North Battleford: full zipper, black sleeves and a kind of shifting blue body; very nice.

Except for two weeks in Notre Dame Hospital, I had never slept anywhere but in a log house in the boreal forest where the single bit of modern technology was a battery radio. Despite all my reading, I did not yet imagine that I would live my entire adult life in cities.

## 7.

# CHIEF

~

To ride a train was beyond anything I had experienced. Forget about horses and wagons on dirt roads, or a slow car or jerky bus grinding over gravel, lurching around holes and mud; this amazement of leaning back in a cushioned seat beside an immense window while the world whirled past without so much as a bump or twitch, you could choose it coming at you or going away, fast as lightning, always the shoulder of the railroad embankment at the lip of the window and the hard clickity-click of steel coming faster and then, suddenly! you flew off a cliff, there was no earth under you, the train ran out on air—the North Saskatchewan, that must be it!—far below the thick and braided river, wide water, and in a flash poplars there bristling like weeds and wuhh! cliffs leaped up into solid earth under you again and the steel sound ran deeper, carrying you faster—all this just leaving the river hills and bush of North Battleford. Vancouver beyond mountains by the ocean would be—your eyes were too full to imagine. Just look.

Day into night, coppice and parkland and rolling hills, farmyards and long fields, towns, grain elevators barely glimpsed and gone, sometimes five or six of them shuddering past, the sprawl of Edmonton lights slower and slower until you stopped completely, the twisted milky rivers sometimes boiling as it seemed under the wheels and sometimes far, far below, moonlight and hours of trees, swamp, muskeg—snow, there would have been snow, always in my Speedwell years there was massive snow and here through the train window it covered the startling mountains against the night sky. For two days and a night—or was it two nights?—we must have tried to eat and sleep on the day coach seats, but I do not remember that as I do the flying-gable roof of the Jasper CNR station, and from its platform the crested mountains spread out along distance like a knobbly hand, pointing. I realized I had not at all been able to imagine mountains from pictures in books or calendars, nor even when, with my fingers, I tried to push them together for the dough landscape Nettie Enns and I made in geography.

"There, you can see it," Mam said. "God's wonder of creation."

One morning our long train curved to a stop on the side of a mountain where there was neither station nor siding; all the passengers were allowed to climb down to the gravel shoulders of the narrow grade and stare across the valley. There, shouldering out of range upon crumpled range, stood the unbelievable face of Mount Robson. The highest peak in the Canadian Rockies, they said, and maybe the highest sheer cliff in the world. God had made that in Canada too.

There were no dome cars on passenger trains then, nor could we, with the cheapest tickets, have entered one if there had been. I have only a single memory from inside the train: the big man who came to sit across the aisle from us a day before we reached Vancouver. He had flowing hair that curled at his broad shoulders and a large gold ring hanging from a smaller one stuck through his ear lobe.

Pah said, very quietly in Low German, "If he had that in his nose, he might be tame enough to lead."

I didn't dare laugh, but I watched him. The man read, dozed, got up to walk down the aisle and returned again as if he were normal. God had made him too—but the hair and the ring were his own doing.

~

Monday, November 5, 1945: Arrived in Van.
10 A. M. had a good time all day.

Brant Street, Vancouver, British Columbia: Gust had built a small house there covered with tarpaper on a lot at the edge of an old cherry orchard. The original Rice orchard house was still there, tall, two-storeyed with two brick chimneys on busy old Nanaimo Road, but new Brant Street was a dead end, only a block long with barely built houses on either side and a cement sidewalk up the short slope to 27th Avenue. The world that crammed my head was so strange now that I could not look at the blocks of houses spread down the valley to the edges of the mountains: I was outside, alone, and I wanted to play with Tony's wooden wagon, hold a handle I could feel in my hand. Tony would be home from school soon, just stay off the street, Tina warned me, and I pulled the wagon up the sidewalk looking at the smooth concrete under my feet, pulled it up, rode it down the incline, again and again.

So the first thing Tony did when he appeared at the top corner of the street was laugh at me riding with my legs splayed wide on either side of the wagon. Like a baby, he said.

"You kneel on the right leg and push with the left going up, and then you come down the same way—push! really get up speed."

Okay, so I did, and came down twice as fast as before and dumped myself into the street, wheels spinning. The pavement scrape on my knee did not bleed very much, but the hole ground through my pants bought for the trip was worse: a patch to wear the rest of the winter.

As for Tony, even though I was taller and two grades ahead, it was obvious he would always know more than I and be better looking. He had the lean face and sharp nose of a Fiedler, not my mother's round Knelsen stubbiness.

I began to recognize this strange world. North of 4160 Brant there were no houses: the grass field of the former Rice farm sloped down to the B.C. Electric tracks. Two- or three-car trams climbed up there from downtown on the rising wooden trestle to the Nanaimo Road station, two shelters perched on steps above the street overpass, and from there continued, they said, on to New Westminster or Chilliwack. Beyond the tram line the city sprawled

into the valley to the CNR tracks and Grandview
Highway and then up over the next line of long hills:
you could see a gleam of ocean inlet and the North
Shore Mountains blazing in the low winter light and
the air came up from the sea moist, like nothing I
had ever breathed, a faint tinge in your nostrils. Salt,
said Tony the know-it-all, and rain, Vancouver never
had snowdrifts, it just rained, you never needed a
parka. A city surrounded by snowy mountains but
with no snow on the streets in winter, and really, still
part of Canada? You'll find out, Tony said.

Vancouver was vaster, louder than I could think.
Wherever we travelled, by tram or bus, in Gust's
almost-new car, or on trolleys singing from wires,
there was forever more of it and more people, how
could there be so many people on earth? I could not
know that Vancouver was one of the most beautiful
cities in the world, its great muddy river branches
and long fingers of the sea, delta and hills always
green with trees and the perfect cone of Mount
Baker south in the United States trailing wisps of
smoke from its volcanic crater; what I saw at first was
unending houses and cement sidewalks and street
lights, and houses, cars and immense fir trees—
they're not spruce, Tony said—and more people and
more houses in which even the smallest, while they
were being built like Gust and Tina's, had electricity

and hot water pouring out of a tap. And no Betjhüs to find in the dark somewhere among the gnarled cherry trees.

Overwhelming as it was, Vancouver was in a way ridiculously simple: nothing to do for light or heat or water, just find a switch or sit on a toilet and everything happened. Gust's car even had a starter inside it, you got in, stepped on the starter and the motor turned over, there was nothing to crank. It was a Schlarafenlaunt, a fool's paradise, my mother said, all you needed to live here auls eene Mohd emm Schmäah, like a maggot in fat, was money.

And of course we had none. We intended to visit only for a few weeks, but suddenly we did not feel like leaving immediately, even though the little house was more crowded than our house in Speedwell when the entire family came home. And we stayed five months, because one day in November Pah walked across Nanaimo Road to the long foundry that belched smoke and blazed fire pounding steel opposite the Rice house and to Gust's astonishment, for Pah spoke only a few words of English, the foreman understood what he wanted and gave him a job. Shovelling up messes on the foundry floor, helping lift what needed to be lifted: anybody could tell him what to do and he'd do it; exactly the kind of work my father would do well and faithfully, forever.

The job paid enough for us to live and save for the trip home, so Pah helped Gust finish the frame-and-tar-paper addition to the house where we could have two rooms to ourselves. One bathroom for ten was a dream for Speedwellers; true, the three-burner propane camp stove in our rooms was no wood oven spreading thick heat like a blessing, but it cooked, no wood-carrying for me, and we had enough to live and could pay the doctor, only a tram ride away, to help Mam with her strange, continuing stomach illnesses. Whatever they were, we children knew no more than the various pills and medicine bottles now standing on the shelf above the sink where we washed dishes and also our faces, with a twist of the wrist the water poured out, hot or cold, and not a slop bucket in sight. Despite the chill of our tarpaper rooms, and the cold I had to crawl into on my iron cot—which seemed so . . . thin, so alone, not deep, thick straw with Dan, already asleep, a muscled, breathing heater beside me under the quilt our mother had sewn with wool we all helped to card—despite that, Vancouver was continuously amazing. Drizzle, shifty fog, the creek in the ravine between Brant and Gladstone always running a brown stream under dark brush clotted with moss, snow that sifted through the air but melted on your hand or as it touched sidewalk or street, wet but never icy—when the sun shone in the sharp air, November, January were unimaginable. City, sea, golden snow mountains.

~

Tony and little Eldo, grade two, led Liz and me to Lord Selkirk School a block west of Brant. Down a dip and over a small ravine bridge, then along 27th Avenue and there it was on Gladstone, four storeys of brick, shingles and enormous windows, with separate entrances for boys and girls, high double doors with long opening handles—no latches here, nor even knobs—and more than six hundred kids, maybe a thousand, how could I tell. There were any number of grade six rooms, you had to remember your code because each had a teacher all to itself who taught only your class, except when you went up to the auditorium in the top floor for gym. Several classes would be there at once, throwing balls, kicking them against the wall right inside the school! Some boys in grade six were really big, and the girls had so much curly hair you'd think they were women; and longer bare legs than I had ever seen. When the sun shone at recess, it seemed more children than there could possibly be on earth were playing in the schoolyard.

And across Gladstone Street, directly in line with the concrete walk from the school's entrances, was a small store. Tony showed it to us first, even before we heard the school bell buzzing like an enraged wasp and we had to go line up. The store's two front windows were packed with chocolate bars.

I had seen them for years. In Speedwell the maps of Canada and the world often hung down unrolled; even when you concentrated on the teacher, on the rim of your vision crouched the subliminal presence of haunting words:

Neilson's, the Best Chocolate Bars in Canada

and:

Neilson's MILK CHOCOLATE—
The Best Milk Chocolate Made

Not just words, worse, pictures of the chocolate bars themselves, four different kinds, floated on the blue of both Canada's and the world's oceans; only the unmarked, spinning globe, which both Miss Hingston and Miss Klassen insisted gave us the true picture of our earth in space, could stop us imagining that the entire Arctic Ocean above Canada and Alaska was overlaid by a monumental Neilson's JERSEY MILK bar, all of Siberia by a Neilson's JERSEY NUT. The ornate capitals were embossed in gold—really, how could you doubt it?

We believed, fervently, but throughout four years of war we never actually saw a single one of those map bars in Schroeder's or Harder's store or even in the rare spaces of Jacob Rempel's store in Fairholme or Dart's in Glaslyn: not one bar to touch, leave alone taste.

The Martens twins always claimed they had eaten a Neilson's Milk Chocolate bar, once when they were very little. You had to peel away the white-and-golden paper to a skin of solid silver, unfold that and the deep brown chocolate revealed itself: divided into beautifully ridged rectangles so each person would have an exactly equal share, just count, nothing to quarrel about. And taste, it was . . .

Taste could not be described, especially by the twins, but for this I wanted no words; chocolate longing was a white-and-gold wash on the world's blue oceans. Cocoa was listed in our ration booklets and there were times when a yellow tin of Fry's Pure Breakfast Cocoa, complete with its royal coat of arms, stood momentarily on a shelf behind a store counter. If by a miracle it arrived in our house with the ninety-eight-pound sack of Robin Hood flour and Mam spooned that ineffable emanation into fresh, hot milk and stirred—a resurrection out of the brown dust! In a church Christmas bag I had once found a brown bud. "Don't chew!" Liz yelled at me, "suck, make it last!" And in June 1944 when Speedwell had a closing school picnic at Turtle Lake and in our class race I came in second by half a step to a snotty brown girl from Turtleview School—she must have practised for weeks running on the hard, ribbed beach—I had the choice of either half a Sweet Marie bar or half an O Henry. I'd never seen or heard of either, and I didn't like my second name so I took half the Sweet Marie and the older boys snickered at me taking the "girlie" prize. Who cared, my mouth was full, as I showed them, and they were swallowing spit. The crunch, the texture, the taste— I would have eaten Sweet Marie again if they had named it Stalin.

But Vancouver didn't need Neilson maps in school: the bars themselves lay piled up in the store window. All you needed to eat them was money.

They cost five cents. Which was the price of a quart of milk, my mother told me, delivered at the door, and the bigger bottles with the bulb on top for settling out the cream were eight. Dad earned twenty-five cents every hour in the smoking foundry.

There came a day when I persuaded Tony to let me help him deliver his weekly flyers in exchange for half a nickel; he bought a Neilson's Milk Chocolate for the two of us to eat hidden in the ravine, away from Liz and little Eldo. The Martens twins were right: you could divide it exactly, rectangle by rectangle laid out on the silver paper; nothing to quarrel about. As for taste——even in all the years of staring at ocean and Siberia, I had not imagined it.

~

Mam was a superb worrier, and in Vancouver that's what she did for Dan suddenly left alone to take care of everything for the whole winter on the farm in Saskatchewan. She wrote him many letters of course, which have not survived, but there is one city photo which she sent Dan with a German note on the back: "Here you can see a picture of when we go into town on Saturday, they come on the street as we walk and take our picture."

The street photographer from Souvenir Snaps, 512 W. Hastings St., caught three of us in mid-stride. Mam with her best black hat and imitation fur coat buttoned up to her scarf; Pah on her left, wearing his Sunday suit, and me on her right, bareheaded and mouth open, something half-eaten in my right hand. As I explained in blotchy ink after Mam on the back of the picture: "I was just eating a bar."

Pah walks as I remember him: eyes shaded by his hat-brim, mouth shut and head down; life and his place in it is what it will be. But Mam is smiling, in fact she looks truly happy, and it is possible she is. I don't know when the picture was taken; perhaps the bright light on the clustered store signs stretching behind us and me capless means it was an early spring day, perhaps the cherry trees along Cambie and behind our house were already in full bloom and soon we would have saved enough and be on the train travelling back to our Saskatchewan home in the snow where Dan, oama Betchla, poor bachelor, had worked so hard alone all winter.

Where we also belonged. As Mam always said, "Speedwell es goot jenaug fe daut Läwe daut wie läwe." Speedwell is good enough for the life that we live.

But it may also be she truly liked Vancouver, that she liked the grey sea at English Bay as much as I did when we walked there. The long changing rooms below the street were of course closed, no one swam under glowering clouds, the swimming rectangles and diving platforms were heaved up on the beach for winter just below the enormous logs that lay about everywhere, some of them almost as thick as I was tall. Sometimes long dark men in nothing but swimming suits leaned against them, or lay sleeping in the pale sunlight. Soldiers, Tony said, they're resting after the war.

The sand was hard, but yielding too, you ran sinking deeper than at Turtle Lake into bits of shells and seaweed and unrecognizable creatures stirred by the shifting edge of the sea. Giant posts stood out in the bay, a grey-and-white bird always crowned every one, motionless as a totem, and though I had seen lake water disappear into horizon, this greyness was alive in a different way; the heavy, dark sky and the sea created a smell where they touched, something breathable on the surface between them, there where you placed your naked feet; and the waves had no pattern, were tiny spurts and riffles to the headlands of the bay and far mountains, like snow flickering over the surface of a drift, yes, almost tiny pointed animals playing under the flexible skin of the sea.

But on the outer rim of Stanley Park, down on the shingle below Siwash Rock, the sea's calm riffles swelled and smashed against the boulders, with foam cresting in tiny curls and fading away, innocently but heaving up to crash again. A huge bird dingy white flew by—a gull, Tony said, they eat anything—then slid sideways at me on the wind so close I jerked back, if I had lifted my hand its yellow bill would have gouged me. The blunt lines of ships perched far out between cloud and sea.

Perhaps my mother liked the sea, and also our many visits with Widow Pauline Fiedler, who lived now without her August just past the school on Gladstone with three unmarried sons, and her daughter Olga Racho with her five children settled nearby. Their father Gustav Racho had been left behind in Coaldale, Alberta, living, it was said, alone like old George Stewart in Speedwell, but not begging; he was no possible king of England.

Pah visited Mrs. Fiedler with Mam, but sat silent, nodding his head as he drank coffee—the Fiedlers in Vancouver certainly no longer drank home-made Pripps—perhaps ruminating on Old August's mantra: "Leave Speedwell, there you can kill yourself working in the cold and you'll still die with nothing." Old August had known how to turn things, he always landed on his feet despite being so stout that he walked only with difficulty; and even after a brief time in Vancouver he had not died with nothing: Mrs. Fiedler had a very nice insulated house sided with cedar shingles—not big and expensive like some you could get here, nah! but good—on a good street without running outside for anything.

I sat in a soft armchair in that comfortable living room, listening with barely half an ear. Son Fred worked far away, logging, and Julius and Alvin were much too old for me to visit, but Liz, who was almost fourteen, regularly wrote in her diary "In the evening went to Fiedlers and had a swell time with Alvin haha"—whatever that "haha" reminded her of. And I begged to go too because in the Fiedler living room I had discovered Zane Grey.

Four books on a shelf beside a fireplace they never used—what, still carry wood into the house?

with a furnace in the basement and a coal chute?—
each book cover had a man embossed in black, holding a gun in an alert posture, sometimes mounted on
a horse, and Mam, unable to read English and necessarily judging any book I opened by its cover, insisted
I was not to read Schund, trash, garbage, like older
boys often, sadly, did. But I argued, carefully trans-
lating titles, that the Fiedler boys weren't Lobes,
they wouldn't read really bad books, these were just
about cowboys and hunting, cowboys had to protect
their cattle from thieves like Mormons and Indians
in *Riders of the Purple Sage*—I didn't mention the
stolen women they were viciously fighting about—
and I'd only read the books there, sit quietly and
read. My mother did not quite trust the reading taste
of the remaining Fiedler boys; they didn't go to
church like Emmanuel, the perfect son-in-law even
if Mary was never the perfect wife, always so sharp-
tongued and crabbily annoyed about something, but
the living room on Gladstone was warm and seemed
innocent, me buried in a book as usual, so there I ran
deep into the savage Ohio forests of 1777 with *The
Spirit of the Border*, a book I would never find in a
public school library. I read swift as falling the over-
written he-maleness of Wetzel "assume gigantic
proportions . . . a magnificent statue of dark men-
ace" before he "plunged into the forest" on the trail

of the hideous villain Jim Girty. And "as he disappeared, a long, low sound like the sigh of the night wind swelled and moaned through the gloom." I could only shudder with ghostly anticipation, flip the page to Chapter XXIV.

And Liz in the wide arch beyond the Fiedler dining room—they had a separate room just to eat in—playing Chinese checkers with Alvin and looking up, her mouth open to laugh at me: Haha I'm your big sister and there's nothing you can do about it haha!

The fingers of my small, rounded mother made her four steel knitting needles flicker in the electric light, a wool sock growing in her hands while she visited: there was nothing I wanted to "do about" her. One glance from her and "Le vent de la Mort," the bloody revenge and re-revenge of Zane Grey seemed too grotesque to page through, much less read—though of course I kept on reading—the known warmth of my head cradled in her lap, her fingers sometimes brushing my hair, her light hand sheltering me the way a hen in a thunderstorm covers her chicks with her body though she is beaten by ice. My loving mother prayed "without ceasing" to an infinitely loving Father in Heaven, yes, but also, I knew, to a terrifying one. Perhaps that was another reason she liked Vancouver.

~

Mam's favourite verse in the Bible said, "For God so loved the world"; that was her life motto. And the evangelists that she, Liz and I went to hear in the various halls and churches of Vancouver almost every weekend—Pah sometimes too, but he said he couldn't understand English well enough; neither could Mam, but for her that didn't matter—the evangelists began their sermons with that phrase too, all the time. But they immediately rushed on from there as if love was just the quick opener to a far more significant aspect of God's character, as if "For God so loved the world that he gave . . ." was merely a plank sticking out over the huge lake of your life that you ran up as fast as you could and it was only at the last instant, when you were about to leap high and dive off the plank of love, that you realized the Lake of Life all around you was actually horizonless, depthless, Wrath.

The molten steel wrath of God; no one, neither Jacob Enns nor the travelling summer Bible teachers ever preached like this in High German at the Speedwell Church. They were reassuring, comforting, God wanted all sinners to repent and none to perish; but this was THUNDER: "You cannot stop at verse 16! You have to read to the end of the chapter!" For there, after the magnificent declaration that God loved the whole world and all that is in it, John the Evangelist, the disciple whom Jesus particularly loved, concludes:

> he that believeth on the Son hath everlasting life,
> and he that believeth not the Son shall not see life;
> but the wrath of God abideth on him.

That was the verse the English evangelists in Vancouver rushed towards, where they spent most of their sermons elaborating every horror text they could find in the Bible, every example in the history of the world or in their own personal stories which were always full of shameful sin, dreadful suffering: God's wrath is like that, only worse. And not only worse, but it also "abideth on you for-ev-er."

Since the stranger had passed through Speedwell and left his red words on our fences and roadside stones, "wra-a-ath" had been a lovely sound in my mouth, yet I could not understand it. I knew anger, I had occasionally been punched and knocked down, I had been in fights and given as good as I got; I had been spanked a few times—by Mam, never by Pah, that was never necessary my mother said, because it was not in my father's nature to strike anyone unless he was totally enraged and that was not good discipline, Mam said—but those were brief school or home emotions that came and went, everybody got mad at someone sometimes and it went away. But Wrath? No one had ever beaten me, certainly not in a continuous rage, and this sounded a lot like that. In the Speedwell Church, when sin, sinners and judgment were preached about, der Zorn Gottes, the Wrath of God was, at most, mentioned in passing; rather, the sermons dwelt on suffering and its consequences because of sin, sorrow, a deep sorrow at the blindness, disappointment at the wilful bullheadedness of rejecting God's love.

"Zorn" did not sound so dreadful to me. In High German sermons the text from John was "der Zorn Gottes bleibet über ihm," which I understood to mean *the dark anger of God abides over (not "on") him*, sort of like a black cloud hovering above you, following you all your life and always raining a bit, or like having poor luck because you weren't an August Fiedler who knew how to turn things over and over and always make a little more than sufficient money happen. Sometimes I almost thought about my father this way: he worked very hard but we never seemed to have quite enough money; when Dan went away to work or ran the farm with Mam everything seemed to be easier—but surely my father was too mild and good to suffer Zorn, leave alone Wrath.

Good as it felt in mouth and ear, the English word was dreadful. And I didn't want to live in a High

German world; after Hitler everything German was despicable.

So just stay on the plank Domma'john, idiot, why jump in the lake! No! the evangelist thundered, you have to jump! And then you will be saved if you believe on the Son! It says so right here, John 3 verse 36, and you prove you believe by jumping, because when you believe and jump, the lake that looks like God's Wrath to the sinner, for the believer it becomes the Lake of God's Love the instant he hits it! We have warned you, the evangelists repeated, the soft piano lifting the Percy B. Crawford Male Quartet to their feet and into the relentless, double-edged hymn,

Almost persuaded, now to believe;

sing the mellifluous harmony right to the bitter end of the third verse,

Sad, sad, that bitter wail, "Almost—but lost!"

"Come," whispered the evangelist. "Come now."

They called this "the altar call," and I had never seen it in Speedwell either. It went on and on. Stand up now and come forward to the altar, come here with all who are coming, and kneel. Repent. Not the Lake of Fire forever.

Some people always walked down the aisle, going forward, but never enough to suit the evangelists.

And I was thinking: until you actually hit the lake, how could you tell? I did believe, I wanted to believe, I did, my mother wanted us all to believe and Liz was tilted forward on the church pew praying with her hands clenched and Helen looking down on us from her Heavenly Glory . . . what about Stalin?

The most horrible person on earth was de Kommunist Stalin, every Russian Mennonite story I ever heard listening to our families visiting told me that. He was even worse than Hitler, who murdered people quick and he was dead now, but Stalin lived on, and as long as he lived every Mennonite knew he tortured you as long as he could keep you alive, first by starving, then with armies and robbers raping, sabring, then he took your land away and your Bible, you could never go to church again, all your men began to disappear, the ministers first, and the teachers, and then one night when you were asleep the secret police, who everyone knew arrived every evening and sat in their Black Maria at the edge of your village, sat and smoked and waited, faceless in the gathering darkness—until one midnight those Onn'jeheiare, monsters hammered on your door and then you saw their stone eyes, heard their terrifying

Russian and your father and your brothers were gone, or your whole family to the smallest child dragged into the night while your neighbours stared through their window curtains terrified, their turn tomorrow, and if you survived cells and midnight torture and cattle cars you would be in a Vorkuta or Siberian taiga camp, you wouldn't know where, digging a canal or chopping down trees in snow, starving and worked to death. Forever? No, not even Stalin could do that. Only until death in its mercy came, as it always does, our mother said, and you went to heaven. Not even Stalin himself could create a Lake of Fire for All Eternity.

The evangelist explained very quietly, during the altar call, that All Eternity was a bird coming to Mount Robson every thousand years to rub its beak against the rock. When, from that rubbing, Mount Robson was worn level with the prairie, then one minute of All Eternity would have passed.

And it hit me: I believed and that was fine, but if you didn't believe, God would be inexpressibly worse to you than Joseph Stalin.

Could I believe that? I didn't want to. How could Mam? How could Jesus be good if God was really like that?

I noticed the evangelists never talked about "the wind blows where it wills," or "the light shines in

the darkness," which were there in John chapter 3 as
well; I noticed how they skipped over "for God sent
not his Son into the world to condemn the world" so
fast I'd have forgotten it was there if I hadn't looked
for it in my English Bible in my bed at home. But I
had no philosophy to grapple with their simplistic,
pounding dualism, no ability yet to puzzle over the
strange doubleness, the "both/and" feelings I felt—
black or white! no or yes! that's all there is to
believe!—though the marvellous world and its stunning intricacy of creation made me wonder.

~

And particularly the organ music.

The evangelistic campaigns we attended in
Vancouver were sometimes held in huge churches
whose dark balconies circled over wooden pews and
faced great silver organ pipes. When these pipes
were played, which was only occasionally but it was
enough to hear them even once, I was inhabited by
sounds beyond comprehension: could that be a
hymn? Could you sing words with that, even loving
ones? You could certainly never make an altar call for
people to walk forward and kneel at the feet of the
evangelist in repentance. The held bass of the organ
shivered the bench and the floor under you, until you

felt it marinate your bones, soak like golden, molten rock into your head. An organ made you forget everything but sound.

And once, only once, an Indian chief wearing feathers around his head and down his long back like a picture book stood behind the pulpit in front of those magnificent organ pipes. He raised his arms, wide, so the long fringes of his white leather jacket swayed gently, and told us he had been invited to visit King George and Queen Elizabeth in Buckingham Palace. While he was there he had asked them if they believed in God. And the Queen had told him, "Yes. We do."

The enormous church exploded into applause, cheering, whistling! I had never heard such a sound in a church before, but this was so amazing I may have joined in: in London, England, the great capital of the British Empire that had been victorious in the greatest war ever fought in history, London where Mr. Winston Churchill spoke and Big Ben kept on tolling throughout the world, throughout the war, there in Buckingham Palace the Queen and the King believed in God! How could a little Baulch of a Saskatchewan Mennonite bush brat like me not believe?

This Canadian Indian chief stood below me on the podium in the church of St. Giles, patron of cripples, and he had talked to them, and I suddenly knew that if this man asked them a question like that, they could only answer truthfully. He didn't walk around the platform waving his arms and shouting, he spoke calmly with a profound dignity that had no need to either yell or threaten like evangelists; he told you what had happened to him and then you knew. He had asked, the Queen herself had answered. "Yes."

~

The man in St. Giles Church looked nothing like the Cree men slumped in their wagons slowly driving past our yard on the Speedwell roads in spring, women and children staring over the sideboards. One of our talky neighbours, who always knew everything, told us road allowance Indians were as quick at stealing as any Russian Bashkirs, when they're heading for Turtle Lake or digging seneca roots or picking saskatoons just make sure your chickens are behind the barn and your dog tied up; they'll take dogs too if they're hungry enough. Sure, you need the dog to warn you they're coming, just don't let him run out to the road.

Do Indian people eat dog? Katie Martens and I didn't know any Cree to ask when in grade four we prepared our "Historical Indian Project" on the wide table in the Speedwell School basement—it was a real basement with poured cement walls, not simply a hole in the ground like the cellar with its barrel heater under our church—and I liked to hear her talk about anything, whether she made it up or not. Katie easily stitched a piece of flour sack over the three peeled sticks I leaned together for the teepee (I didn't know enough about the Cree to bring four) and Katie said it was too bad the Indians didn't live in teepees any more, they were so poor now, and I told her I couldn't understand why their horses and wagons looked so miserable, worse than ours who were refugees, and especially their clothes. The school books said they'd been here since before anyone and lived wherever they wanted everywhere in Canada, why were they so poor? Katie didn't know any more about why than I did, but she thought a teepee would be fun with a campfire burning in front of it so we added that, wood splinters over shredded bits of red crepe paper, and our camp did look very neat among the flour-and-papier-mâché hills and spruce tips standing on them with strands of blue wool creek winding by over the cardboard earth. The basement was empty except for us two working and Katie laughed her cheerful bubbles of a laugh; we could be chief and squaw, she said.

I remember that project, and her words, as exactly as anything in my childhood. We were below the tiny northwestern basement window, where afternoon sunlight fell brightest, away from the open plank stairs onto the earthen floor. We could hear Miss Klassen walk overhead among school children slurring their feet. We never had classes in the basement, not that I recall; it was a freezing cave in winter where the risers for the annual Christmas concert stage lay stacked along with broken desks and the kindergarten table we no longer needed upstairs because there were fewer children. The entrance above the stairs was a heavy lid you had to heave up and lean against the wall where the boys hung their coats. But once Katie and I were down there working together on an "Historical Indian Project."

~

When the Indian chief in Vancouver had spoken, he lowered his arms. He looked around at the people in the lower pews, and then he lifted his face to us in the circled balcony. He turned fully towards me clenched onto the brass railing nearest him over the pulpit, and stopped. His face was folded and gentle, like my mother's, but also hard, not threatening but fixed; like a hillside boulder exposed during the building of a road, deeply immovable.

Silence filled the church like prayer. Then he turned and walked back to his chair. The black tips of his feathers almost touched the floor between his tan moccasins. Before he could seat himself the piano began plinkering a frill, the evangelist had uncrossed his legs and was riffling his Bible in anticipation and the male quartet already stood breathing, stretching their mouths open. For me it was over.

That evening, beautifully, there was no Vancouver rain. Riding home on the trolley I recognized that the city had both names and numbers for its night streets. And so much light: night barely gained a shadow between blazing lights. I saw myself in the trolley window, and through myself the brightness of the street lights outside where they labelled the corners, first with tree names—Spruce, Willow, Ash—and then suddenly Yukon, Alberta, Manitoba, Ontario, Quebec; they skipped Saskatchewan probably because they couldn't spell it, as no one in grade six at Lord Selkirk School could, except me, and then the trolley was singing its wires down the light corridor of Kingsway bright as day, the driver droning "King Edward" and "Victoria Drive," and I waited and pulled the cord for Gladstone because that was closer to Brant than Nanaimo Road, only four short blocks, but running ahead on the concrete I saw that the lights of the city were doubled against the hanging clouds overhead and night was a thin, bent line between two immense blankets of light reaching to the unchangeable North Shore Mountains with their pale silhouette of stars. Where was the moon? Tomorrow, Saturday, I would help Tony distribute the weekly flyers in his area along Nanaimo and then we would follow the creek ravine under the train trestle to Trout Lake and build a log raft and paddle out onto the lake and in the evening we might take the trolley to the evangelistic campaign again, but the Indian chief would not be there, he had spoken tonight and that was sufficient. I ran faster through the shadows and light of the street wishing there were no bright windows beside me, wishing for the heavy darkness of a trail worn between poplars to run into but there was none and I was happy, very happy.

Tony and I did push ourselves out onto Trout Lake next day, too far out, and after some time we believed we would drown because several logs got away from our raft and our poles were too short to find bottom in the mud and we gradually sank so deep we could only hand-scoop ourselves by submarine inches towards the nearest swampy shore. Sometimes Tony, sometimes I crouched in cold water over our shoes trying to balance. I knew I hated water, there was no trusting so much water and though this was not the ocean it was close enough and it would be even colder the deeper you sank and we would most certainly sink. But we didn't drown, not quite, and in the general relief at our coming through the door we were no more than yelled at for the soaked clothing and mud we brought home, and next morning we went as usual to the Sunday service at the Mennonite Brethren Church off Fraser Street. Gust took all ten of us in his car.

This church gathered underground; only the basement was completed, with heavy roofing paper and tar where the floor would be when they had collected enough money to build more. From the top of the outside steps you could look south down the slope of city houses to the Fraser River flats, the grass and silos of dairy farms on Lulu Island (now Richmond and Vancouver Airport) and far beyond to the pale blue snow of Mount Baker across the border in the United States of America. No one simple name for that country would do, it had to have a title. I wondered what changed, what new world happened when you stepped over the line drawn so straight on maps; if you stood with one foot on either side would you suddenly split because the USA could do anything it wanted? But, close as it was, we never crossed to find out.

Everything in the basement church was High German, as was proper for Russian Mennonites in Canada then, especially those who, with the war ended at last, were beginning to move into the crowded city from the isolation of their stony immigrant homesteads on parkland and prairie. As usual I sat with the other boys on the backless front bench of the men's side, directly below the pulpit. My legs were now long enough to comfortably triangle myself to the floor and I could sing all the hymns from memory—it seemed I knew hundreds of them—but Tony beside me didn't sing, and neither did Gust. Tina had a beautiful soprano, like our mother, but she could never sing duets with Gust like Mam did with Pah when they were working together in our bush home, or outside in the garden, or in the cattle corral milking or anywhere on the farmyard: if they were within earshot of each other my father would lift his lyric tenor to her soprano:

O mein Jesu du bist's wert
Dass man Dich im Staube ehrt,
Dass man Dich beständig lobt und ehrt.
Niemand ist so gut wie Du,
Meine Seele jauchzt Dir zu,
Meine Seele jauchst Dir freudig zu.

O my Jesus you are worthy
To be honoured in the dust,
To continually be honoured thus.
There's no goodness like to you,
My soul lauds and praises you,
My soul shouts to you for happiness.

When together they sang such a soaring hymn, carried by heart for centuries across continents and oceans, they sounded like lovers, though I do not remember seeing them kiss.

~

During my evenings in the Fiedler living room Zane Grey had, by means of brutality, tried to confirm what Emmanuel told me running in the snow behind our caboose: love between a man and a woman was stronger than death. In his books nothing, not even the most vicious, relentless violence, could break it. I never associated Zane Grey love with my parents—they were too old, too Mennonite fixed for that—but I tried to see if something was perhaps happening in Liz on the verge of fourteen, so vivid and alert, so laughing when we all played softball in the Rices' grassy field in the warm March (March!) sunlight when the cherry trees, not the spruce, were as if dusted with snow; the way she ran into Alvin Fiedler trying to get back on base before he could touch her with the ball in his hand. Though if that happened it seemed fine too, she'd grab his hand and wrestle him for the ball and finally whirl away from him and throw the ball to the pitcher, laughing. Alvin was as tall and handsome as he had to be, but often he looked merely dour, grumpy like his aged father often had, and happy, passionate Liz seemed to be laughing at the wrong guy. Julius maybe, but he was far too old, over twenty. Even when Alvin tuned her guitar—Liz took guitar lessons and I violin because our mother insisted that in a city with music teachers we each had to learn to play a good, portable instrument—Alvin never told funny stories like his brother Emmanuel did. When I teased Liz with, "You really like Alvin, huh?" she wrinkled her nose and contorted her usual sisterly aphorism, "That's for me to know and you not to find out."

The Fiedler–Racho–Wiebe gathering was our only community for five months in Vancouver— the Lobes had scattered across Saskatchewan and Alberta cutting lumber and trucking, not even Mrs. Fiedler knew exactly where most of them were— and I do not remember visiting anyone else. After we tired of spring softball in Rice's field, we ate ice cream. No endless churning in a bucket filled with crushed ice, no slurping a semi-liquid mess, you could buy a miracle of ice cream bricks at any store on Nanaimo frozen hard as stone and cut them with a knife and let chunks melt off a spoon freezing your tongue. Vanilla or strawberry or chocolate, or all three at once, striped Neapolitan, whose layered existence was impossible to imagine until you actually ate it. Chocolate was best. I couldn't know that chocolate revels were still to come.

~

Not a face or a name remains from Lord Selkirk School, neither student nor teacher; or from the church we attended every Sunday, or of the storekeepers on Nanaimo or the doorways where Tony and I laid our weekly flyers—what were they for, groceries? One person I do remember: a young man with fierce black hair who came leaping down cottage steps on Brant Street and yelled at me over their fence to stop standing there staring in their living-room window! Doubtless I was staring, but the curtains were open and so I assumed it was invited. That happened on the day we arrived, before Tony came home from school and found me riding his wagon up and down the sidewalk. I had never before seen the inside of a fancy city house—as it seemed to me then.

I must have passed that house hundreds of times in five months and looked through its huge single-pane window every time, but I never stopped walking and I remember nothing at all of what was inside.

Lord Selkirk had an auxiliary building with a high half-timbered peak set at right angles to the school where groups of classes were sent to watch movies. I had never seen a movie before, though by 1945 I was allowed to listen to "Lux Presents Hollywood" every Monday evening on radio station CFQC Saskatoon. I'd never heard the clicking flicker of a projector, seen the beam of light in a shuttered room and shadows twitch and tumble over a screen. Sometimes I watched the pupils, over a hundred of them on stacking chairs, every face turned to that rectangle of light, every face as grey as the faces they watched. Shadow stories for eye and ear. Both smart and simpler, somehow, and never to me as fascinating as written words. When you told movie stories to someone who had not seen them, they seemed flat, even stupid. But the continually reordered alphabet of words: that went far beyond smart or flat, into mystery.

What did we watch in that high, black-beamed hall? Tony tells me on his seventieth birthday that he remembers clear as today seeing a magnificent *Prisoner of Zenda* with Ronald Colman as the

Prisoner and Douglas Fairbanks Jr. as Rupert of Hentzau, whereas I retain nothing but a possible Mickey Mouse or *Snow White* cartoon. But most certainly I saw plenty of "Our Gang" films (The Little Rascals); the big-bolted rafters of the hall rang with laughter at the Gang's endless bad antics. I find now that 221 "Our Gang" films were made between 1922 and 1944. We may even have seen Our Gang number 197 (1941), in which Mickey's mother is pregnant for the fourth time and Mickey becomes very worried because he's read that every fourth child born in the world is Chinese. Whatever we saw, Liz and I told our parents nothing about it, they might have forbidden us such worldliness; which may be another reason I've forgotten them so completely.

And I remember a song very well, "The Teddy Bears' Picnic"—was that in a movie?—and the marvellous lines,

> If you go down to the woods today
> You're sure of a big surprise . . .
> You'd better go in disguise . . .

What an evocative word, "disguise": your reality concealed, perhaps cancelled, shape-shifted. A profound word for a writer, I could feel that already, though not yet know it; not then.

The war was over, and slowly the world was changing. Wood carefully carpentered was no longer needed to cover a house: Gust simply nailed wide slabs of red asphalt pressed to look like bricks over the tarpaper walls and brown asphalt shingles on the roof and instantly our poor house was disguised into class. Every afternoon the *Vancouver Sun* arrived at 4160 Brant thicker than ever—the surrender of Japan certainly didn't end the news!—a mass of paper folded neatly into itself and tossed onto the wooden deck along the front of the house where one March Sunday we lined up after church to take our last Vancouver family pictures. Mrs. Fiedler agreed to join us.

The one *Sun* front page I remember was a large picture of a woman in high heels at a bus stop, standing on one leg with the other bent up high and bare, pulling on a stocking. The caption read that she had bought the first pair of nylons for women ever sold in Vancouver—price $1.75, when a quart of milk cost 5 cents—and she could not wait to get home to put them on. Her usual lisle stockings lay puddled on the sidewalk beside her shoe and her skirt was flipped up so high, if you looked long enough it was possible you might see the two nubs of her garters against her long, naked thigh.

"That's how it is in the big world," Pah said. "Ohne Shomp." Completely shameless.

~

I had tried to fit a three-quarter-size violin between my chin and shoulder and fingers for several months; it was a stubborn, squeaky thing. On Monday, April 1, 1946, we left Vancouver without it. Mam said Speedwell was where we belonged, uns Tüss, our home.

The CNR passenger train steamed east through the Rockies, over Alberta hills and through the long parkland forests into Saskatchewan smooth as a dream, and then the bumping Meadow Lake bus.

North of North Battleford, Highway 4 dragged itself up between the round drumlin hills surrounding Cochin until the great ice sheet of Jackfish Lake lay below, slowly softening under the sun. In April 1946 I was eleven and a half years old, and I had no idea we were travelling alongside large Indian lands (at that time reserves were not allowed to declare their presence with highway signs) nor had I the faintest premonition that 120 years before, the brilliant Plains Cree leader Big Bear had been born here to a Cree mother whose name is forgotten and a Plains Saulteaux chief named Black Powder, born right here, on the shore of this lake, only forty kilometres from my own birthplace as the raven flies. But there was no raven to fly an omen across the spring sky which I could then have comprehended: that Chief Big Bear, who died on January 17, 1888, would someday inhabit half a century of my personal, my writing, life.

## 8.

## ASPEN

~

It was in the sewer of Paris that Jean Valjean found himself. . . . The wounded man on his shoulders did not stir, and Jean Valjean did not know whether what he was carrying away in this grave was alive or dead.

E arly December, 1946. In front of the wide windows of Speedwell School, on a temporary stage built by the school board secretary, Dave Heinrichs, the girls from grades five to eight are practising "Good King Wenceslas" for the Christmas concert. There are only five of them, and the school has no piano or pump organ—nor could anyone have played it if there was one—but Miss Siemens' voice anchors a note here and there, her waving arms guiding the girls along the melody so that momentarily they sound like one, full and clear as an evening owl among the trees gliding over the little bump of "gath'ring winter fu—ooo—el." Miss Siemens wants a bit of harmony whenever possible, and on several lines Katie Martens and Nettie Enns, who have sung in our church longer than they can remember, slide into an alto that deepens, broadens their sound into another colour, while Annie Sahar and Vera Funk and Helen Trapp can only remain true on the melody, softer then, almost a hush in your ear.

I am scrunched sideways in a desk, leaning against the warm galvanized surround that guards the gas-barrel heater in the centre of the room. It may be I have just stacked it with split poplar because the heat of wood burning fondles me, heat unlike any other I know, having lived for five months with propane in mouldy Vancouver, thick wood heat you can smell in waves even before you feel it nubble your body like dense fur. As usual, I am thoughtlessly chewing my fingernails as I sit with a book opened into the low winter sun red between the sheets draped over wires around the stage.

The book is Victor Hugo's *Les Misérables*. The wavering carol of cruel cold and snow and deep footprints—so Canadian bush—and the beatific heat, the level light are so brilliant, I hear Javert's conscience finally split and burn crimson on the page,

> "Javert, what are you going to do with this old man?"
>
> "Why, I'll arrest him and he'll go down to the galley prison at Toulon. . . ."
>
> "What! The man who saved your life today?"

Indelible childhood. I cannot know that fifty years from now I will literally walk in the Seine River sewers of Paris with this song, this warmth, this story light my shadow still, walking with me.

And at barely twelve I am not quite reading Hugo's massive novel either; I am reading Solomon Cleaver's drastic diminution of it into *Jean Val Jean*, a sanitized text approved for Canadian children by both the public and the Roman Catholic school boards; in it, the thirty pages of *Les Misérables*'s intricate cloacal history is eviscerated to one subordinate clause:

> Standing in the great sewers of Paris—some of whose mighty tunnels are ten feet in diameter

and which, like the giant trunk and branches of
some hollow tree, stretch mile after mile under
the city streets—[Jean] gazes into the black darkness, wondering if he will ever find a way out.

Hugo summed up his cloaca chapters with the
Parisian proverb, "To descend into the sewer is to
enter the grave," and, "The sewer is a cynic. It tells
all." Such understandings become in Cleaver simply
an image of "some hollow tree, stretching for
miles"—hollow tree, horse apples! Even in 1946 that
doesn't fool me for one second. I have lived in a city;
after my lifetime of plopping outhouses I have studied the spiral of water in a toilet bowl swirl my turds
down into the bowels of sewers—but I never
dreamed sewers could be huge enough for a man to
walk in, much less carry a body.

I do know that, no matter how large the sewer,
what Jean Valjean will be wading in is no sweet rain-
drop seeping through a hollow tree. Five years later
when I find my first good summer job helping build
the water and sewer system under Coaldale, Alberta,
population 800, the biggest pipes we will lay are
barely large enough for a slim teenager to slither
along on his toes and elbows; and I will spend half
a day's wages buying the Modern Library of the
World's Best Books edition of *Les Misérables* and

read its 1,222 pages from first to last. I will come home brown and sweating from shovelling, hoisting pipes, measuring levels in the prairie summer sun and the long section of "The Intestine of Leviathan" will fascinate me, not only because of the clay sewer pipes I wrestle with every day in the deep trenches below the streets of my hometown, the houses of my neighbours, but also because by working on that construction crew I am forced to wade, all day, every working minute, in what to me are the sewers of the English language. I will be forced to understand that a head-on *shit* or *bugger* or *fuck* are the least of our superb language's intricate, endlessly branching combinations of filth to smear on every conceivable human experience; especially on town girls I know from school and church passing on the sidewalk in their summer shorts.

Nevertheless, while gobbling down Charles Wilbour's turgid translation of *Les Misérables*, through prairie heat and aching, growing muscles and the quickly boring profanity of a Coaldale construction crew, the soaring thread of those five girls' "ble—e—ssing" will sing some quiet and peace, some clarity in my head. Also remembered sadness.

Because in 1946–47 Speedwell was going away. Leaving. Not its land of course, not the long eskers of hills laid down by glaciers grinding and melting forward and back over the earth, the meandering swamps and creeks, the immovable erratics sticking up wherever you chopped down and uprooted trees to pile them in windrows, all your children helping clean up branches and brush, throwing them as high as possible so the windrows would later burn like long hills of fire leaping against the snow and winter sky, against the drift of northern lights flaming down upon you.

In our small district more cleared land than ever nudged into the boreal forest, there were better houses and even, amazingly, a hip-roof barn built of lumber—but the depression of the 1930s was past and World War II was fought and won and over, Gott sei Dank, thanks be to God, and Canada offered much more than this labour subsistence in ice and mosquitoes and rocks and seneca roots. The neighbours who had already left wrote us that everywhere south in Canada there was a livable climate, there was electricity, there was work, there was money to buy a tractor, a car. The post office informed us of everything—so many letters from friends now gone and the Eaton's and Simpson's catalogues thicker than ever and weekly newspapers, the *Winnipeg Free Press* and the *Family Herald* and *Weekly Star* from Montreal and the *Western Producer* from Saskatoon—as we ourselves had seen that world during all those months in Vancouver.

And one Sunday Gustav Biech, for whom Dan often worked in winter feeding cattle, and who had built up the best and largest farm in the district, east of Jack Pine, close to the highway, one summer Sunday Gustav and Lydia Biech drove a pale grey 1946 Plymouth into the church yard, a vehicle that shone in the sun; that cost over a thousand dollars, it was said. Obviously only people in Sunday clothes would dare get into it.

A car. It is clear that over a year before, in May 1945, Dan came home with a car. It can be seen in a picture taken in our hay corral of me and my nieces Carol and Anne and five multicoloured (mostly Hereford) calves after I returned home from the North Battleford hospital: in the distant background, beyond the sod- and straw-roofed barns, between the usual small mountain of firewood, our buggy and the corner of our house, stands a roofless car. The engine is hidden by a corral post, but the straight, rectangular windshield is clear, as are the two front seats and the board box built behind them, between the high back fenders and their narrow wheels with wooden spokes.

~

Is there a yeast in memory that grows, knits our past into the timeless shapes we desire? Or do I now know

events and times only from what I see in accidentally
retained pictures, the exact Kodak instant focused on
crimped paper, and I gradually remember . . . because
in my hand I recognize I'm wearing my homecoming
present after having survived my appendix: a bright
yellow shirt, my favourite colour, with a gleaming
black collar and button-line down my chest. And
behind us children standing in our hay corral yard is
Dan's car: a worn, tattered roadster worthy of being
a Depression Bennett Buggy.

But despite its absolute uniqueness in our Speedwell life, I don't remember ever riding in it, nor
whether Dan still had it when we returned from
Vancouver. The nearest gas pump, cash only, would
have been in Fairholme ten miles away—though
John Harder must have had a barrel for his 1942 Chev
truck hauling cream twice a week to Medstead—but

for a car to be useful in Speedwell, even one with a platform for hauling sacks or boxed animals, it would have to be manoeuvrable on dirt roads and able to keep moving between all the mudholes. And a car would be completely helpless in winter snow, to say nothing of the radiator bursting in freezing temperatures. You could crank it till you were dizzy and it would still be a frozen dead machine; covering its hood with a horse blanket wouldn't help any more than trying to build a house out of three walls. In Speedwell you could always lead horses to your well, stuff them with hay you cut in your own sloughs for nothing except sweat.

And I find my mother's Gothic script on the back of another snapshot, "abgenommen den 28 Maerz 1947," taken the 28th of March, 1947, six weeks before we left Speedwell for good, which shows

Dan and me seated not in the car but in our creaky cutter in deep snow with his pride team of grey Fox and dappled Silver, their necks arched to race us out of there. Dan wears his dress overcoat, I shade my face against the sunlight with gauntlet gloves, I remember them now that I see them, my pride in those huge leather cuffs but I know all their warmth was in Mam's knitted liners. Behind us the spiky spruce of the muskeg across the road allowance from our house.

I cannot doubt my mother's handwriting. But where were Dan and I going in our Sunday clothes on a winter Friday morning?

We were the only Speedwell Wiebes ever—though it's the second most common Russian Mennonite name on earth—one small family and still proud of our magnificent horses that could run us to church or post office or town through any mud or snow, harness bells ringing. In the picture you can see the bells on Silver's breeching. But people were leaving; by March 1947 the Speedwell–Jack Pine districts were three-quarters empty of people. People had come and gone since before I ever noticed, especially young people going away to work—spring sugar beets, summer railroads, fall threshing, winter lumber camps—or to Bible school in Hepburn, but even if they married and moved to isolated village mission churches, they always came back to visit and remained part of their local family. True, before the war whole families had moved away permanently, but other families arrived then to take over their log houses and sod-roofed barns, to break larger fields out of the poplars. But that changed during the war; now whole families—the Henry Friesens, the Paul Poetkers, the Wilhelm Voths, the Otto Dunzes, the George Koehns, the John Schroeders, the John Dycks, the David Loewens, the Jacob Rempels, the Peter Bergs, and then by 1942 the entire Fiedler–Lobe–Racho–Dunz–Leischner–Biech clan (except stubborn Gustav Biech) had left for the southern prairies or British Columbia; trucks heaped high, growling slowly away on our stony roads; and not a single family came to take up the empty places.

Their farmyards stood bare; log buildings leaned, sank, collapsed into their cellar holes. Sometimes the farmers nearby would not even bother to work the laboriously cleared land; poplars sprouted along the edges of fields and soon the only crop you could find there were patches of early summer strawberries, wild and tiny as hidden drops of blood. I was no good at picking them, though my sisters could pluck a syrup pail full in an hour: I had to brush over the weeds and leaves with my fingers to reveal their berry shape before I could see them.

Leaving, the air of all seasons was filled with leaving. A rumour in church or at the post office this week was a fact the next, and when we four Wiebes arrived back from our unexpectedly long Vancouver stay in April 1946, Mrs. Sam Heinrichs and her family too were gone. For four years Liz and I had hiked the mile and a half to their yard and then the last mile and a half to school with Wilfred and Louise; in fact, Wilfred and I had scouted out the shortest possible route to school and had even convinced the girls to use it, despite their fluttery shudders about "bush animals!" What animals? "Maybe a cow, a squirrel, a slinky weasel!" Their apprehensions of course made us merely braver and we followed the Heinrichses' field trail northeast from their yard to cross a corner of Jacob Rempel's big field, where we picked up a cow path tramped deep between the tall poplars, angling through Grandpa Daniel Lobe's bush—the old man's grave was in the church cemetery, a perfect white picket fence around it with the tips and corner posts curved into bright orange—until we found the bare height above Grandpa Lobe's creek and followed that down to the slough and skirted its swampy edge, where there were always lots of spring frogs croaking, their gelatinous egg masses floating in brown water, and blackbirds building nests in the bulrushes, singing relentlessly as the stalks bent and wavered under them; finally, we came out between the willows just across the road from the school. The trail saved us half the walking—well, maybe a third—through Dave Heinrichs' yard and past Old Stewart's decaying cabin, though you couldn't ride a horse on it, too many rusted barbed-wire fences. Now the Sam Heinrichs family was gone and the house where we often sat around the kitchen table talking and looking out of its unique bow window was empty; no one took the windows for salvage because no one was building anything. The blacksmith shop door hung on one leather hinge, the forge with its smoke canopy gone, nothing but a whiff and crunch of coal near the blackened wall. On the path between house and barn, where Sam Heinrichs' coffin had leaned open with the family mourning around it, only a deepening mat of chickweed was growing quick.

And Mam's best remaining friend, Gilda's mother, the Widow Anna Heinrichs who was the finest seamstress in Speedwell, now talked British Columbia as well. After all, Bill Poetker and Rosella, her oldest daughter, had left several years ago to run a big dairy farm in B.C., on Lulu Island, and they wrote it was getting bigger—what was it like there by Vancouver? Mam and Pah had of course visited the Poetkers and could explain what *big* was, black-and-white cows the size of bone-hipped horses dragging udders like

bulging barrels. But rumour in Speedwell had it
that the Widow's oldest son Arlyss—where did they
find such a name?—liked Speedwell teacher Sarah
Siemens very much; the big question was, how
much did she like him? She had boarded at the
Heinrichses' for a year, she should soon know. And if
they did get married, would they stay so she could
teach another year? No one had ever taught in our
school three years in a row, but Isaac Braun had
stayed for four at Jack Pine after the school burned
down—it was said that George, the youngest son of
the Jack Pine School chairman, Joe Handley, had
started the fire, though no one knew why young
George with his handsome, often scowling, face had
done it and Mr. Handley had the school rebuilt so fast
in the middle of winter it hardly caused a problem,
perhaps wasn't even reported. What Joe Handley did
to George was beyond Mennonite rumour, but
George joined the Regina Rifles before he was eighteen and was severely wounded, they said, fighting in
France—but Ike Braun had stayed in the district
because he married Doris Heinrichs and now they
had a beautiful little girl, Gwen—where did they
get those names?—so anything was still possible.
The Widow Heinrichs might stay and if Arlyss and
Sarah got married they might stay and then the
Brauns probably would stay too and Doris continue

to be a Sunday school teacher (she had been mine when I was a little kid) though there were now so few children in church left to teach. Even in Speedwell School there were only twenty-three pupils in eight grades to perform the Christmas program.

Friday, December 20, 1946. A heavy winter night, the two Coleman mantle lamps were hung high on their hooks, hissing brightly; the stage curtains were closed and the ceiling radiated twisted crepe-paper streamers, pink and red and white, centred at the stage by a large crepe-paper bell. I must have done something on the program, perhaps many things because, except for Edward Funk and Jackie Trapp, at twelve and in grade seven, I was the oldest boy in school. But I remember nothing.

Or . . . it may be I do. The title of a school play hovers in my Speedwell memories: "Wanted: A Housekeeper." If it was performed in 1946, I would have played one of the two ancient bachelors who advertise for a housekeeper, but the only words I recall are those of the first applicant for the job; she can cook nothing but "Cabbage soup and fried pork," words repeated throughout the play to great laughter. Would Miss Siemens drill us in a bumpkin comedy for Christmas?

I remember so little of that last year. After the city noise of Vancouver, did I long to be gone? I don't remember that either, not like reading *Jean Val Jean* beside the school heater. But by some fortuitous family exchange after Mam's death in 1979 I have seven box-camera photos of that time, and four are labelled in my mother's handwriting. One says: "den 1 Januar 1947." It appears that on New Year's Day, a Wednesday, Reverend and Mrs. Jacob Enns and their family visited us and the photo shows the four parents in front of the winter-shredded plaster of our house where snow is banked up for heat as high as the living-room windows. Pah and Mr. Enns stand on the outside in vests, suits and ties, while Mam and Mrs. Enns, who is even broader than my mother, stand between them wearing scarves and collared winter coats. The sled I use to haul wood from the woodpile sits behind them, half loaded, and beyond that the snow slopes across the garden past the well to the grey poplar knoll at the horizon. There is driven snow on the roof and on the windowsills behind my father's right elbow but, strangely, the windows themselves are unclouded by frost. In fact the glass is so clear that the looped window curtains can be seen inside; and also something deeper, it may be shadows on the glass thrown by the bright sunlight or a presence standing there, peering out.

Three of the people in the photo smile directly at the camera; perhaps because they are good friends;

perhaps because they have decided that this year, or next year at the latest, they will leave Speedwell for good; perhaps because they have already told each other as much. Only my father does not smile; he squints into the winter sun, searching distance as if he has already gone south, far away.

~

The tiny spaces of Liz's five-year diary (which began as Helen's) are, for the first few days of 1947, filled with details of a teenage girl's life no memory could retain:

January 1, Wednesday: Dad, Rudy & myself went to church. Mom made dinner [i.e., the noon meal]. For dinner all of Enns were over, after dinner Heinrichs kids came, we took some snaps.

January 2, Thursday: Rudy went to Aaron Heinrichs today cause we want to butcher pigs tomorrow. Dad is getting everything ready. Rudy brought books home.

January 3, Friday: Today is a very busy day for all. Enns and Heinrichs are here butchering. I washed dishes almost all day, at night we drove to the mail in moonlight.

January 4, Saturday: Didn't do very much Sat. work today except clean up a little and iron a bit.

January 5, Sunday: We were all at [Abe] Fehrs today, went skiing and did we ever tumble & had lots of fun. We kids did the chores then went to church [hill] & toboggan.

January 6, Monday: We were washing today and I was reading "Stately Mansions", I surely enjoyed it too & hope I can be a girl like Garnet some day.

January 7, Tuesday: I did up my hair for church tonight. Had quite some adventure in the [church] cellar to, a nice chat after & a lovely ride home in the moonlight.

January 8, Wednesday: I ironed all day long today. Read some in bed at night. I also washed my hair and curled them.

January 9, Thursday: Did some more ironing today & and finished for once. In the evening we all went to church except mom, had a nice service.

January 10, Friday: Today has been a rather dull
day, a storm out & Mom got sick. When the
mail came I was glad to get [from Eaton's?] a
good pair of stockings & print dress. Oh diary,
I bawled for Helen tonight.

January 11, Saturday: Moms feels better today
for which we're very thankful, washed floors
and cleaned up. Took a nice bath at night.

January 12, Sunday: We went to church and
came home where we were all day. Listened to
the radio & slept part of the day.

January 13, Monday: Cold today, went to the
mail with Rudy, came home & went to bed. Had
my first knitting lesson today.

Liz leaves the next twenty-two daily spaces blank,
until abruptly:

February 5, Thursday: We cleaned up part
of the wash today. At 3:30 we turned to
N. B. [North Battleford radio station CJNB?]
and heard Dan's voice, it was too good to
be real.

February 6, Friday: We heard that Dan was
coming home today, was I ever glad. Dad got
him from the highway.

February 7, Saturday: Today is a day like others
except Dan's home, he's so swell too. Played
Chinese checkers.

February 8, Sunday: Today Rudy & I went to
the church. Came home, had a good dinner,
played Chinese checkers. Went to church for
Y. P. M. [Young People's Meeting]

Liz made only two more 1947 diary entries in
Speedwell:

April 27, Sunday: Today I'm (sweet) sixteen. We
went to Fehrs, played ball and in the evening
had a bonfire at our place. Boy I'll never forget
my first real kiss & Leslie.

April 28, Monday; Seems very gloomy adays
The weather warm Les. was over for hay got
only one smile sort of blue today.

What books did I bring home from the Aaron
Heinrichses'? Five church meetings in twelve days

to begin the New Year, getting the mail twice a week, visiting the Abe Fehrs, playing Chinese checkers, listening to the radio—CJNB North Battleford must have had a community message program for Dan to speak on, to let us know he was coming home from wherever he was working; a marvellous service in that bush country without telephones or electricity—and for Liz washing floors, endless ironing, learning to knit. But also a book dream of growing up beautiful, nice dresses, and above all an actual "real kiss." And Leslie Nord? A cousin of Isola and Troy Fehr, tall, hardworking, well over twenty—really too old for my sweet-sixteen sister, but there was no teenage boy left in Speedwell to dream about. How often did Liz cry, alone now in her bed under the rafters, for Helen with whom she might have talked about real kissing? Helen, who may never have kissed any boy, though she dreamed of John Koehn after the Koehns left Speedwell in March 1944.

Through all of March 1947 Liz's diary is blank, though the Speedwell Cemetery records show two funerals within a week of each other, the first since Helen's death two years before. One was for Maria Dorn, an ancient, wrinkled lady who lived with her daughter Katerina (wife of Dave Heinrichs), and who had a superb goitre under her chin—what a tantalizing, gurgling word, "goitre," not like the Low German "Kropp" as harsh and ugly as "chicken gizzard," which it meant too—a goitre large and smooth as if she had swallowed a great turtle and it remained permanently moored in her neck.

The goitre memory may be misplaced. Katerina and Dave Heinrichs had no children, but Dave had been on the school board since his brother Aaron died, and if he was in the yard when we crossed on our way home from school he would wave, sometimes call us in for a sweet, flavoured drink in that time of wartime sugar rationing, or perhaps a cinnamon roll. Dave's big, permanently bowed body and rock-bottom bass anchored every hymn, every choir that sang in Speedwell Church; and I remember the wake packed two or three chairs and benches deep around their kitchen table, with Katerina Heinrichs seated there, mourning her aged mother while the community women served Tweeback and coffee—it may actually have been Katerina who had that moving, unforgettable, neck.

The second March death was sadder: Abe Fehr, only forty-seven years old, gaunt and handsome husband of Katie and father of Orville and Isola and Joyce and Troy and Delano and Mildred and Carolyn, a man who played western or Hawaiian guitar with a sliding silver bar until your body shivered in rhythm, who sang his singing family into country gospel harmony the radio Carter Family could barely match. But he always had weak lungs, they said, and he died of tuberculosis. So my only friend left in Speedwell, Troy, who once explained the ways of dictionaries and forced a devastating translation from stallions and mares to Emmanuel and Mary upon me, Troy, only fifteen, his face shattered, was partnered at the head of the coffin with his big brother Orville who had been a soldier in the Canadian Army, carrying the heavy body of their father through the snow around the leafless poplars to the graveyard with four other Fehrs and related Nords. I remember one summer day behind all the teams tied up at Harder's General Store when Troy shot his pressured urine higher and farther than any boy in Speedwell, an arc of sunlight over three grain wagons: it was no contest, and for a few years he kept up, as it were, a standing challenge. Who could have guessed that such a tough boy, who already seemed to know everything on the edge of manhood, could also cry.

During Abe Fehr's burial, Helen's white grave-stone was photographed. Mrs. Katerina Martens, Katie's mother, stands with arms folded on the left, and the tall, stooped shape of Leslie Nord bends away from it towards the new grave they are filling.

Abe Fehr died on March 27. In that March 28 picture which Mam carefully labelled in ink, it may be that Dan and I were going to the Fehrs to help them prepare for the funeral. Within six weeks Dan and Isola Fehr, who had once given Helen her own new, unworn dress to be buried in, would be married: on Mother's Day, May 11. Four days later Pah, Mam, Liz and I would leave Speedwell for good.

My mother labelled two other pictures in March 1947, but neither of them is of the funerals. They seem typical homestead work pictures, but as I study them over days they change, they begin to slip from focus to focus, as if these ordinary Brownie Box snaps were shape-shifting.

One was taken in our yard; half the picture is blank snow and a quarter is poplar and spruce sticking up into blank sky; on the narrow band between the two lies a long pile of logs, as high as a man, which is being sawn into firewood. Six men labour around a stationary steam engine that plumes a white cloud against the far spruce: two men lift each log, pass it to two others who shove it against the saw-blade, while the fifth seizes the cut block and throws it behind him on the growing heap of firewood; the sixth man—from his shape and the cap pulled low over his ears it must be my father—seems to be coming towards the camera, walking away from the workers. My big brother Dan, legs wide apart and arms cocked in lifting, is unmistakable against the white burst of steam. Who the other men are or who owns the saw outfit I don't know.

The saw blade, hidden by the working men, would be a metre in diameter and spinning so fast one cannot see its teeth. On and on through the winter afternoon its screams burst in the wood. The sawdust heaping up below will be used to cover the fresh ice already cut and hauled from the slough and stacked in our ice cellar dug into the ground behind the house to keep our cream cool for shipping throughout the coming summer; the woodpile Dan will split block by block—Pah will be gone, looking for work and a house in Coaldale—in the lengthening light of spring thaw, and Liz and I will stack the pieces in neat rows to dry. Next winter this great mound will all be burned, it will warm the house for Dan and Isola throughout the bitter cold: it will become fire, this white poplar, *Populus tremuloides,* trembling aspen.

You can hear trembling aspen leaves shiver. At the slightest breeze the dark green leaves flicker into their underside paleness and a sigh like great sorrow flows through the forest. In that distant picture of the long stack of logs being sawn I feel something strange, a perception that refuses to focus, but in the close-up of the other picture my mother labelled in 1947, a gradual recognition emerges.

Our strongest horses, mismatched grey Silver and brown Jerry, their heads cocked to hold the traces taut on the whiffletree, are hitched to a bobsleigh piled high with poplar logs. Dan balances forward on the logs, tall and powerful with the two reins in one fist and the other arm bent, ready to lift; behind him our father stands tilted sideways, peering down, content as ever to be a labourer on his own land, expecting nothing.

But now, looking, it is the thick, knobbly logs with their axed ends thrust at me, each of them moments before living trees, chopped down by my father and brother as they stood with their sap frozen in their veins waiting for the spring sun, it is the long poplars with their tips dragging in snow behind the sleigh that quiver in my mind. This is more than simply the endless human labour of survival in the Canadian boreal forest: poplar forests grow from Canada to Russia to England and Israel (*Populus alba*, or *libneh* in Hebrew), and ancient legend has it that aspens around the circle of the earth have been trembling since that moment when the hands and feet of Jesus were nailed to a poplar cross, when his flesh was smashed against its wood. No aspen trunk will ever again grow straight enough to form a cross, and the heart-shaped leaves on their narrow stems will never again stop shivering, for shame, for endless, endless sorrow.

Stories create feeling beyond reason or guilt; in story we understand, even as we hear and sense it, that wind can be an image of the divine moving within us. When wind runs high in the crowded aspens, we see them bend their thin, pale bodies down again and again like homage, like worship, and we hear and see their flat-stemmed leaves shiver as they turn their whiteness into sighing, groaning together. The long sound of creation, grieving. And sometimes too they do not straighten up again but remain bowed; the youngest, tallest, will grow year after year bent round until their tips touch the earth. And even stooped in such sorrow, in shame and respect and adoration, they also declare themselves unendingly alive: chop down as many poplars as you will, clear any field to the last stick or twig from the surface and out of their roots searching everywhere through the earth new shoots will push up; year by year you will have to labour to contain them at the edges of your field. In fact, scientists tell us that clones of a single aspen seed can occupy up to eighty hectares of land, literally thousands of trees growing through thousands of years from one seed on land first exposed to sun and wind when the Pleistocene ice sheet melted here 12,000 years ago.

The aspen in Canada's boreal forest are the largest living organisms growing on the earth; every one a link in our boundless circle of life.

Perhaps that is why—who can explain how—the death of Jesus for me always was, and will always remain, indelibly more than an historic act of brutal execution. When aspens bend, sighing pale, my body feels fact beyond any sight, or hearing; or denial.

That contradictory, unfathomably comforting awareness: the fire that burns in the soul like ice, the ice like fire.

~

It may be that one of the books I brought home from the Aaron Heinrichses' on January 2 was *Elsie Dinsmore* by Margaret Finlay; that 1869 classic of the faithful Elsie who, after the death of her angelic mother, tries desperately to live the thirty-eight godly character traits (I read the book, but never tried to list the virtues) while her godless father, who does not attend church but amuses himself reading novels (!) on Sunday and whom Elsie is forced to love and honour because he is her father and yet reject because he is so grievously godless, tries chapter after chapter to break her adamant Christian resolve. All at the age of eight. It is the kind of book Aaron Heinrichs could have brought along when he emigrated to Canada from Colorado, to benefit his four growing girls learning to read English.

But perhaps, thanks to Arlyss, I also found a few Zane Greys there, more of those eighteenth-century Ohio forest whites and savages, of the "long low sound like the sigh of the night wind moaning through the gloom." Except for Grey's unrelieved brutality and killing—which, oddly enough, was one of the easiest aspects of adult behaviour for me, a loved and innocent child, to imaginatively slide over without discernment; I had no sense that Speedwell forests were dangerous—Grey's forest world was as close to mine as any I had yet found in a book. And during the final winter of 1946–47 I was alone in it even more than usual.

That year I became the only child going to school from the southwest area of the district. The Lobes and Heinrichses were gone, and Liz had completed grade eight so there was nothing left for her to do in Speedwell School. Three miles twice a day, going and coming home through the trees and

around the swamps and across the empty farmyards;
I walked, rode, and in the dark winter morning I
harnessed Prince and drove alone in our smaller
cutter with an oat bundle under the seat to feed him
at noon in the school barn. Our single track, which
Prince had to break again and again all winter
through the clearings and their shifting blizzard
banks of snow, was the only trace on the trail.
Sometimes I walked ahead of him holding his bridle
with my left hand, so light in my felt boots I could
walk on the hard drifts, but Prince never could; his
big hoofs broke through at every step and he would
be panting white jets under my arm, his nostrils and
slobbering lips hoared thick with frost. If I could
walk on the drift, the cutter could ride over it too, but
Prince always had to muscle through, poor beast.

Prince was sturdy and amiable, but I didn't actually like horses. Few farm kids did, as I remember; the
horses we had were so big and slow, so stupid, too
immovable for our childish whims and shifts of mind.
I remember riding Bell to school, who once crushed
me as I ran under her belly, and getting so enraged at
her unalterable pace when I wanted her to trot that I
beat her as wildly as I could with the reins over ears
and head until I was exhausted. But she simply shook
her head and plodded on; there was nothing I could do
to make her move faster than she had decided. At a

certain point she stopped moving altogether and stood, with me lying stretched out on her broad back crying in fury. I know exactly where it happened: on the road allowance north along the top of the hill above Jake Dorn's place, beside the long mudholes in the road that Dan finally banked up and repaired with a two-horse earth-scoop, to pay a bit of our land taxes.

The winter before our leaving: in our snowy yard I am about to unhitch Prince. I wear my first fur-trimmed parka, breeches, knee stockings and winter boots. Our last dog—black Carlo is dead, what was this one's name?—faces the camera and the single poplar beside our well beyond Prince seems to be growing out from between his ears like an immense spine of black antler. Behind me lies the wooded knoll with a scraggly jack pine where I disappear when I don't want to do some chore; where one spring after the snow had disappeared from the thickest bush I was stunned to find, under the leaves, two heavy rifles.

Gust buried them there before he and Tina moved to Coaldale in 1942; half a century later in Lethbridge he will still remember them exactly: a double-barrelled shotgun and a bolt-action .43 Mauser, the kind used for almost a century by armies from Europe to Chile to South Africa, especially in the German trenches of World War I and, Gust tells me, he did not dare take it along to Coaldale—a German-speaking person with such a gun? But for me they became exciting toys I played with every day, especially the heavy Mauser with its steel barrel grooved in brown wood and big enough to stick my finger down. I played from tree to tree aiming at our weed-sprouting barn or board granaries—never the house—and our slab toilet barely visible in the bush, snapping off shots and sprinting to dive around cranberry and rose bushes, from tangled saskatoons, aiming at our road gate in case a huge car with its top down should appear there and Joseph Stalin in the back seat smiling that smile under his Schnur'boat, moustache, and just when the chauffeur got out to open the barbed-wire gate I would pick the Beast off, I had the sights lined up dead on, a between-the-eyes shot . . .

Would God's wrath abide on you forever for shooting Stalin?

I played until I was, inexplicably to my mother, dirty and sometimes scraped bloody; until my father discovered the rifles where I hid them too carelessly and they were gone. I never dared ask and never knew until fifty years later, when Gust told me, that Pah had buried them to rot in the spruce muskeg across the road allowance, buried them off our land. He never said a word to me about it, nor was one necessary. I knew I had to keep them hidden because my parents refused to allow a gun on our place no matter what a Fiedler or Dan, when he owned the farm later, might do. Guns did nothing but kill people.

That spring our teacher Sarah Siemens must have arranged the annual Speedwell School picture for early May, before we left, because I am in it. Twenty-one pupils huddle around the flagpole with her, and one family, the Doerksens, makes up seven or perhaps eight of the total. This family appeared from somewhere and settled into our Franka place after we moved to Gust's homestead for its well in 1942. The Doerksens were handy bush-farm people; the eldest in school, Glen, told me his dad and brothers had made a two-horse bobsled that winter using their axe, a saw and the kitchen butcher knife

for carving holes in the runners to set uprights. Every morning I raised the Union Jack on the pole which disappears above us. Children of the stony field and boreal bush, we look like ragamuffins, though everyone—except perhaps tousled Barbara Trapp—seems to be wearing some sort of shoes. I am still there, but barely: only my hair, forehead and the edge of my eyes are visible in the fold between Nickie Sahar's and Helen Doerksen's heads. Helen has a white patch over her right eye, and everyone else's face is completely visible, especially Annie Sahar with her towering hair on my right and lean Edward Funk on my left; he is taller than Miss Siemens.

The school's peak roof rises over us, the mud plaster between its logs almost completely washed away by weather. One railing on the steps is broken away and the door stands open, inward. You can see through the west window to the shadow of the hill behind the school where in winter we slid down on home-made sleds and occasional board skis, or wrestled and had snow fights and rolled down when pushed hard enough, pretending to be logs, spruce and birch and deadfall poplar we had known intimately all our brief, thoughtless lives.

I am almost gone; not even my grin is left under the Speedwell flagpole. But on the outside edge of our grey huddle, away from the school, there Katie Martens stands complete, hair pompadoured high, mouth open, white blouse and black bell-bottom slacks. She will not disappear meekly. When her family leaves Speedwell in 1948 she will walk away exactly as she pleases and everyone will see her do it plain as day.

~

I am lying on the bed where Dan and I sleep, under the angle of our house rafters beside the steep steps that open to the kitchen below; Liz sleeps alone in the other half of the attic, beyond stovepipe and a white sheet. I am reading, lying on Dan's two-thirds of the bed to be nearer the tiny gable window. Outside is brilliant May, the towering clouds barely interrupt the sun, but I am lost in a book—is it another Elsie Dinsmore book, or a Zane Grey, or *Rock of Decision* again, which over a year ago Helen and I read to each other? A book read out loud is very different from one read silently, especially with Helen, and it may be I miss her to the point of tears and that is why I am rereading it alone, aloud would be too much—

"Sonny!" my mother shouts from outside through the screen door. The slough frogs are croaking, it's warm enough for mosquitoes.

More likely I am avoiding her with the last book I haven't read in the Speedwell School library, so thick with its heavy cover: *The Toilers of the Sea*, by Victor Hugo. After Jean Val Jean and the winter ocean of Vancouver, I have to read this Guernsey book standing on the narrow shelf—had anyone ever touched it?— set on an island hidden against the map outcropping of France. It is thunderously boring but I plow on, words in books exist to be read, and for six decades I have forgotten everything except the last scene, which I remembered as a man chained to a post on an immense beach and gradually the tide approaches, rises as he struggles, roars his terror until the sea swells above his gaping mouth and he disappears. However, when I scan the book now, I discover my memory is almost totally reversed: there is no external power of post or chain in the last chapter. Rather, the protagonist Gilliatt seeks out a natural declivity among the ocean cliffs, seats himself there and waits until the woman he loves—can only the French love this way, absolutely and forever?—sails past with the man *she* loves, and he remains seated, rock upon rock, watching the ship vanish as the tide slowly rises to his waist, his shoulders, his neck, until, when the vessel fades on the skyline, "the waters covered the head of the watcher, and there was nothing visible but the waves of the sea rippling against Gild-Holm-'Ur."

Perhaps I am fortunate that my closest memories cannot be overturned so easily in a used book store.

~

My mother is calling, and at a certain point even I, her reading avoider, am ashamed to ignore her. Work must be done, the whole bright day cannot be wasted following words.

Mam, in the long dress and apron she wears all day, sits on our plank front step, cutting potatoes for planting.

"Etj lauss de Bibel," I tell her. I was reading the Bible.

She concentrates on the cluster of eyes in a red potato, turning it in her broad, worker hands. "Don't lie."

"The Old Testament, one of the killing stories."

"You're not too big yet for a thrashing," though she has never really vedrasht me.

I laugh. "It's not lying if you know it's not true."

"What is it then?"

"A joke," I tell her, and add in English, "a story!"

She absolutely refuses "joke"; she will not so much as permit herself to smile, though her lips twitch. "Du enn diene Jeschijchte. You and your stories. Sometimes I don't know if that's what they are."

"Then it's your fault," I say, picking up the pail with cut potatoes. "Catch on."

"Soo eenfach es daut nijch," she says. It's not that simple.

But to me then, an impatient, impulsive boy, it seemed she was the simple one; for her everything seemed to be ent'wäda ooda, either or, black or white.

Either or: anything anyone did, in all of God's creation, it was always black or white—with the black most likely to come first. I then thought of my mother's life as contradiction: her abiding fear at the immanence of divine, eternal wrath, yet she herself lived a life devoted to goodness and love—perhaps not a contradiction as much as an inexplicable dissonance, a disharmony so powerful I recognized it like an echoing revelation a decade later in Münich's Alte Pinakothek where the Renaissance paintings of the life of Jesus presented him in magnificent wealth, an opulence so stunning it rivalled any possible Medici: the Son of Man who in biblical story walked the dry earth of Palestine with lepers and described himself as having nothing, no, not so much as a place where to lay his head. Either or. Black or white. Where, I wondered, were the brilliant colours of God's rainbow that arched all together? Only promised, occasionally, in the sky?

I had been too young to notice earlier, but after Vancouver it seemed to me there was no avoiding it: the world was enormous beyond all comprehension, certainly beyond only black or white. But what my mother actually meant when she said, "It's not that simple," was still beyond me.

Along the bush on the far side of the garden Dan is plowing with four horses, seated on our two-share plow. His big arm works the depth lever, threading the plowshares along the line between shallow grey-wooded soil and the underlying clay. I walk the furrow bent low, nudge the cut potatoes into the soil, tight as I was taught years ago, so the next round of the plow will cover them to an exact depth and then we will mark the long rows with pegs and rake the surface smooth. A winter's worth of good food, to be eaten in all the ways Mennonites prepare potatoes, but best they are sliced and fried in Jreewe'schmolt, rendered pork fat with bits of red meat, we call it "cracklings," nothing can taste better after a day outside in February than these potatoes browned deep and fat between your teeth. In garden ground my bare toes bump into stones, curl in pockets of sand scattered like bits of antediluvial beach in the tan clay, sand so moist you can shape it momentarily between your toes—actually in the sunlight the varied earth feels more intriguing than any book. That was one stupid thing about winter: the early dark is good for reading, but your feet and hands are always wrapped in something heavy—bare feet and hands know things too, especially in sunlight; they are the four opposite corners of your always inquiring body and they can know things far beyond your hard head.

In this garden our food begins; and in our farmyard where the chickens graze, in the sloughs where cattle forage along the edge of mossy water, in the boreal bush where saskatoons and cranberries and chokecherries grow, wild strawberries on deserted fields; and miles north of Speedwell School, beyond the fire cutline where forest fires begun by lightning burned years before I was born, over the sandy jack pine and poplar hills grow wild blueberries, square miles of them bunched in drops bluer than sky, which we pick in August to fill five-gallon cream

cans, and Mam boils them in the hot summer
kitchen and I carry them down the ladder into the
cellar below the house and set the preserves in rows
of purple, red, blue and black sealers: winter jam for
bread and berries for Plautz and for whipped cream
desserts with just a ration sprinkle of sugar.

Standing barefoot in the turned soil behind our
house, I know: Of this earth my cells are made.

~

I have felt remembrance beyond words when I
returned to the boreal place where my sister is
buried, where my mother conceived and bore and
fed me.

But such remembrance also happened when,
after six decades of life, I walked in places where I

had never before physically been: in Russia, the former Mennonite village once called Number Eight Romanovka, north of the city of Orenburg, driving up the great steppe hills that stretch into horizons, the village cemetery where my parents met beside my grandmother's grave and where gravestones overgrown by grass and lilac bushes still say "Wiebe" in both German and Russian; and also two thousand kilometres west of Orenburg in Ukraine, in the former Mennonite village of Neuendorf, now Shirokoye, just west of the huge Dnieper River city of Zaporizhzhia where my father was born and where the bricks of the village school he first attended are falling from the walls in broken piles among wandering chickens; and in the town of Harlingen on the North Sea coast of the Netherlands where my blood forebears were forced to begin their wandering, where in 2003 the registration clerk at the Hotel Anna Casparii recognizes my Frisian name Wiebe and asks when our family left Holland and I tell him, "Almost four hundred years ago."

And then, when I step back out onto narrow Noorder Haven Street in Harlingen, I have a sudden, overwhelming, sense that this water glittering in this canal passing this hotel door and being pumped up into the North Sea, is, molecule for molecule, cycle for cycle, the very water my ancestor Wybe Adams van Harlingen last saw here in the town of his birth, when he sailed away to Danzig in 1616.

It may be that our bodies, despite our minds, retain what we have neglected to notice; or even undermine our ability to forget what we long not to know about ourselves. For a survivor of the fire-bombing of Hamburg, the sudden drone of a plane overhead can convulse the body in shudders; a midnight pounding on the door awaken a Gulag survivor into uncontrollable screams. Even when all facts seem lost, the bodily effects remain, as the poet Dionne Brand details in her memoir, *A Map to the Door of No Return*. When she lists for her grandfather the names of all the African peoples she knows, he tells her none of them are their people, but "he would know [the name] if he heard it." However, he never does remember and because of that, Brand writes, "A small space opened in me . . . a tear in the world. . . . It was a rupture in history, a rupture in the quality of being. It was also a physical rupture, a rupture of geography." It seems that when you have lost the place on earth where you come from, when your ancestral name has been ground out of existence, you suffer damage.

Memory as psychic and physical evanescence. As I wrote and rewrote these words, gradually a memory of my Speedwell nightmares returned to me. A betrayal by sleep: the child life I lived somewhere in the Land of Sleep would on occasion be ripped open, exposed frightfully in my physical bed. There were many nightmares, beginning, I know, when I first began to walk because my mother would awaken to pick me up in my wanderings and lay me back in bed, but now I first remembered knowing the name. Not Low German, which is simply a modification of Droom, dream, like beesa, bad, or gruselja, repulsive, frightful, but English knew better: "nightmare," a gigantic horse that suddenly burst with you into darkness, you were clinging to its bare back, no reins or even a halter shank, its neck too huge for your arms to reach around and you could only clutch the short tufts on its withers as it rushed you into terror. Like Bell, always uncontrollable and now gone suddenly berserk.

The shape of only one nightmare came back clearly, a smeared apparition from the spring of our leaving. I had to do something, Right now! and it was of course already too late, I would burn in Hell from all ages to endless ages for this, fire and ice burned the same, there was no difference, but someone was pounding on the door downstairs and I had to answer, Now! I was out of bed and backwards down the ladder stairs in the darkness and something tried to stop me, someone and someone else, but I was fighting them—*I have to do this!* and the door opened to no one on the porch, I could see, so they must be waiting in the yard, a wagon and a team of horses, a car! I am outside in the spring night burning my feet like ice and fire and past the summer kitchen through the slab fence gate, *Etj mot!* I have to! and I'm halfway down the empty slope to the barn,

> And I feel that "I" is too little for me!
> There's somebody fighting his way
> Out of me!

But it is my mother, out there. Even as I lunged from the house I had sensed something double, I both knew *I had to!* and also that there would be nothing to do—there never had been—and my mother clasps me tight around the shoulders and I am afraid and enraged at the same time, I *should* have done something but there *is* nothing, I am barefoot in the cold night yard in my spring underwear, my warm Mam murmuring in my ear and I shake her off and walk back past Pah at the slab gate doing nothing as usual, just watching, I hate them for seeing me act so stupid again, I love them, there *was* someone and *I had to* and I'll show them, I'm Tüss, home, I'll go upstairs and sleep. And I do it.

Years later I found those three lines of split image for being inside a nightmare, "And I feel that

'I' is too little for me . . ." in the long, raging poem by the Georgian/Cossack poet Vladimir Mayakovsky called *A Cloud in Trousers*. A close friend said to me, "You're always reading Russian writers, are you sure you're not half Mennonite and half Russian?" and I could only mutter, "To be so lucky."

~

With every passing day our memory is what we can still find in it, or cannot avoid, and no doubt Gao Xinjian is correct when he comments in *Soul Mountain* that losing particular memories is a form of liberation. But there are many we would wish never to lose: the more precise they are, the more they comfort us. Liz wrote nothing in her 1947 diary after her sixteenth birthday, not even of Dan and Isola's wedding on May 11, but suddenly on Thursday, May 15 she recorded these facts:

> We arrived in Coaldale about 7: o'clock p.m.
> Had a very pleasant welcome at Voths with a
> warm supper, after supper Ed. [Voth] took us
> to our new home.

The former Speedwell storekeeper Wilhelm Voth with his removable teeth had returned to our

Saskatchewan bush for hire in a dusty car to carry Pah, Mam, Liz and me 470 dirt and gravel miles (756 kilometres) to Coaldale, Alberta. We held no public auction, that community burial of all things farm and family, gathered bit by bit in the fourteen years—almost to the day—of our Speedwell living. Rather, we shipped a few household possessions by train, packed in two wooden boxes Pah built, and left the farm, all its animals and machinery to Dan and his marvellously good natured wife, Isola. Mam went to Helen's grave on Wednesday and we started at sunrise on Thursday to drive it in one day and save ourselves overnight expense. On Friday, before Mr. Voth took us to Lethbridge to shop for furniture, I washed the various layers of my wind-and-sun-hardened travel vomit from below his right car window.

Coaldale was the first stop east of Lethbridge on the railroad originally built in 1885 by Sir Alexander Galt's business consortium to haul the coal they mined along the Belly (now Oldman) River below Lethbridge to the new transcontinental Canadian Pacific Railroad at Medicine Hat. In 1947 Coaldale's main street, where Highway 3 led us from Medicine Hat, ran parallel to the track and its stores and houses clustered around three grain elevators, but our "new home" was in Nortondale, an outgrowth on the town's west side.

There were two streets of Nortondale houses and, though I did not recognize it at the time, Second Street Nortondale—now Coaldale's west Twenty-third Avenue—was as close to a Russian Mennonite village as my parents ever found in Canada. With two exceptions, all the thirty-odd families living there had arrived in Canada during the 1920s and spoke Low German. Our small lumber houses set on two-acre plots faced each other across narrow irrigation canals on either side of the gravel road; each yard had a huge garden and many, like ours, had small buildings where we could raise chickens and feed a pig or sheep for butchering. By fall Pah had even bought a milk cow, which he staked out to graze on our back acre or along the irrigation ditches like other families since there was of course no Russian herdsman to take our animals to a communal pasture. I did not realize that, until I left for the University of Alberta six years later, it would be my daily chore to milk that cow morning and evening in the small shed that hid our family outhouse from the street. She was a good cow, Guernsey at least in her soft beige colouring, and we sold the extra milk to neighbours for ten cents a quart.

Standing on the high bank of the main irrigation ditch whose muddy water flowed east just beyond the houses and plots on the south side of the street, I could look over farms, fields and pastures leaning up the vast slope of the plains to where the Front Wall of the Rocky Mountains appeared and vanished again into mist beyond the Milk River Ridge. The ridge separated the continental rivers flowing south to the Gulf of Mexico from those flowing north to Hudson Bay. Over it the square peak of Chief Mountain hovered like the snow and granite profile of a man lying on his back. But it was too distant for me to discern clearly, nor had I any notion yet of the Blackfoot stories about Old Man and Thunderbird surrounding that awesome place.

Coaldale was not landscape for Mam; it was cautious hope. Though not quite fifty-two, her years had been too difficult for outright optimism. Her life's mottos had always been "Harre auf Gott," wait for God, and "Den Mutigen gehöert die Welt," to the courageous belongs the world, and now, by moving to southern Alberta, it seemed her patient hope gradually was becoming more than a glimmer in the distance. Here there were steady wages for Pah, he no longer needed to struggle with farming decisions—let Dan do that in Speedwell, he was much better at it and could explain himself in English—and for her last two children there was a huge church with over a hundred Christian young people to become friends with, to attend Sunday school and sing in choirs. Indeed, the Coaldale Mennonite Brethren Church offered a fine three-year Bible school and, even more amazing, also ran an Alberta Department of Education—approved separate high school on the north edge of town. Here, in Coaldale, it might very well be possible, Mam thought, for both Liz and me to be saved from the endless, subversive temptations of the post-war world. And there were many older Mennonite women for her to talk to: they understood this Canadian world in ways she never would.

Pah did not waste time staring across southern Alberta prairie which looked so much like the steppes where, as a boy, he had carried lunch to their

Bashkir herdsman grazing the village cattle in the Number Eight Hills. He was happy for the well-shingled house—though it had no foundation, it merely sat on stones in the brown earth—happy for the street with its ditch of running water, the huge Coaldale Mennonite Brethren Church north of town, his job on a dairy farm where every day someone would tell him exactly what to do.

"Hia oppe Stap woa wie aundasch läwe," he said. Here on the prairie we'll live differently.

And my lengthening bones knew he was right; truly aundasch, different.

# THE COMING WIND

~

1947. Monday, May 19: Dad went to Lethbridge
today to work. Rudy went to school and mother
and I worked in the garden. Then went to town
a little bit yet.

The town of Coaldale was dominated by English
names like Graham, King, Handley, McCann,
Foxall, Greer, Fairhurst, though there were a few
main street businesses with Mennonite names like
Martens and Thiessen on their false fronts. In Mrs.
Jinty Graham's classroom of thirty-seven students
Principal Roy Baker assigned me the end corner desk

nearest the cloakroom door: as if I'd slipped into grade seven very late, perhaps accidentally, and might be gone if someone noticed me. That was fine with me; my seat was beside the tall windows and I could look out through the huge branches of the cottonwoods to the gravel street, where cars passed and people walked in shiny leather shoes on wooden sidewalks even when it rained.

And soon I discovered that I was totally unique in school for wearing blue denim farm overalls, particularly since the buttonholes at my hips were so worn the metal buttons did not hold the side flaps closed as they should. Though school ended in a few weeks, there was more than time enough for the poetic English class wits, playing with "Rudyard" I think, to cross-label me "Barnyard." A particular fit for the more general names like "bohunk" or "schmo."

As Big Bear says, "A word is power, it comes from nothing into meaning." I could add that some words are so powerful they are fixed in us beyond any possibility of forgetting.

The Frank and Helen Wiens family lived beside us in Nortondale, eight children—four in their teens like Liz and me—Mennonite neighbours happy to help us learn how to live and work in hot summer Alberta. The oldest son, Abe, farmed eighty acres of land east of town; they had a contract with Canadian

Sugar Factories for sugar beets and soon we joined them hoeing the endless rows, those straight, flat lines etched by bright threads of irrigation water reaching, as it seemed, beyond the treeless horizon.

Before the fifties, beet seed was still unsegmented: the tiny sprouts came up in clusters and they had to be thinned to single plants one hoe-width apart so each beet could mature into a thick, swollen root. Actually, hoes were fine for weeds but not much help for thinning: only on your knees with your bare fingers could you properly single them down. Bent down into long acres of sugar beets, you gradually became a distant bump, nameless under the scorching sun.

Coaldale's sweet gold. In the forties it was the Japanese Canadians, forced inland by the Canadian government from their Vancouver homes during World War II, and the immigrant Russian Mennonites, adults and children alike, who provided most of the labour that nurtured 30,000 acres (12,150 hectares) of beets grown in the Lethbridge district. As Joy Kogawa, a grade behind me in Coaldale School, would later write in her novel *Obasan:*

> . . . the heat waves waver and shimmer like see-through curtains over the brown clods and over the tiny distant bodies of Stephen and Uncle and Obasan miles away. . . . then on my knees, pull, flick flick, and on to the end of the long long row . . . it will never be done. . . . It's so hard and so hot that my tear glands burn out.

I whined but never wept, though I know my mother did: the pain in her misshapen bunioned feet, her bent back. Between beet hoeing sessions we children picked green and yellow beans when they matured in late July and August. All along the Nortondale streets were small plots of "cash crop" assigned by the Broder Canning Company, on our back acre as well. One cent a pound for first and second picking, two cents for third, but you had to strip your row carefully, and clean, no tearing up plants or grabbing clusters from other rows. Sometimes a day in a good field paid almost $2— imagine that, when before the war Dan worked that long for fifty cents.

In September Liz entered grade nine (not a word in her diary) and for me in grade eight "Barnyard" revived immediately. But I had begun to learn something about clothes and walking away from names in silence. And Murray Robison, one of the finest teachers I ever had, further undermined the label by grading me between seventh and ninth in the class of thirty-five, not so far behind Bob Baker, the lanky, good-natured son of the principal who was invariably first. Other vestiges of bush-farm bumpkin disappeared when, as a spring drama event, Robison had us stage A. A. Milne's delicate one-act fluff, *The Princess and the Woodcutter,* and to my happy astonishment assigned me to play the Yellow Prince, the most garrulous and foppish of the three princelings vying for the Princess's hand. It was performed in our classroom, for ourselves and families, in full costume.

Of course the Woodcutter ultimately wins the Princess, and I'm not sure whether we prairie plodders captured much of the upper-class English filigree the play is meant to convey, but the Yellow

Prince is there with the Woodcutter—Shirley Smith, the prettiest girl in class—looking over his (her) shoulder at me with classic-profile disdain while I, in the yellow knee pants and vest Mam had sewed from a dyed flour sack, flick my hand at him (her) in whatever princely condescension I can manage.

Personal problems sometimes fade as simply as they arise in an enjoyable, learning classroom. That we Wiebes were a poor worker family on the edge of a hardscrabble prairie town dominated by several influential businessmen and wealthier irrigation farmers did not yet register very strongly. Our life was so different from isolated bush Speedwell—with electric lights, coal delivered by truck, a cistern storing irrigation water, which we hand-pumped in the kitchen (it never tasted as good as our former well). There was a huge church of over seven hundred adult members, a brick school, streets, stores and houses in what seemed to me a crowded town—life was so changed that I barely noticed we had no car or telephone, and it would be four years before anyone in Coaldale had running water, sewage services or natural gas. The euphoria of leaving a dreadful war behind and the end, at last, of the Nuremberg trials, smudged wealth and class distinctions, especially among teenagers. We were told the world was clean and new for us, we began to think we could do, could become, anything we wanted: "Work hard, the sky's the limit!"

And in fact Alberta's enormous "sky" was expanding. On February 13, 1947, just south of Edmonton, Leduc No. 1 Discovery Well blew in with an enormous explosion of gas that rained oil on ecstatic, dancing drillers; the first of thousands of wells in hundreds of square miles of deep Alberta oil reefs. For most of us the fifties and sixties would grow far beyond any teen imaginings.

But more than obvious opportunity, Coaldale Consolidated School proved to be a daily Canadian multicultural manifestation more than twenty years before Ottawa named that an official policy. In 1948–49, when I was taking grade nine, I see in my yearbook that Coaldale Consolidated High had 108 students; of these, 37 were of Russian Mennonite ancestry (22 of them girls), 23 were British, 17 Japanese and the remaining 31 a potpourri from everywhere, largely central Europe. When the new aluminum-covered R. I. Baker School was opened in March 1950, some one hundred students from twelve grades performed a rainbow "Pageant of the Nations" written by English–French teacher Edna McVeety and directed by Murray Robison. Greetings were printed in twenty languages and twenty-two different nationalities made presentations, often wearing traditional clothing. We Mennonite kids together sang "Glaube der Väter," "Faith of Our Fathers," in four-part harmony.

Gaining some peer acceptance and good marks were not the most memorable benefits of living aundasch, different, in Coaldale. More significant for the solitary kid I gladly remained—I discovered how to disappear in a crowd—more crucial were books. The 1948–49 CCHS Yearbook was prescient beyond all wit when it analyzed Rudy Wiebe's ambition as "To own a library" and his "Weakness: Fiction." The latter has obviously proven to be a lifelong pun.

Shelves of books from floor to ceiling in the school library, and also in the new (1945) public library on Main Street. Between them these small rooms contained perhaps two thousand volumes, but after vacant Speedwell the very sight of so many book spines was both miraculous and evocative. The public library even allowed you to take out two books at a time, almost enough for a weekend.

And beyond books there was the land: open, visible to every long circle of horizon. The earth, the sky, the unfailing wind. Anywhere in southern Alberta you could see for miles, nothing to bristle from the green vistas of land except trees planted in careful rows, lonesome shelterbelts or windbreaks as they were called, huge cottonwoods lined up along streets or protecting farmsteads, and sprouting alone on the elevations or in the hollows of irrigation canals, but they always stopped abruptly, turned square at corners like leafy walls. Nowhere were there overwhelming spruce or aspen forests hiding the land completely, bending in groves to the muscle of the wind, no whitening flicker to the sad sigh of their leaves. In contrast to the world where I was born, or the river and forested mountains of Vancouver where we briefly lived, on the prairie everything man-made—houses, farms, towns, elevators, even the small city of Lethbridge along the edge of the Oldman River coulees—was exposed, poised on a long, open cliff of often staggering wind, a wind that could run ice in summer with hailstones, or hot in the depths of winter to lick every flake of snow into mud when Old Man sent the "snow biter wind," as the Blackfoot people called it, of his winter chinook blowing up over the incline of the Rockies and sweeping east down the frozen prairie.

A seemingly endless land forever open to the visitation of wind. Bracing myself into that breathing wind, I would grow to feel it: a land too far to see, fathomless to the looking eye—but, perhaps, touchable by words. Words strung out with utmost care, like the thin, high steel of the railroad bridge at Lethbridge stretching itself across the immense canyon of the Oldman River, words forged and bolted together into the living architecture of story.

# ACKNOWLEDGMENTS

~

Childhood memory is always a family affair, especially in an immigrant Mennonite family. Abram and Katerina Wiebe had seven children, and in 2006 only three of us remain. Therefore my first and most heartfelt thanks are for my brother Dan Wiebe, Grande Prairie, Alberta, and my sister Elizabeth (Wiebe) Uren, Lethbridge, Alberta, and for the stories we could tell each other. In particular, the five-year diary which, for several years, Liz continued intermittently after Helen's death, has helped me pinpoint events with a precision far beyond any possible memory. Thank you, dearest Liz; I know you will be understanding where my remembering, as given here, bears little or perhaps even no resemblance to your own.

Thank you also to the following: Tony Fiedler, Lethbridge; Gerald Fiedler, Belleview, Alberta; Frances (Hingston) Cotcher, North Battleford, and Anne Klassen, Saskatoon, Saskatchewan; Paul Poetker, Edmonton; Ferne Goll and the Glaslyn committee that published the two huge volumes of *Northern Reflections: History of Glaslyn and the Rural Municipality of Parkdale* (2005); the Speedwell School contingent at the Glaslyn celebrations on July 1, 2005, which included (to give them their Speedwell names) Elsie Koehn, Margaret and Jack Trapp, Hilda and Jake and John Enns, Olga and Nick Sahar, Edward and Vera Funk, Henry and Stella and Margaret Martens; special thanks to Mary (Loewen) Fehr, Kelowna, British Columbia, who sent me her 117-page personal memoir: "My youth, my school, our farm, our church in Speedwell, Saskatchewan," and also Dave Little of Willowdale, Ontario, who discovered and sent me a copy of the application map for a "Pearl Lake School District" made by Aaron Heinrichs in 1930.

In particular, I want to acknowledge the work of Dr. Jack Thiessen, without whose absolutely unique *Mennonite Low German Dictionary*, Max

Kade Institute for German-American Studies, Madison, Wisconsin, USA (2003), so much of this book would have been impossible to write. Thank you, Jack, for making the (for me) instinctive sounds of Low German systematically visible on paper; at last.

And to Louise Dennys, Jennifer Shepherd, Nina Ber-Donkor, Angelika Glover, Scott Richardson, Deirdre Molina and Sharon Klein: you are the people who make publishing with Knopf Canada much more than bringing a book into existence. Thank you.

A NOTE ABOUT THE TYPE

*Of This Earth* has been set in Walbaum. Originally cut by Justus Erich Walbaum (a former cookie mould apprentice) in Weimar in 1810, the type was revived by the Monotype Corporation in 1934. Although the type may be classified as modern, numerous slight irregularities in its cut give this face its humane, old-world manner.